"There is nothing easy about eschatology. Thankfully, Craig Hill has produced a wonderful road map for laypeople and experts alike to follow during the difficult journey through God's time. Hill plays a fine Sherlock Holmes, discovering new insights and fresh clues as to the meaning of the Bible's prophetic and apocalyptic texts. Contemporary events make Hill's treatment all the more compelling and his evaluation of popular biblical interpretations all the more urgent."

— MIKE McCURRY
White House press secretary, 1995-98

"I thought eschatology was just too scholarly a subject for anyone but theologians to think about. Christians who dwelled on it — well, I found them a bit strange. But Craig Hill has proven me wrong. *In God's Time* not only makes eschatology understandable to laity but also explains why it's important to every Christian in today's world. And Hill writes beautifully."

— FRED BARNES
The McLaughlin Group panelist, 1988-98;
executive editor of *The Weekly Standard*

"Hill's study of eschatological thinking in the Bible will come as a liberation to many troubled by forms of Christian belief that are fixated on calculating the time of the end. His explanation of biblical prophecy and its relevance for understanding Jesus is clear and forceful, and his accessible style makes the book a pleasure to read."

— JOHN BARTON
University of Oxford

"This is a splendid, well-written book on a topic of continuing importance for the health of the church. A gifted teacher and a wise guide, Craig Hill explains the Bible's teaching on 'God's time' clearly and judiciously. He doesn't assume any prior knowledge, nor does he duck the awkward questions his readers are likely to have. His book is packed with helpful insights for a wide range of readers. Many will wish they could have read this book years ago."

— GRAHAM STANTON
University of Cambridge

"Thanks to Craig Hill for this powerful and timely word calling the church to take seriously its eschatological beginnings. A must-read for understanding the Christian faith."

— A. KATHERINE GRIEB
Virginia Theological Seminary

"Hill writes for Christians who don't know what (or how) to think about the End Time and what Scripture says about it. He tackles the hard questions and comes up with answers that are both specific and remarkably sane. While completely informed by the best scholarship, his prose is lively, unaffected, and clear. Here is the sort of writing too seldom found — work by an expert who actually says something helpful to ordinary people."

— LUKE TIMOTHY JOHNSON
Candler School of Theology,
Emory University

"Every Sunday Christians confess belief in the 'last things' — the second coming of Jesus, resurrection of the dead, and final judgment. Hill here provides students, pastors, and interested laity with a much-needed guide to New Testament eschatology and its Jewish roots. He includes a helpful guide to reading apocalypses like Daniel and Revelation and explains the origins of contemporary beliefs about 'the rapture.' This book should be required seminary reading. Christians living in the twenty-first century need not abandon the core elements of their ancestors' faith."

— PHEME PERKINS
Boston College

"Craig Hill's book ranges widely over the biblical text to consider the way the Bible hopes. The book is attentive to the many different nuances given the permeating act of hope in Scripture. Hill shows how characteristic and crucial is hope for biblical faith and yet how liable it is to distortion and misreading. His book is an invitation to rethink the odd claim of faith in a cultural context where hope is either impossible or transposed into fanciful escape."

— WALTER BRUEGGEMANN
Columbia Theological Seminary

"This is a wonderful study of the book of Revelation and of Jesus' own words in the Gospels about the End Times. Hill argues persuasively that these texts require neither an ultraliteral 'left behind' interpretation nor the skepticism of the Jesus Seminar, which has dismissed the texts as inauthentic. Hill demonstrates that apocalyptic literature was a popular Jewish religious genre during Jesus' time, a poetic way of talking about God's dramatic intervention in the world on behalf of his people. To the earliest Christians, who were all Jewish, the culmination of that intervention was, of course, Jesus himself."

— CHARLOTTE ALLEN
author of *The Human Christ: The Search for the Historical Jesus*

IN GOD'S TIME

The Bible and the Future

Craig C. Hill

WILLIAM B. EERDMANS PUBLISHING COMPANY
GRAND RAPIDS, MICHIGAN / CAMBRIDGE, U.K.

© 2002 Wm. B. Eerdmans Publishing Co.

Wm. B. Eerdmans Publishing Co.
2140 Oak Industrial Drive N.E., Grand Rapids, Michigan 49505 /
P.O. Box 163, Cambridge CB3 9PU U.K.
www.eerdmans.com

Printed in the United States of America

16 15 14 13 12   10 9 8 7 6

ISBN 978-0-8028-6090-3

Contents

The End from the Beginning

This is a book for people who want to come to grips with what the Bible says about the future. It is not written primarily for scholars, although it is written from a mainstream scholarly perspective. Over the years, I have been profoundly grateful to Christian academics who have made a point of writing for the church. This book represents my first effort to join their honorable society.

But why write on this of all subjects? Books about the Bible and the future are hardly a novelty; scores appear every year. Ought we to welcome even one more of this already superabundant species? Certainly, the world does not require another publication purporting to unveil recent fulfillments of biblical prophecy. You might be relieved to know that I do not conclude that the World Wide Web is a Satanic plot or, despite the loss of part of Chapter Four to a *Windows* crash, that Bill Gates is the antichrist. Indeed, one reason for writing a book such as this is the presence of so many other publications touting such far-fetched ideas.

Eager as I am to reach out to diehard End Times enthusiasts, they are not the primary audience I have in mind. I am particularly interested in writing for those who find this whole issue baffling, off-putting, or troubling. For such persons, I hope to show that the idea of God's triumph is central to Christian faith and that a working knowledge of the concept is essential to an informed reading of the Bible, particularly the New Testament. Working through these materials can also lead to growth in one's faith and to new perception into and appreciation for the faith of others.

I am grateful to Wesley Theological Seminary for providing me the time and encouragement to pursue this subject, to Clare Hall, Cambridge University, where I was a Visiting Fellow during much of the writing of this book, and to Tyndale House, Cambridge, whose biblical studies library was an invaluable asset. I also wish to express my appreciation to Sylvia and Donald Fites, Robert and Ingrid Coutts, Paul Lamberth, Brian Beck, John Barton, George Ramsey, Chad Pecknold, Jeff Dryden, Richard Deibert, Jules Gomes, Rob Wall, Pamela Gable, and Suzanne Gibson Vance, each of whom supported this project in some way.

My partner in this as in all endeavors is my wife, Robin. *In God's Time* is dedicated to our children, Arthur and Victoria, in strong hope of their bright future.

A Note to Readers

One abbreviation used in the book that might be unfamiliar to some readers is "par.," which stands for "and parallels," as in "Mark 2:18-22 par." It is used when a cited Gospel passage is paralleled in one or more other Gospels. In this case, Mark's account of the dispute over fasting in 2:18-22 is paralleled in both Matthew and Luke. These other versions of the story are not cited because they do not add substantially to the argument. Similarly, two parallel lines, "//," are used to indicate that two passages are parallel, as in "Matt. 7:24-27//Luke 6:47-49," a reference to Jesus' saying about hearers and doers of the Word, which is found in both Matthew's and Luke's Gospel.

With rare exception, all biblical quotations are taken from the *New Revised Standard Version*.

CHAPTER ONE

Are We There Yet?

Every year brings its share of dashed hopes and frustrated expectations. In 1988, the Denver Broncos were defeated in Super Bowl XXII, Tom Hanks came up short at the Academy Awards, Gov. Michael Dukakis of Massachusetts lost the race for the U.S. presidency, and the world's armies failed to end human history in catastrophic battle at Armageddon. The last disappointment belongs primarily to the twenty million or so readers of Hal Lindsey's 1970s bestseller *The Late Great Planet Earth*. Lindsey had argued that the world was poised for cataclysm, literally "of biblical proportions," after which Christ would return to reign for a thousand years. He calculated that these things ought to occur within forty years — a "biblical generation" — of the founding of the modern state of Israel in 1948. "Many scholars who have studied Bible prophecy all their lives believe that this is so."[1]

It is not so. 1988 came and went with nary a whiff of sulfur. But prophetic interpretations are malleable as playdough and resilient as cockroaches. Post-1988, there is no end to the writing of such books, both by Lindsey himself and by his many imitators, including Tim LaHaye, whose dark End Times novels, the *Left Behind* series,[2] have sold tens of millions of copies to date. In fact, the *Evangelical Studies*

1. Hal Lindsey, *The Late Great Planet Earth* (Grand Rapids: Zondervan, 1970), p. 54.
2. The writer of the series is actually LaHaye's "co-author," Jerry B. Jenkins. LaHaye's views are discussed in "Not Left Behind," a short appendix to this book.

Bulletin recently named LaHaye "the most influential Christian leader" of the past quarter century.

Even in today's sluggish economy, prophetic interpretation is a growth industry, what Robert Jewett calls the "doom boom."[3] Volumes predicting the Second Coming line the shelves of Christian bookstores, competing for space with Last Days videos, charts, tracts, and novels. Search the Internet for terms like "apocalypse" and "return of Christ," and you will be directed to tens of thousands of websites. Clearly, a lot of people are intensely interested in what the Bible has to say about the future. Why? Surely curiosity plays a big part, as does a sincere desire on the part of many to understand the Scriptures. Less laudable motives also are in evidence. For a community that prizes the Word, a knowledge of biblical esoterica can bring crowds, status, and authority like nothing else. It is no accident that many well-known Bible teachers regularly offer new, idiosyncratic interpretations of prophetic texts. "Profounder-than-thou" competition is very real in Christian circles. Last Days preaching is also used to generate fear, most frequently employed for the sake of evangelism: "Turn or burn! Fly or fry!" Enthusiasm for the end shows no sign of ending anytime soon.

But that is not the whole story. For every Christian captivated by the subject, there are many others who either ignore or dismiss it. Their reasons are plentiful. The matter may seem peripheral at best, incomprehensible at worst. Biblical language about the end strikes some as vindictive and offensive. Many find the whole thing an embarrassment. What generation has not read itself into the biblical texts, only to be proved wrong? Worse still are the myriad of silly, sometimes grievous acts that have been committed under the intoxicant of prophetic expectation. (Think Marshall Applewhite and the Heaven's Gate community.) Regrettably, the book of Revelation in particular has a lamentable history as the favored text of miscreants and dupes. (Think David Koresh and the Branch Davidians.) For still others, End Times belief is an unwelcome inheritance from the family's primitive past, an uncouth relative who should have been shown the door long ago. Ancient ideas about a "new heaven and a new earth" are so time-bound as to be irrelevant. Indeed, some modern biblical scholars have taken consider-

---

3. "Coming to Terms with the Doom Boom," *Quarterly Review* 4, no. 3 (1984): 9-22.

able pains to construct a "historical Jesus" respectably free of such barbarity (see Chapter Six).

Extremism is often the easiest but seldom the truest course. The unquestioned embrace and the unqualified rejection of the biblical hope are equal but opposite errors: in the first instance, faith is robbed of reason; in the second, faith is deprived of substance. Those most enthralled with prophecy seldom ask difficult and uncomfortable questions about the context and worldview of the biblical authors, the extent to which their expectations went unfulfilled, and so on. Those quickest to reject these same texts show little grasp of the historical and theological difficulties triggered by their dismissal. So it is wise to avoid, as it were, both uncritical infatuation and overhasty divorce. Still, each side has a point. On the one hand, it is important to recognize that Christian faith is grounded in hope of the triumph of God. To give that up is to jettison the core of historic Christian belief. On the other hand, it is dishonest not to admit the problems inherent in the biblical expressions of this hope. To avoid the hard questions is to retreat into a naïve and ultimately unsatisfying faith. These texts are troublesome, but they have something vital to say to contemporary Christians. What is needed is an approach that takes seriously both possibilities and problems and so encourages both a faithful and a thoughtful response. What follows is one small attempt to meet this challenge.

Eschatology in Two Words

Those conversant with this subject use a lot of words — "millennialism," "dispensationalist," "pre-trib/post-trib" — that have little meaning to anyone else. In the pages that follow, I shall try to keep jargon to a minimum. There is one term, however, that is worth introducing right at the beginning. The word is *eschatology* (pronounced with a hard "k": *es ka tol' o gē;* not to be confused with *scatology,* which is something else altogether). The word is built on the Greek *eschatos,* meaning "last," and refers to that branch of theology that concerns itself with "the last things." More broadly, eschatology is about the fulfillment of God's plan for human history.

Eschatological systems can be bewilderingly complex. Ironically, that is part of their appeal. Who doesn't like to be in on a mystery? When all is said and done, however, the essential point of eschatology is quite simple. In two words: God Wins. God's purposes ultimately will succeed; God's character finally will be vindicated. At heart, all eschatologies are responses if not quite answers to the problem of evil. Are injustice, suffering, and death the final realities in our world? Is human history, both individual and corporate, purposeful? Is all this talk about the goodness, love, and justice of God just pie in the sky? Eschatologies differ in how they conceptualize God's triumph, but they are essentially alike in asserting God's victory as the supreme reality against which all seemingly contrary realities are to be judged.

Christianity is irreducibly eschatological. As Karl Barth put it, "Christianity that is not entirely and altogether eschatology has entirely and altogether nothing to do with Christ."[4] Jewish expectation of a Messiah (literally, an "anointed one") was an eschatological hope. The early Christians saw Jesus as the anointed one through whom God's purposes for humanity were realized — now in part, but later in full. This belief pulsates through the New Testament; apart from it, there would never have been a Christianity. One representative passage is the speech credited to Peter in Acts 3:18-21:

> In this way God fulfilled what he had foretold through all the prophets, that his Messiah would suffer. Repent therefore, and turn to God so that your sins may be wiped out, so that times of refreshing may come from the presence of the Lord, and that he may send the Messiah appointed for you, that is, Jesus, who must remain in heaven until the time of universal restoration that God announced long ago through his holy prophets.

The obvious objection is that eschatology, Christian or otherwise, is just wishful thinking. We would like to believe that God exists, that creation is purposeful, that human history is meaningful; nevertheless, all around us we see suffering, evil, and futility. So faith allows us to pretend that the world really does make sense. Eschatology in particular sounds like fantasy, a tidy imaginary world in which everything

---

4. Karl Barth, *The Epistle to the Romans*, trans. E. C. Hoskyns (Oxford: Oxford University Press, 1933), p. 314.

turns out as it should, where everyone, at least everyone in our group, lives happily ever after. It may be harmless escapism or it may be reprehensible deception; in either case, it is not reality.

That is a tough critique, and I can offer no guarantee that it is not accurate. As the apostle Paul wrote, "Hope that is seen is not hope" (Rom. 8:24). When all is said and done, faith in God remains faith. That is its nature. But that does not mean that Christian faith is baseless. The reason for the exuberant eschatological faith of the early church is not hard to discover. It is the resurrection of Jesus.

Many first-century Jews believed that God would raise the faithful to eternal life at the end of the present age. This belief in resurrection of the dead needs to be distinguished from both resuscitation of the body and immortality of the soul. A person who died and was brought back to life only to die again at some future date is said to have been resuscitated. This is what is envisaged in the raising of Lazarus and similar biblical stories (John 11:1-44; 1 Kings 17:17-24; Matt. 9:18-26; etc.). Immortality is the belief that people are not truly *mortal,* that is, that their existence does not actually end at death. Usually this is based on the notion that each person has a soul that occupies his or her body. At death, this eternal spirit is disembodied; it goes to heaven or hell or some other suitable locale. (Gothic-style houses and creaky wooden ships seem the preferred destinations.) More characteristic of both ancient Judaism and early Christianity is the belief that the person is a psychosomatic whole. No soul exists independent of a body, so when the body dies, the person dies. Death as the penalty for sin (Gen. 3) is so devastating because it is so final. It would take an act of God to be rescued from death. Exactly: "For the wages of sin is death, but the free gift of God is eternal life in Christ Jesus our Lord" (Rom. 6:23). Resurrection is not a given; it is a gift. At the time of resurrection, persons will be given new bodies capable of eternal existence. (But what sort of body? I refer you to Paul's discussion in 1 Cor. 15:35ff.)

In his resurrection, the early Christians saw the vindication of Jesus, who despite crucifixion was shown to be God's Messiah. Even more, they saw in his resurrection the vindication of God. All of this talk of future hope, of God's final justice and triumph, really is true. They knew it would happen to them because they had already seen it happen to Jesus. 1 Cor. 15:20-24:

In fact Christ has been raised from the dead, the first fruits of those who have died. For since death came through a human being, the resurrection of the dead has also come through a human being; for as all die in Adam, so all will be made alive in Christ. But each in his own order: Christ the first fruits, then at his coming those who belong to Christ. Then comes the end, when he hands over the kingdom to God the Father, after he has destroyed every ruler and every authority and power.

The conviction that Christ had been raised by God animated the early Christians and gave great dynamism to their faith. Christians claimed that in the resurrection they had seen the end of history placarded in the midst of history. So theirs was not a weak, "Gee, I hope it all works out" expectation. They had powerful assurance that the things they wished to be true really were true, and in that confidence they led thousands of others to faith.

Is there any proof that they were right? It is hard to know what such proof might look like. One cannot test their claims as one would test a scientific hypothesis, that is, through replication. Christ's resurrection is an unrepeatable act. What about historical proof? Strictly speaking, there is none. Historians *prove* nothing; instead, they gather evidence and formulate more or less convincing arguments about the probability of events. That does not mean that historical study is pointless; it does mean that one should be cautious about its limitations. We have a judicial system that trusts jurors to weigh evidence and so to adjudicate between rival accounts of some disputed event. We make provision for their verdicts to be overturned because jurors sometimes get it wrong. With respect to the resurrection, history permits us to say at least one thing with a high degree of confidence: the early Christians themselves were convinced that it was true.

When I was a teenager, a friend offered to take me to a faith-healing service at a nearby church. I had my doubts, but the opportunity seemed too intriguing to pass up. I went expecting a flamboyant figure, rather like Steve Martin in the movie *Leap of Faith*. Instead, the preacher was a rather average-looking, average-acting character who seemed to be in no hurry to get around to the real business of the evening. After an interminable sermon, he invited members of the congregation to come forward for prayer. He laid hands on one individual who said that he had a chronic back problem. After praying, the minister asked, "Are you healed?" The poor fellow, apparently in some pain, did not know how to respond. The preacher clarified matters: "If you believe that you are healed, you really are healed!" "Uh, I guess I am healed," said the man. Now it was patently obvious that he was not healed. Had the man truly been cured, what would he have done? Allowing for regional variations, he would have jumped, danced, and shouted "Hurray!" The point is that, after a fashion, the early church jumped, danced, and shouted across the whole of the Mediterranean Basin. They behaved the way people would behave who were convinced that Jesus really had been raised. They were assured, joyous, and bold witnesses, often in the face of repeated and even deadly opposition. They knew what was at stake and were clear about their reasons:

> If Christ has not been raised, then our proclamation has been in vain and your faith has been in vain. . . . If Christ has not been raised, your faith is futile and you are still in your sins. Then those also who have died in Christ have perished. If for this life only we have hoped in Christ, we are of all people most to be pitied. But in fact Christ has been raised. . . . (1 Cor. 15:14, 17-20)

Theirs was an *eschatological* faith grounded in the resurrection.

No End in Sight

That was then; this is now. Eschatology occupies a tenuous place in contemporary academic theology. The de-eschatologization of Christianity has been challenged in recent decades by a number of prominent scholars and theologians, such as Jürgen Moltmann, J. Christiaan Beker, and Wolfhart Pannenberg. Important progress has been made; nevertheless, Christianity's eschatological inheritance is by no means secure. Scholars continue to launch countless missions to rescue Jesus from the clutches of (so they imagine) his eschatologically deranged kidnappers — the New Testament authors. I have heard hundreds of Sunday-morning sermons in "mainline" churches; I cannot recall one that dealt squarely with the subject of the future. Why flee eschatology? A few reasons, such as embarrassment and incomprehension, were mentioned above. Another powerful motive is the desire to reconcile faith with science. While that goal is laudable, how and on whose terms it is to be effected are real sticking points. In many cases, what is promoted is not accommodation to scientific discovery but capitulation to "scientific" rationalism. Eschatology is about God acting in and through human history. For some, that possibility is ruled out in advance. What can God do? Again, the litmus test is the resurrection. It is understandable that some people cannot believe in the possibility of resurrection. They have that right, and I respect it. But if there was no resurrection, then really there is no point in talking about *Christ*ianity. Jesus is not the living, vindicated *Christ* (Messiah) who is and will be God's agent for the realization of God's purposes. The usual fallback position is to focus on the ethics of Jesus, but calling the result Christianity is, at least technically, a misnomer. Moreover, it is clear that Jesus' ethic itself is eschatologically grounded: because the coming reign of God has a certain character and value, says Jesus, one would be sensible to respond to it in certain specific ways. "The kingdom of heaven is like a merchant in search of fine pearls; on finding one pearl of great value, he went and sold all that he had and bought it" (Matt. 13:45-46). If there is no "kingdom," then what is the point? In that case, the gospel scarcely qualifies as good advice, much less "good news." Paul, quoted above, had it right: "If Christ has not been raised, then our proclamation has been in vain."

Three related but somewhat less acute problems also are raised by science. The first concerns the early Christians' limited view of the cosmos. They knew little about the immense expanse of universe around them; therefore, the framework within which they thought about eschatology was severely restricted. For example, they believed that the earth was the center of the universe; thus a re-creation of the earth was essentially a re-creation of the entire physical cosmos. It is a little harder for people today to conceptualize "a new heaven and a new earth" (Rev. 21:1), at least one that might arrive next Tuesday, not in tens of billions of years.

Which leads to the second problem. The early Christians had a limited view of human (much less geological) history. They did not know about the great expanse of time that came before them. They thought of history in terms of a few thousand years at most; hence it was possible to think of the "ages" as relatively brief periods. Again, the framework within which they thought about eschatology is seen to be quite narrow and antiquated.

The third problem concerns creation. Although eschatology is technically about the "end," most eschatologies are heavily dependent upon a doctrine of creation. The end will be as the beginning; the creation will return to its pre-fallen state when evil, sickness, and death did not exist (see Gen. 3). The problem is that most of us no longer hold literally to the biblical account of creation (six days and all that). A lot of living and dying occurred prior to the arrival of *homo sapiens;* those *T. rex*es had six-inch teeth for a reason. Moreover, one might find it difficult to believe that humans ever existed who were free from the universal biological propensity toward self-interest, which is the basis for so much of what we rightly consider sinful. What works in a coral reef ecosystem (philandering with multiple partners, eating one's enemies) can wreak havoc in the average suburban neighborhood. There is truth in Katharine Hepburn's famous statement in *The African Queen:* "Nature, Mr. Allnut, is what we are put in this world to rise above."

A different sort of problem that needs facing is the failed expectation of the first-century Christians. Obviously, Christ did not return in their lifetime. One might well ask, "Shouldn't we just admit that the whole business is a wash and move on?" Even more perplexing is the attitude of Jesus himself. Some evidence suggests that Jesus too expected the end in the near future. Was Jesus wrong? If so, what does that mean for Christian faith?

So it is not surprising that for many believers eschatology has taken a back seat to other concerns — or, more accurately, that it has been tossed in the trunk or pitched out the window. Christians are right to be occupied with a hundred other things, worship and the promotion of justice, to name two prominent examples. But theologies are like organic systems in which a change in one part affects every other part. Microorganisms might seem inconsequential, but they are essential to all of life. If they go down, the whole system eventually goes down with them. Eschatology is similarly basic. Its elimination undermines all of Christian theology.

Is eschatology salvageable? Yes, but not without some hard thinking and difficult choosing. The criticisms mentioned above need to be confronted forthrightly. In no small part it is the aim of this book to encourage and to equip readers to engage this task for themselves. At minimum, that requires a working knowledge of the issues and a basic familiarity with several key texts. Toward that end, we shall look at the history of future expectation and the role of prophecy in the Old Testament (Chapter Three), the rise of apocalyptic Judaism and its significance for Christianity (Chapter Four), the two biblical apocalypses — Daniel and Revelation — which have exercised unparalleled influence on the church's future hopes and expectations (Chapter Five), the views of Jesus concerning the future (Chapter Six), and the way in which the church, both ancient and modern, experiences and anticipates God's reign (Chapter Seven). First, however, we must deal with the contentious issue of the nature and authority of Scripture. The great majority of books on eschatology are written from the side of Christian fundamentalism. I am a Christian but I am not a fundamentalist, which means that I approach these texts with somewhat different questions and assumptions than many readers may have come to expect. Because so much hangs on the matter and because I want to be clear about my approach (I shall try for persuasive, but clear will do), I have included a short essay on the Bible as the next chapter.

Biblical eschatology is not a simple topic. Its study is rewarding but also challenging. Coming to grips with the historical background of the biblical texts is the part of that challenge most often ignored by eschatology books. For that reason, I have tried wherever possible to fill in the gaps, to include information that helps to put the Bible in context. The references in Chapter Three to ancient Babylonian and Canaanite prophecy, for example, will be of more interest to some readers than to others, but the time it takes to consider such material is time well spent. To interpret the Bible in isolation from its context is usually to misinterpret it.

This book is written primarily but not solely for Christians. I teach in a seminary whose student body is diverse in almost every way imaginable. Not all of my pupils identify themselves as Christians; nevertheless, most seem eager to understand "what is really going on" in the Bible. One does not have to be a Christian to find the New Testament interesting and valuable, but one does need to understand eschatology to understand the New Testament. Additionally, a knowledge of eschatology helps to clarify — and to some extent to explain — contemporary theological differences both in and outside of Christianity.

What follows is by no means an exhaustive study of biblical eschatology; nevertheless, I hope that it will move us a step or two in the direction of understanding. In truth, we may already be "nearer now than when we first believed" (Rom. 13:11).

CHAPTER TWO

First Things First: The Bible

I often listen to Christian radio, an exercise that is by turns inspiring and infuriating. A striking feature of many programs is the frequent qualification of the word "Christian." Broadcasters take pains to inform listeners that they are "born-again" or "Spirit-filled" Christians. Clearly, they want to assure us that the opinions being expressed are those of *real* followers of Jesus Christ. An especially popular qualifier is "Bible-believing." Taken literally, this label assumes a contrast between Bible-accepting and Bible-rejecting Christians. Granted that Scripture is approached and interpreted in differing ways, is it possible wholly to discredit the Bible and yet to believe in Christ? Surely not. Such "faith" would be entirely without content. In any case, those who reject the Bible outright are not the "Bible believer's" true foil. The assumed contrast is instead with those who claim to be Christians but who do not subscribe to the doctrine of biblical inerrancy, which is the belief that the Bible contains no theological contradictions, historical discrepancies, or other such "errors." Implicit in this assertion is the idea that the Bible speaks with one voice on every subject. That means, for example, that all of the Bible's eschatological passages are presumed to be equally valid and entirely compatible with one another. Thus an inerrantist looks not for this or that expression of eschatological hope conditioned by this or that historical situation, but for the individual parts of the one uniform biblical eschatology. This is the approach taken by most popular books on eschatology, whose authors set for themselves the task of assembling the great End Times puzzle, discerning how this piece of Daniel fits with that piece of 1 Thessalonians or Revelation. Of course, real puzzles have but one solution, whereas eschatological reconstructions are as plentiful as the eschatologists who devise them. Unfortunately, Bibles, unlike puzzles, do not come packaged with the answer pictured on the box. In reality, this process is more like the creation of a mosaic: myriad representations are possible, each owing as much to the artisan as to the medium.

It is telling that so many people today regard inerrancy as the litmus test of authentic Christian faith. Among other things, it demonstrates how thoroughly the debate over science, especially evolution, has shaped modern American religion. We now find ourselves in the absurd position in which Christians may judge one another on the basis of their opinion of Cretaceous life forms. After a recent speech, someone pulled me aside and explained that fossils had been planted by Satan to trick humans into questioning the Bible. Personally, I would prefer a world with Velociraptors to one in which the devil has the power to mess about with geology. I certainly would favor a world in which Christians did not divide an issue that has so little to do with the truthfulness of their faith or the quality of their character.

Is belief in the Bible an all-or-nothing-at-all proposition? Our answer to that question is foundational to our understanding of all biblical teaching, not least on the vital subject of the future. It is a matter that requires our serious attention at the outset of this study.

I Was a Teenage Fundamentalist

During my freshman year of high school, the evangelist Leighton Ford conducted a crusade at our local armory, one result of which was the founding of a Christian coffeehouse called The Lighter Side of Darkness. "Lighter Side" was a perfect late-60s–early-70s period piece, complete with purple walls, cushions for seats, and empty wire spools for tables. (The common practice of referring to the coffeehouse by its initials, *LSD*, did little to endear it to already suspicious parents.) A number of my friends began to attend Lighter Side, and eventually I went along as well. It was like nothing I had ever experienced. The confident faith, the joyous worship, and the sheer drama of the place (one of the leaders was a former drug dealer with reputed mob ties) easily overshadowed anything I had witnessed at my United Methodist Youth Fellowship. I attended Lighter Side throughout the remainder of my high school years.

The principal activity at Lighter Side was Bible study. Every Tuesday, Friday, and Saturday evening one of the coffeehouse "elders," a fellow in his early twenties, would lead us through a passage or a series of verses related to some topic. The unstated assumption was that Christians believed everything the Bible taught without question or equivocation. It was easy.

I vividly recall the day that it got difficult. I was reading a portion of Matthew's Gospel as part of my daily devotions. Noting the cross-reference in my *Thompson's Chain Bible,* I turned to the parallel account in Luke. I was surprised to find significant differences between the two versions of the same story. No interpretive contortion, and by then I possessed an extensive repertoire, seemed capable of reconciling the details of the two accounts. Unsettled, I phoned one of the elders for guidance. I explained the conundrum, but he too was unable to fashion a satisfactory solution. "So, what do you do when you encounter this sort of problem?" I asked. His answer: "I just try not to think about it." That was advice that I could not take. Too much was at stake.

More than twenty-five years and three theological degrees later, I am still a Christian. The core of my faith has not changed all that substantially, but my understanding of the Bible has. In the short space of this chapter, I want to outline what I think is a reasonable and faithful alternative to both inerrancy, on the one hand, and skepticism, on the other.

A Pair of Paradigms

1. Deductive vs. Inductive Reasoning

Let me suggest two paradigms or models that might help us to get a handle on the Bible. Admittedly, these are generalizations; they cannot account for every complication and exception. Still, they are true enough to be useful, provided one sees them as broad patterns and not as comprehensive descriptions.

The first paradigm builds on the distinction between deductive and inductive reasoning. Deductive thinking involves the application of a general truth to some specific situation. Let us say that the general truth is the excellence of my wife's memory, for which I am perhaps not as grateful as I should be! Were Robin to inform me that I have a doctor's appointment at 3:00 p.m. tomorrow, I would not phone the physician's office for confirmation. I know that she has a reliable memory; therefore, I deduce that she is likely to be accurate in this particular reminiscence.

Inductive reasoning works in the opposite direction, from the specific to the general. When I first met Robin, I had no idea that she was gifted with such a good memory. Over time, through countless, often embarrassing experiences, it became clear that her memory was superior to mine and ought to be trusted. In the process, I formulated a general truth: Robin has an excellent memory.

People who believe in biblical inerrancy tend to think deductively about the Bible. The general truth is God, who is known to be perfect and all-powerful. What sort of book would such a God "write"? Obviously, one that is without error, since it is God's nature to be perfect, and it is in God's power to produce whatever result God wants. Let us then turn to specific texts, for example, to the dozens of stories found in all three of the Synoptic Gospels (Matthew, Mark, and Luke). (These Gospels are *synoptic,* or "viewed together," because of their many similarities.) What are we to make of the differences among these accounts? Since this is a perfect book authored by a perfect God, we know in advance that no *actual* discrepancies can exist. Case closed.

Deductive Reasoning

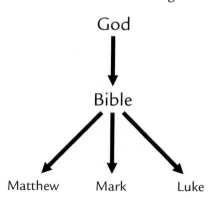

God

Bible

Matthew   Mark   Luke

The argument is usually bolstered by an appeal to the King James translation of 2 Timothy 3:16: "All Scripture is given by inspiration of God, and is profitable for doctrine, for reproof, for correction, for instruction in righteousness." Without entering into a complicated argument about Greek syntax, let me note that much has been read into this verse that is not there. The most probable translation puts verses 15 & 16 in parallel:

15: "the sacred writings which   are able to   make you wise
                                                         unto salvation. . . .
16: All inspired writings   are *also* profitable   for teaching. . . ."

The main point of the passage concerns the usefulness of the Old Testament, the early church's Scripture, not only for evangelism but also for Christian teaching and admonition. These verses were written at a time when the OT's status in the church was very much in question. In the author's view, the Old Testament should continue to be read as Scripture by the church. The word *theopneustos,* "inspired" or "God-breathed/blown," was used elsewhere (e.g., in the Greek author Plutarch with reference to dreams) as a claim of divine origin, something God caused to be, without specifying the *manner* of origination, e.g., "dictated" by God. In practice, this belief functioned very differently from modern-day theories of inerrancy. Paul, for one, was extraordinarily free in his use of Scripture. In many of his 89 biblical quotations, the original text is reworded to suit his argument, sometimes greatly altering its original meaning.[1] A similar problem is evident in the New Testament's heavy reliance on the Septuagint, the Greek translation of the Old Testament, often at points where the text differs substantially from the original Hebrew.[2] Which Old Testament is inerrant, the original or the version quoted by the New Testament? In short, it is anachronistic to cite 2 Timothy 3:16 in support of inerrancy. Ironically, this is one of many instances in which the Bible is misread in defense of its accuracy.

1. See the careful analysis in Richard Hays, *Echoes of Scripture in the Letters of Paul* (New Haven: Yale University Press, 1989).

2. For example, in Acts 15:13-21, James's argument is dependent on a quotation from the Greek version of Amos 9:11-12 (vv. 16-17). A related problem is the unlikelihood that James would have quoted the Septuagint to the Jerusalem church.

One admirable aspect of this way of thinking is the seriousness with which it takes the Bible. Indeed, the Bible may be regarded as the very *Word of God*, a title borrowed from prophecy (e.g., Isaiah 1:10: "Hear the word of the Lord . . .") and generalized to include all Scripture. It should be noted that the Bible actually contains many types of literature, only a fraction of which could be described literally as "Word of God" speech. I shall never forget being in a worship service in which Psalm 137 was read, which ends, "Happy shall they be who pay you back what you have done to us! Happy shall they be who take your little ones and dash them against the rock!" True to form, the pastor then said, "This is the word of the Lord," to which the congregation dumbfoundedly responded, "Thanks be to God!"

The apparent simplicity of inerrancy is appealing. "God said it. I believe it. That settles it." By comparison, other viewpoints may be dismissed as hopelessly complex and irredeemably subjective. Many defenses of inerrancy boil down to the sentiment that it must be true because God, being God, would not have left us in such an otherwise dicey situation.

Looking at the above diagram, it is easy to see why so much energy is expended in defense of inerrancy. Logically, the smallest biblical discrepancy would impugn the very character of God. Did Jesus cleanse the temple near the beginning of his ministry (John) or near the end (the Synoptics)? By this reasoning, he must have done it twice — that, or God is impotent, imperfect, or worse. But did Jesus celebrate two Last Suppers? According to the Synoptics (e.g., Mark 14:12), the meal occurred on the day of Passover, but John explicitly dates it earlier (13:1-30; 18:28). One could go on and on enumerating such difficulties. The point is that inerrancy is a gloriously imposing yet exceedingly fragile construction. All is at stake in every part; as with a balloon, the tiniest puncture threatens annihilation.

On one level, there is no point in arguing with inerrancy. The idea is thoroughly circular; its conclusions are written into its premises, so there is nothing to prove and nothing to doubt. In other words, all contrary evidence, such as biblical discrepancies or contradictions, is ruled out in advance. Unless one is willing at some point to think inductively, to weigh and to test, the general truth is unassailable. It reminds me of the story of the man who was convinced that he was dead. Naturally, his attitude distressed the members of his family, who eventually enlisted the aid of a psychiatrist. After several fruitless sessions, the psychiatrist landed on what he thought was a solution. He asked the man, "Do dead people bleed?" "No," the fellow answered thoughtfully, "dead people do not bleed." The doctor then pricked the man's finger, which bled profusely. "I'll be," said the man. "Dead people bleed!"

At best, this way of thinking produces confident disciples. At worst, it sets those same disciples up for a fall. I took a religion class in college in which the professor walked us through a number of the Bible's most problematic texts. The exercise was devastating for some of my classmates. The Bible is wrong, they concluded, and so their faith is invalid. Just like that, everything that they had believed came tumbling down. Others fought back, urgently and resourcefully defending the Bible. Ironically, however, both responses originated in the same mindset, based on the conviction that belief in God is inseparable from belief in inerrancy.

My initial encounter with biblical difficulties did not lead to an immediate change of mind. Not by a long shot. I still accepted the idea that all true Christians were inerrantists. But the issue was on the table and would not go away. Only later, after some years of study, could I admit that the doctrine of inerrancy does a poor job of accounting for the Bible that it so ardently defends. In passage after passage, I saw that otherwise intractable problems would disappear if only I would admit that real human authors in particular historical settings with specific theological concerns had authored them. Let me give two of literally hundreds of possible examples. These will be much easier to understand if you follow along in a Bible.

Mark 6:1-6 records the story of Jesus' speaking and subsequent rejection in the synagogue at Nazareth. Matthew tells the same story at the same location in his narrative (13:54-58) with only minor variations, but Luke puts the story elsewhere, not in the middle but at the very beginning of Jesus' public ministry (4:16-30). An interesting consequence is the disciples' absence from the story; according to Luke, they have not yet been called. One could harmonize all three accounts only by fudging significant details in each. One could say that the event occurred twice, but that is hardly likely. But if we look at the story from the point of view of Luke's historical situation and purpose, everything falls neatly into place. In all likelihood, Luke has moved the story to the beginning of Jesus' ministry because he wanted it to serve a programmatic function. Note the addition of 4:17-21, the reading from Isaiah 61 that will serve as Jesus' "job description" throughout the remainder of this Gospel. Contrary to Matthew and Mark, the people at first received Jesus' words with gladness (v. 22). Their rejection came later, only after Jesus had spoken of God's favor toward the Gentiles (vv. 25-30), another detail found only in Luke. In fact, Jewish rejection and Gentile acceptance are two of Luke's central concerns,[3] so it makes perfect sense that he has told the story in this way. Nothing could be more Lukan (see Luke 2:25-35). To fret over the historical differences between this account and that found in Matthew and Mark is to miss the point entirely.

A second case is the story of Jesus in the synagogue at Capernaum. This time Mark and Luke are quite similar (although, again, not identical; cf. Mark 1:21-28 & Luke 4:31-37). Matthew omits the story entirely — or does he? Compare Mark 1:22 and Matthew 7:28-29; the two sentences are almost identical:

> *Matthew*: ". . . the crowds were astonished at his teaching, for he taught them as one having authority, and not as their scribes."
> *Mark*: "They were astounded at his teaching, for he taught them as one having authority, and not as the scribes."

Again, what is happening? The explanation is simple. The great majority of scholars think that Mark was the first Gospel and that Matthew and Luke both used Mark as their principal source.[4] (See Luke's acknowledgment of other "Jesus books" in Luke 1:1.) In this particular case, Matthew followed Mark until he came to the statement about the astonishment of the crowds. Note that Matthew 4:18-22 reproduces the immediately preceding passage, Mark 1:16-20, with only minor changes. He appears to have liked the verse so much that he deleted the story to which it was attached, reserving it for something better: to serve as a description of the crowd's response to the Sermon on the Mount. To understand this move, it helps to know that Matthew was concerned to portray Jesus, in deliberate contrast to the Pharisees, as the true and authoritative teacher of Israel (e.g., Matt. 23:8-10), whose teaching is sum-

---

3. This is true both in the Gospel and in Acts, also written by Luke; note, for example, the crowning declaration in Acts 28:25-28.

4. A number of scholars believe that the Gospel used by Luke and Matthew was a somewhat earlier form of Mark than that contained in our New Testament.

marized primarily in the Sermon on the Mount. Once more, we see a "problem" in the narrative that actually makes complete sense when viewed within its own historical and literary context.

One shelf in my office is given to books written by inerrantists attempting to explain away such difficulties. It is instructive reading. One of the largest volumes purports to examine every significant discrepancy. That is a startling and revealing claim since the author has missed at least ten difficulties for every one that he has spotted. The truth is that most of us read the Bible devotionally, not historically or scientifically. We come to it to find solutions, not problems, and so it is understandable if we fail to notice, for example, that Jesus sent out the Twelve with "nothing . . . except a staff" in Mark 6:8 but with "no staff" in Luke 9:3. It is not the sort of observation that the average Bible study program trains one to make.

Does the existence of such problems mean that the Bible cannot be trusted, that it is false? Many have jumped to this conclusion, but it is by no means necessary to do so. Let us return for a moment to the example of my wife's exceptional memory. I said that it is reliable; I did not say infallible. Knowing what I know about Robin, I would need a very good reason not to think that she is right about that 3:00 p.m. doctor's appointment. But what if tomorrow morning she left me a note saying that the appointment is at 3:15? I would not think her entirely wrong; the appointment probably is at 3:00 or so. I certainly would not call her a liar because of the obvious "contradiction." In much the same way, I would assert that discrepancies in the Bible are not so extensive or essential as to require that we dismiss it out of hand. If the Bible disappoints us, it is more because of our inappropriate expectations than because of its limitations. The Bible is a powerful, precious, and irreplaceable witness to Jesus Christ, but it is not itself a proper *object* of our faith.

Of course, these are my own statements of general truth, arrived at by inductive, not deductive, reasoning. As we have seen, the inductive approach begins with the particular and then moves to the general. In this case, the study of individual texts (e.g., the Synoptic Gospels) eventually leads one to formulate opinions about the entire Bible. Ideally, this way of thinking enables one to ask open-ended questions. It does not presuppose a result to which the Bible must be made to conform, and it is not threatened by contradictions or differences. That does not mean that it

Inductive Reasoning

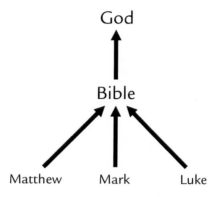

requires that there be difficulties; in practice, persons can be found using this approach across a considerable theological spectrum, from fairly conservative to very liberal. Of course, that breadth of interpretive possibility raises the specter of subjectivity. What is to stop me from finding only what I want and constructing a god to suit my purposes? Are we not venturing out onto the slippery slope of relativism?

The short answer is that all of us, including inerrantists, are already there. None of us can escape entirely the historical situation in which we are located. Each of us comes to the text with a prior understanding of reality, with assumptions about what is true and what is possible, with unexamined self-interest and unacknowledged self-limitation. Having made this admission up front, we have the chance to construct a system of interpretive checks and balances that tests our individual readings against the readings of others within the broader communities of faith and learning, both across cultures and through time. For all its weaknesses, this way is infinitely to be preferred to the pretension that we simply "read" but do not interpret the Bible. Else how does one account for hundreds of "Bible-believing" denominations that champion conflicting readings of the same texts? Let me be clear: I am not saying that any one interpretation of the Bible is as good as any other; however, I do assert that our apprehension of the truth is always relative and conditional. Given our finitude, no one of us is going to be entirely right, although some will inevitably be more right than others. These limitations do not seem to bother us in other spheres of life; neither should they bother us with respect to religion.

2. Conforming vs. Modeling

Our relationship to the Bible is complicated by a number of factors, not least the considerable chronological and culture distance that exists between us and the biblical authors. This relationship is graphed below with time as one axis and culture the other. The New Testament (for now, it will simplify things to focus on the NT) is represented by the box, and our position is marked by an asterisk (*):

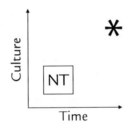

We can use this graph to depict two quite different understandings of the Bible. The first approach is perhaps the more common and, at least on the surface, the simpler and more direct. What is our relationship to the Bible? In a word, conformity. We read the Bible so that we may believe what it teaches and do what it says.

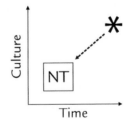

Some who take this approach simply ignore the gap between themselves and the New Testament authors, assuming that what they read is self-evident or that the Holy Spirit alone will lead them into right understanding. Others consult commentaries, Bible annotations, and other guides to help them make sense of the New Testament in its original context. In either case, the object (to borrow from Tennyson's

Charge of the Light Brigade) is "to do"; "Theirs not to make reply; Theirs not to reason why."

Not surprisingly, this approach fits hand in glove with the doctrine of biblical inerrancy. If one is to do whatever the Bible instructs, then the Bible had better always be right. The strength of such thinking again is that it encourages people to take the Bible seriously. For many, Bible study is as essential as prayer. Let us give credit where credit is due: the commendable emphasis on Bible reading in fundamentalist congregations puts most of our mainline churches to shame.

Attractive as it may be, there are severe problems with such thinking. Anyone who studies the ancient world quickly learns to respect the gulf that stands between us and it. Equally daunting is the fact that the New Testament embraces *multiple* first-century perspectives. For example, the author of Hebrews, likely a Jewish Christian, worked with the Platonic notion of two parallel worlds, the earthly, material, and temporal realm below and the heavenly, spiritual, and eternal realm above. Hebrews assumes that the physical sanctuary and priesthood in Jerusalem has a non-physical counterpart in heaven. Christ, the eternal priest, placed his blood on the heavenly altar, and so effected a perfect atonement (e.g., Heb. 9:23-28). A contrasting example is Paul, a Jewish Christian (ex?)-Pharisee who grew up in Tarsus, a center of ancient Stoicism. When Paul wrote that he had "learned to be content with whatever I have" (Phil. 4:11), he echoed a sentiment familiar to any Stoic. So, are we to become first-century Jewish-Christian Platonists when we read Hebrews and first-century Jewish-Christian Pharisaic-Stoics when we read Philippians? We cannot become both, and, in truth, we cannot become either.

The illustration from Hebrews highlights the fact that the authors of the NT, not to mention the OT, worked with assumptions that made perfect sense in their time but make little or no sense in ours. That is entirely understandable and should be no cause for alarm. The fact is that we are all in the same boat. Were I to ask the members of an adult Sunday School class at my church about their theology of creation, most would respond something like this: "The universe came into being as the result of the Big Bang, but the Big Bang itself had a cause, and that cause was God." To modern types, this is a more plausible construal of the origin of the universe than that found in Genesis 1, which incorporates a view of creation common to the ancient Near East. We might easily forget that our belief in the Big Bang is just as culturally conditioned as their belief in the "Watery Chaos." Five hundred years from now, it might be that no one will believe in the Big Bang. Future sophisticates might well view us with withering disdain: "The Big Bang? What idiots. . . ." In reflecting on Genesis, what matters is not the correctness of the science but the truthfulness of the theology. Using the vehicle of an ancient creation story, the author made momentous theological assertions, for example, that creation is purposeful and good, and that humanity is made in the image of God. Nothing we cobble together will be any truer an account.

A second problem concerns the implicit assumption that the New Testament contains one viewpoint on every issue. In reality, on many questions there is a diversity of biblical perspectives. One example is the New Testament's varied statements concerning the Jewish law. Were Christians still required to obey the Hebrew Bible's many ordinances? The issue was never settled. Disagreement is evident, for example, in the contrasting accounts of the hand-washing story in Mark 7:1-23 and Matthew 15:1-20. The implication of the story for Mark is that "all foods are clean." Matthew drops that phrase and concludes instead that Jewish Christians are free to ignore the prohibitions of the Pharisees about hand washing but not those of Leviticus about food.

A further example is the New Testament's mixed testimony concerning women. The texts that instruct women to be silent and submissive are well known ("notorious" might be the preferred description). Most of these passages are located in books that many scholars regard as "Deutero-Pauline," that is, secondary ("deutero") materials written by later authors in Paul's name (e.g., Ephesians & 1-2 Timothy). The only lines in an undisputed Pauline letter that instruct women to be silent are found in 1 Corinthians 14:33b-36, a passage whose authenticity is questionable for a variety of reasons, including its varying location in ancient manuscripts, its appeal to the law, and its flat contradiction of known Pauline practice. On the other side of the ledger is the indisputable fact that some women did exercise leadership roles in the Pauline churches; note, for example, the rules for women prophets in 1 Corinthians 11:2-16 and the many women included in Paul's lists of Christian workers, as in Romans 16. Galatians 3:28, also written by Paul, stands as a rallying cry for Christian equality: "There is no longer Jew or Greek, there is no longer slave or free, there is no longer male and female; for all of you are one in Christ Jesus."

The Protestant Reformers were right to insist that the whole counsel of Scripture ought to be consulted, but their dictum "Scripture interprets Scripture" all too easily becomes a license for harmonizing according to one's prejudices. How often have we selected the biblical view that we prefer and then used it as the key for interpreting out of existence the views with which we disagree? Challenging or controversial texts are dodged; in the process, the theological distinctiveness and integrity of individual biblical authors are lost.

There is no uniform New Testament view of the law or of women. That can be frustrating, to be sure, but it is not the impossible obstacle that some imagine. In practice if not in principle, even the most conservative of biblical interpreters manages to navigate safe passage around these problems. Of course, it is better to make such interpretive choices consciously, but doing so requires a different conceptualization of our relationship to the Bible. If "conformity" is incorrect or even unworkable, what is an appropriate alternative? I suggest that we ought to consider modeling ourselves after, not conforming ourselves to, the Bible.

Believers today are employed at the same essential task as the New Testament authors, namely, the attempt to make sense of their world in light of God's self-disclosure in Jesus. I call this the "But in Christ" project. Like us, the writers of the NT were located at particular moments in time and in specific cultural environments. Like us, they accepted much of their situation as a given; however, at certain points they realized that their world was challenged by what they had seen of God in Christ. Those are the "But in Christ" moments. Yes, first-century this and first-century that about women, *but in Christ* "there is no longer male and female" (Gal. 3:28). I would contend that it is precisely at these junctures that the New Testament is most important and most revelatory.

Using our graph, I would picture the relationship in this way:

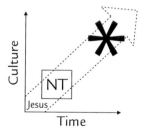

The addition of Jesus is deliberate. Those who operate according to the previous model may love and worship Christ, but, from the point of view of biblical authority, they do not require him. The text itself is the Word of God; it does not derive its authority in any obvious way from Christ. This model is different. It presupposes that Jesus himself is God's primary revelation, and that all Christian thinking is subject to the test of Christlikeness (as in Phil. 2:5). The arrow is the theological trajectory that passes through the New Testament and, we hope, through us. Some parts of the New Testament simply reflect first-century culture (e.g., the acceptance of social hierarchies), and are outside the dotted lines. Likewise, Christian thinking today lies both in and outside of the trajectory.

A compelling example is the New Testament's treatment of slavery. To *conform* literally to the New Testament is to allow the owning of slaves, a point not lost on nineteenth-century American slaveholders. Nevertheless, much New Testament teaching is in tension with the institution of slavery. Paul's letter to Philemon is especially instructive. Paul did not argue against slavery *per se;* realistically, it is too much to expect him to have done so. He did not live in a democratic society that tolerated social reform movements; in any case, he anticipated the early return of Christ, who himself would overturn the old order. Nevertheless, Paul powerfully asserted the slave Onesimus's equal standing with his owner, Philemon. Furthermore, he hinted in v. 21 that Philemon ought to set Onesimus free. Clearly, most of the New Testament is on a trajectory toward egalitarianism: in Christ "there is no longer slave or free." On a profound level, the Bible does side with the abolitionists, who said "But in Christ" to the ongoing institution of slavery.

Does the New Testament retain any authority in this scheme? To quote Paul, Yes, "much, in every way" (Rom. 3:2). For one thing, we would have little idea of who Jesus is or what he taught without the New Testament. Occasionally, I encounter someone who speaks of Christ and yet is blissfully unconstrained by the available evidence: "My Jesus would never have taught about God's judgment." Can one bypass the New Testament and get directly to Jesus (see p. 27)? Only if one is content to find a projection of oneself. To know and to listen to Jesus necessarily means knowing and listening to Matthew and John and Paul. The New Testament books are irreplaceable guides into an otherwise inaccessible territory; they are the gold standard against which all claims about Jesus must be tested.

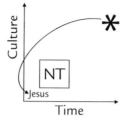

The biblical authors have also provided us with the archetypes of Christian thinking and living. As persons of the first and early second century, they stand in a historical relationship to Jesus that we cannot duplicate. Their responses to Christ, their "But in Christ" conclusions, are our primary models. To be faithful to Hebrews does not require becoming a Platonist; it means following the example of faithful thinking and acting laid down by its author, and in its verses meeting and being challenged by the Christ who met and challenged this individual nearly two millennia ago. In my experience, this method encourages a more sympathetic understanding of the biblical authors. They are remarkable persons and yet not so different from ourselves.

Let me suggest an analogy. As an adult, I have come all the more to appreciate my parents. Looking back at the times when we disagreed, I can see that they usually were right. Their instruction and example are reliable guides that I would do well to follow. Indeed, I am in regular conversation with the internalized voice of my parents. Long after they are gone, they will continue to direct me toward what is good and true and worthy. That is not to say that my parents are perfect. Like all good people, they are most likely to misstep when failing to live up to their own ideals. Fortunately, those occurrences are comparatively infrequent, and they justly deserve respect and admiration. By analogy, the Bible, even with its imperfections, is still our good parent whom we should imitate faithfully but not uncritically. It is a voice with which we should remain in lifelong conversation. Where it seems self-contradictory, it must be tested against its own best, most Christlike self, even as we continue to test ourselves against it.

Of course, this approach does not produce uniform or certain results. The Jesus by whom we judge the text is himself a product of our reading of the text, and therein can lie great mischief. Granted that there is a trajectory of theological truth running from Jesus through the New Testament to us (and, let us not forget, present before Jesus in the Hebrew Bible), on what basis do we plot the angle of that trajectory? Certainly, the more individualistic and idiosyncratic the interpretation, the more it ought to be balanced by the interpretive tradition of the larger believing community (that is, the Synagogue and Church through time and across cultures). Beyond this consideration, one is well advised to look both to reason and to experience as checks on the private interpretation of Scripture. Nevertheless, even these will not lead to unanimity and certitude. We have to face reality: different persons will interpret Scripture differently. That does not mean that all interpretations are equally valid, nor does it free us from the requirement to interpret the Bible carefully and rigorously. On the other hand, it does mean that we should hold our beliefs with a fair measure of humility and with charity toward the beliefs of others. A further implication is that no one interpretative school will convince everyone. Our cultural backgrounds, social locations, schooling, and experiences are too varied to allow for universally accepted interpretations. What is credible to me will not always be credible to you, and vice-versa. In such cases, tolerance is not only ethical, it is sensible.

How properly to interpret and to apply the Bible are matters far beyond the scope of this brief chapter. For those wishing to read more, I recommend three fine books: Paul J. Achtemeier's *Inspiration and Authority: Nature and Function of Christian Scripture* (Hendrickson, 1999); Richard B. Hays's *The Moral Vision of the New Testament* (HarperCollins, 1996); and Frederick Tiffany & Sharon Ringe's *Biblical Interpretation: A Roadmap* (Abingdon, 1996).

What does all of this have to do with eschatology? The lessons that I would draw include these:

1. We should not assume that there is one, uniform biblical eschatology. Disagreement is not presupposed, but neither is unanimity. In contrast to most popular interpreters of these texts, we will be cautious about harmonizing apparently disparate perspectives. Conflicting eschatologies, where they exist, deserve to be treated with fairness and integrity.

2. There is nothing wrong with a perspective that is anchored to a particular time and place. Indeed, all viewpoints are so conditioned.

3. The truth of an assertion does not arise from its uniqueness, nor is truth an all-or-nothing-at-all proposition. The creation accounts of Genesis are profoundly true even though they were influenced by other cultures and were conditioned by their historical location.

4. Neither is our own interpretation unparalleled or unconditioned by its circumstances. This realization compels us both to modesty and to diligence: the understanding that we might get it wrong urges us to work conscientiously to get it as right as possible.

5. Modern believers are engaged in the same essential task as the biblical authors whom they study, namely, understanding the impact of God's self-disclosure on their world, identity, and actions. In this respect, matters of Christian faithfulness and theological insight are of greater significance than questions of historical or scientific accuracy. It is interesting to enquire about Revelation's view of the timing of the end of history, but it is more important to ask what Revelation teaches us about faithful discipleship and how its perception of Christ might properly be applied to our world.

6. The Bible does not belong solely to fundamentalism and neither should eschatology. To abandon either is to saw off the very limb on which we are sitting.

Much as a democracy requires an educated citizenry, a non-fundamentalist church requires an educated congregation. To weigh, discern, and test what the Bible says takes knowledge and effort. It is not easy. Sometimes it is even painful, especially when the text challenges our preconceived notions or disappoints our expectations. The Bible comes to us like the angel to Jacob (Gen. 32:22-32), wrestling with us, and both wounding and blessing us in the process. Jacob would not have become Israel apart from this encounter (v. 28); neither can the church know its identity without wrestling long nights with Scripture. It is the Bible that would compel us to understand ourselves in the context of our future, and so it is to the biblical future that our attention now turns.

CHAPTER THREE

The History of the Future

The future has a long and colorful past. For untold millennia, human beings have contemplated what lay around the next bend, or season, or lifetime. Indeed, the ability to imagine and plan for the future is fundamental to our intelligence and essential to our survival. Our forebears were hardly the most imposing species to trek the African plain: without fang or claw for attack, without speed or camouflage for defense, humans needed all of the forethought they could muster. Add to the mix consciousness — and with it, a voracious appetite for meaning — and it is easy to see why people have looked to the future as a way of understanding their world and interpreting their purpose. Although true eschatologies (systems of belief about God's ultimate victory) probably came on the scene fairly recently, that is, only about 2,500 years ago, their antecedents are much more ancient.

Of course, not all interest in the future springs from lofty purpose. Knowledge of the future is valuable in countless practical ways. So farmers listen to weather reports and investors read market projections. Those who possess, or at least are believed by others to possess, reliable information about the future control a vital and desirable commodity. This truth has not escaped the notice of a thousand generations of diviners, seers, mediums, oracles, and other prognostic professionals, to which one could add modern-day economists and "futurists." (The examination of birthrates and income trends seems a tad more rational than the analysis of entrails, but both pay the rent.) Moreover, knowledge of the future is a much wished-for antidote to the nagging, sometimes paralyzing uncertainty of life. A trip to the local Tarot card reader or equivalent may assure anxious souls of future happiness. Some seek to dodge personal responsibility by offloading important decisions onto others: "No, I can't visit Grandma today. My horoscope plotter warned me not to leave town on Thursdays." It may well be that much knowledge of the future is not good for us, encouraging passivity, resignation, and moral infantilization.

The idea that we can know the future and the conviction that the future is inevitable are closely related. Each opinion naturally but not necessarily leads to the other. (I have heard it argued that God exists beyond space and therefore also outside of time; therefore, God may have foreknowledge of events that, technically speaking, are not predestined. I confess that such matters are beyond my small powers.) Not surprisingly, belief in both prediction and destiny was widespread in the ancient world. Modern readers are often struck by the fatalism they encounter in Greco-Roman texts. The world had a given structure, individuals had a station in it, and that was that. Often this attitude was reinforced by a cyclical view of history modeled on the endlessly repeating pattern of the seasons. In short, history was not going anywhere and neither were you. Much of the moral philosophy of the day taught that it is best to learn to be happy where you are. After all, the lowliest slave could be inwardly free and content, while the mightiest king could be enslaved to passion and beset with worry. (Of course, I might choose to be a free and contented king, but that option was not suggested.) Wrote Epictetus, the Stoic philosopher, "I am without a home, without a city, without property. . . . Yet what do I lack? . . . Who, when he lays eyes upon me, does not feel that he is seeing his king and his master?"[1] Those who sought a better fate — a destiny upgrade, so to speak — could pursue various forms of popular religion or magic (incantations and charms, not tricks with rabbits) in hopes of altering the course of future events. The classic expression of the conflict between fate and choice is Sophocles' play *Oedipus Rex*. Oedipus was told by an oracle that he would kill his father and have children with his mother. This was disquieting news, to say the least. He fled, but in his very attempt to outrun fate, Oedipus raced toward fate's terrible conclusion.

1. Quoted from Abraham Malherbe, *Moral Exhortation: A Greco-Roman Sourcebook* (Philadelphia: Westminster, 1986), p. 37.

Against his will and yet by his choice, he fulfilled his destiny. What's a good tragic hero to do? Apparently nothing. Though the future may be ours to see, "whatever will be will be."

Unlike most first-century religions, Judaism and Christianity linked piety toward God with morality toward others. The human response to God is first and foremost that of behaving righteously, not that of offering sacrifices or performing rituals. This emphasis on right behavior appears to assume a measure of choice, else how could God hold us responsible for our actions? Nevertheless, the impulse toward a belief in predestination is strong in monotheistic religions. To the extent that other beings — whether human, angelic, or demonic — can make things happen, God's power is limited. The difficulty is particularly acute with reference to the existence of evil. If God is all-powerful, why are wickedness and suffering tolerated? One way of dealing with the problem is to postulate a degree of divine self-limitation. God has ceded some authority to others while still overseeing the big picture. I vividly recall a conversation that I had with a woman whose son had been murdered several months before. She left the church after a minister, undoubtedly acting with the best of intentions, consoled her with the news that her boy's death had been God's will. Understandably, she found little comfort in this report and was repelled by the idea that God could have wished her son to be fatally stabbed. I responded by saying that I considered the murder to be a tragedy, not an act of God. I was first startled and then moved as she wept with obvious relief. I had never been so aware that airy theological ideas have tangible earthly consequences.

The degree to which God both knows and controls history has been disputed for centuries in both Judaism and Christianity. Many of the historical books of the Hebrew Bible (another title for what Christians traditionally call the Old Testament) were written from a "Deuteronomistic" perspective in which God rewards good and punishes evil in the here and now (see below). This viewpoint is evident also in the book of Proverbs, for example, in 10:3: "The Lord does not let the righteous go hungry, but he thwarts the craving of the wicked," and 10:22: "The blessing of the Lord makes rich, and he adds no sorrow with it." In other words, God actively governs this world, and humans pretty much get what they deserve. Job is prominent among the OT books that call into question the simple association of prosperity with virtue and suffering with wickedness. Job's accusers suppose that his miseries are proportionate to his sinning, but the reader knows otherwise. Bad things can happen to good people. Similarly, Paul wrestles with the question of human responsibility in the face of divine action (or inaction) in Romans 9:6-29. Protestantism itself is split between those like Calvin who emphasize Providence and those like Wesley who tip the balance to the side of human freedom. (You might have heard the story about the Calvinist who, after falling down the stairs, said, "I'm glad I got that over with!")

It is important to observe that biblical prophecy as a whole is more concerned with influencing the present than with revealing the future. The linkage between right behavior and right worship is central to the Hebrew Bible's prophetic literature. Self-acknowledged "prophets" were two-a-shekel in the ancient world, as the famous conflict between Elijah and the 450 prophets of Baal illustrates (1 Kings 18). When the great Hebrew prophets did foretell the future, often as not it was to *prevent* some impending disaster. "Here is what things will look like if you do not straighten up." Such prophecy called the nation to repentance, warning the people of Israel not to take God's favor for granted. Their future was not inevitable; it was conditional. This sort of prophecy is quite dissimilar to the fatalism of *Oedipus* and quite unlike the determinism of the later apocalyptic writings.[2] Generally speaking, Hebrew prophecy assumed both that human choice could affect the future,[3] and that God's will was beneficent. In time, it also came to view history from a linear perspective, that is, to assume that history is going somewhere, that ultimately the future will be better than the past. The New Testament itself is predicated on this belief. But, as humans are prone to do, we are getting ahead of ourselves.

---

2. "Apocalyptic" means "revelation" or "unveiling." Apocalyptic writings foretold God's cosmic triumph over evil, making use of startling images and multilayered symbolism. The Book of Revelation is the best known Christian *apocalypse*. Jewish and Christian apocalyptic thought will be discussed at some length in the next chapter.

3. There are exceptions. For Amos the destruction of the northern kingdom was inevitable and permanent.

Biblical Prophecy in Context

A prophet is one who speaks for God, whatever the form or content of the communication. The Hebrew word for prophet, *nābî'*, means literally "one who calls" or, possibly, "one who is called." In NT Greek the word is *prophētēs,* meaning "one who speaks for another." Both senses are evident, for example, in Exodus 7:1, in which Aaron is appointed to be the "prophet," the mouthpiece, of Moses. In fact, the Greek version of the OT, the Septuagint, translates *nābî'* as *prophētēs.*

It is common for theistic religions (that is, religions that believe in a god or gods) to affirm the existence of human intermediaries, persons specially equipped to address, hear, and speak for the god(s). This is entirely understandable; a speechless idol might be of some decorative value, but it is of little practical use. Nevertheless, unlike Ray Kinsella in the movie *Field of Dreams* ("If you build it, he will come"), most people do not appear as a matter of course to receive messages from the divine. If they did, there would be no need for mediators; hence Moses' wish in Numbers 11:29: "Would that all the Lord's people were prophets, and that the Lord would put his spirit on them." Even the early Christians, who unhesitatingly affirmed that they possessed the Spirit (see especially Acts 2:16-21), regarded prophecy as a particular endowment given only to certain individuals.[4]

Prophecy is a very ancient phenomenon, predating the birth of Israel by centuries at least. Examples of prophetic texts from other Near Eastern cultures abound. For example, a prophet at Mari recorded this message some 3,800 years ago:

> Am I not Adad the lord of Kallassu who reared him . . . and restored him to the throne of his father's house? . . . Now, since I restored him to the throne of his father's house, I should receive from him an hereditary property. . . . If he grants my request, I will give him throne upon throne, house upon house, territory upon territory, city upon city; even the land from east to west will I give him.[5]

4. E.g., 1 Cor. 12:10; Rom. 12:6; Eph. 2:20; Acts 11:27; 13:1; 15:32; Rev. 1:3.

5. Helmer Ringgren, "Prophecy in the Ancient Near East," in *Israel's Prophetic Tradition: Essays in Honour of Peter R. Ackroyd* (Cambridge: Cambridge University Press, 1982), p. 3.

It is likely that the prophet was associated with the temple, which would be the beneficiary of the king's gift, should he obey the words of the prophecy. I once visited a large "charismatic" church that was in the midst of a building campaign. A handful of people stood during the service to give prophecies (e.g., "Richly give to the building fund, and richly will I bless you") that sounded eerily similar to the above oracle!

Nearly four millennia ago, a woman prophet named Baia of Arbela spoke the following:

Fear not, Esarhaddon! I, the god Bel, speak to you. The beams of your heart I strengthen, like your mother, who caused you to exist. Sixty great gods are standing together with me and protect you. . . . Do not trust men! Turn your eyes to me, look at me! I am Ishtar of Arbela; I have turned Ashur's favour unto you. When you were small, I sustained you. Fear not, praise me! Where is the enemy which blew over you when I did not notice? The future is like the past! I am the god Nabu, lord of the tablet stylus, praise me![6]

Centuries later, an unknown Assyrian prophet spoke this oracle:

Fear not, [King] Ashurbanipal! Now, as I have spoken, it will come to pass: I shall grant (it) to you. Over the people of the four languages (and) over the armament of the princes you will exercise sovereignty. . . . Fear not! As she that bears for her child, (so) I care for you. . . . Fear not, my son, whom I have raised.[7]

We see numerous parallels to biblical prophecy in these three examples, including mention of the authority of God over the king, the ability of God to know and control history, the favor of God toward obedient subjects, the call to put one's trust in God rather than in humans, and so on. It is clear that prophecy was a long-established activity that included conventional vocabulary and topics, much of which is represented in the Bible. Many of the stylized behaviors of ancient Near

6. Ringgren, "Prophecy in the Ancient Near East," pp. 5-6.
7. Ringgren, "Prophecy in the Ancient Near East," p. 6.

Eastern prophets are also found in Scripture, especially in the accounts of Israel's early history. For example, it was common to think that prophets possessed or were possessed by a divine spirit, which was thought to produce the ecstatic or trance state in which they prophesied. Note the rather odd story recorded in Numbers 11:24-25:

> So Moses went out and told the people the words of the Lord; and he gathered seventy elders of the people, and placed them all around the tent. Then the Lord came down in the cloud and spoke to him, and took some of the spirit that was on him and put it on the seventy elders; and when the spirit rested upon them, they prophesied. But they did not do so again.

— and the even odder story in 1 Samuel 19:20-21:

> Then Saul sent messengers to take David. When they saw the company of the prophets in a frenzy, with Samuel standing in charge of them, the spirit of God came upon the messengers of Saul, and they also fell into a prophetic frenzy. When Saul was told, he sent other messengers, and they also fell into a frenzy. Saul sent messengers again the third time, and they also fell into a frenzy.

Music was often employed to induce the prophetic trance state, as, for example, in Exodus 15:20 and 1 Samuel 10:5. (Church choir directors please note.) A particularly fascinating incident is mentioned in 2 Kings 3. Elisha was asked by the king of Israel to prophesy. In response, he requested a musician. "And then, while the musician was playing, the power of the Lord came on him" (v. 15). Compare Samuel's charge to Saul (1 Sam. 10:5-6):

> After that you shall come to Gibeath-elohim, at the place where the Philistine garrison is; there, as you come to the town, you will meet a band of prophets coming down from the shrine with harp, tambourine, flute, and lyre playing in front of them; they will be in a prophetic frenzy. Then the spirit of the Lord will possess you, and you will be in a prophetic frenzy along with them and be turned into a different person.

Of course, the use of music (and dance with it; e.g., 2 Sam. 6:14-16) to create an altered state of consciousness is a practice of many religious people today, from Whirling Dervishes to Pentecostals, perhaps even the occasional Methodist or Presbyterian.

Ancient prophets received their communications in signs, visions, dreams, and words (cf. 1 Sam. 28:6). The first means, which includes the use of omens and divination, is the rarest in the Bible. The clearest example is the priest's use of the Urim and Thummin, what appear to have been sacred dice that could yield a yes-or-no answer.[8] (If the thought of priests huddled over a table throwing dice strikes you as a bit incongruous, you are not alone!) We also hear from time to time about the casting of lots.[9] Other forms of divination, such as the examination of the livers of sacrificed animals, were strongly discouraged or forbidden, as was the practice of magic and necromancy (calling up the spirits of the dead). See, for example, Joshua 13:22; 1 Samuel 15:23; Deuteronomy 18:10-12; and Isaiah 8:19.

Prophetic dreams are mentioned frequently in Scripture,[10] although the interpretation of dreams is usually credited to "wise men," such as Joseph and Daniel, and not to prophets. The distinction between dreams and visions is often vague; typically one speaks of a sleeping person having a dream and a fully conscious person having a vision, but the biblical authors sometimes refer to dreams as visions.[11] The content of visions and dreams is wide ranging indeed, everything from an appearance of God (Gen. 15:1) to the sight of a fiery chariot (Ezek. 1:4-28) to a glimpse of Jerusalem's destruction (Jer. 38:21-23) and restoration (Isa. 40:1-5). The New Testament records its share of visions, for example, the appearance to Peter of the sheet containing unclean animals, which he interprets as a sign that uncircumcised Gentiles (non-Jews) should be admitted into the church (Acts 10:9-29).

It is the third form of communication, the word from God, that dominates the Bible's prophetic literature. The well-known phrase "Thus says the Lord"[12] was modeled on an already existing messenger formula. (See Gen. 32:4: "'Thus you shall say to my lord Esau: Thus says

---

8. Exod. 28:30; Num. 27:21; 1 Sam. 14:41; etc.

9. Lev. 16:8; Num. 26:55-56; Acts 1:26.

10. As in Gen. 20:3; 31:10-11; 37:5; 40:5; 1 Kings 3:5; Joel 2:28; and Matt. 1:20.

11. Job 20:8; 33:15; Isa. 29:7; Dan. 2:19; etc.

12. Exod. 4:22; Josh. 7:13; Judg. 6:8; 1 Sam. 10:18; etc.

your servant Jacob . . .'") Given the number of such statements, it is remarkable how little the Bible actually has to say about the manner in which these messages were received. Occasionally, Scripture speaks of hearing a literal voice of God.[13] Sometimes words are conveyed in a vision.[14] Far more often, we are told only that "the word of the Lord came to" someone.[15]

It is noteworthy that each of the non-Israelite oracles quoted above offered assurance of success to the king (including, in the final case, a declaration of sonship, as in Psalm 2). Many prophets were attached to royal courts, the pre-eminent biblical example being Nathan, who exercised considerable influence in David's government. It was Nathan who announced God's covenant with David (2 Sam. 7) and who, in concert with Zadok the priest, anointed Solomon as David's successor (1 Kings 1). Despite his support for the king, Nathan is best remembered for the confrontation in which he courageously exposed David's guilt in the Bathsheba affair (2 Sam. 11-12). Much less impressive were the many ancient prophets who made their living as professional yes men. 1 Kings 22 tells the amusing story of a meeting between Ahab, king of Israel, and Jehoshaphat, king of Judah, who were together considering whether to go to war against Aram (present-day Syria). Ahab consulted his four hundred court prophets, a group smart enough to know the side on which their bread was buttered. To no one's surprise, they enthusiastically endorsed the king's plan. Unconvinced, Jehoshaphat insisted on an outside opinion:

> "Is there no other prophet of the Lord here of whom we may inquire?" The king of Israel said to Jehoshaphat, "There is still one other by whom we may inquire of the Lord, Micaiah son of Imlah; but I hate him, for he never prophesies anything favorable about me, but only disaster." (vv. 7-8)

Religious centers were the other hub of prophetic activity. Babylonian, Greek, Assyrian, and Canaanite temples had their prophets, as

---

13. E.g., in Exod. 3:4-4:17; Deut. 4:33; 1 Sam. 3:2-14; Mark 1:11; cf. Acts 9:4-7.

14. 1 Sam. 3:1; 15:1; Ezek. 1:3; etc.

15. E.g., in the opening verse of Hosea, Joel, Jonah, Micah, Zephaniah, Haggai, Zechariah, and Malachi.

did, for example, the Israelite shrine at Bethel (2 Kings 2:3). Often these sites were the home of a community of prophets who lived together under the direction of a senior prophet, such as Elijah. These "bands of prophets" (a wonderful phrase) are mentioned numerous times in the Hebrew Bible.[16]

Women as well as men could be prophets, the famed oracle at Delphi being the best-known example. The Hebrew Bible refers to at least five: Miriam (Exod. 15:20), Deborah (Judg. 4:4), Huldah (2 Kings 22:14), Noadiah (Neh. 6:14, a false prophet), and the unnamed woman of Isaiah 8:3. The NT mentions Anna (Luke 2:36) and the four daughters of Philip (Acts 21:9), as well as the mysterious "Jezebel" of Revelation 2:20. 1 Corinthians 11:5 speaks of women prophets in a manner that assumes their regular and active presence in the Pauline churches.

What are we to make of the many similarities between biblical and non-biblical (and even pre-biblical) prophecy? Was Elijah really no different from the prophets of Baal? Certainly, distinctions can be made. The violent and orgiastic behavior associated with Canaanite and some other forms of prophecy is not attributed to Israelite prophets. (1 Kings 18:28: "Then they [the prophets of Baal] cried aloud and, as was their custom, they cut themselves with swords and lances until the blood gushed out over them." I confess that I have never understood how Baal managed to find recruits.) More important are differences of theological substance, first and foremost in the conception of the deity in whose name the prophets spoke. As Hebrew thought grew self-consciously monotheistic, it excluded other gods entirely, regarding pagan prophecy as either demonic or human in origin. Likewise, the biblical prophets were concerned with establishing God's righteousness, not with satisfying a deity's hunger or a king's ambitions. Their quest for social justice set them in fatal opposition to the powers both of court and of temple (cf. Luke 13:33-34, which assumes that it is the lot of the prophet to be martyred). For many, the call to prophecy was a summons to live outside the walls of propriety, order, safety, and status.

It is important to recognize that the practice of prophecy in Israel developed over several centuries. Ideas and images borrowed from surrounding cultures were reshaped into increasingly distinctive forms.

---

16. For example, in 1 Sam. 10:5, 10; 19:20; 1 Kings 20:35; 2 Kings 2:3-7; 4:1, 38; 5:22; 6:1; and 9:1.

1 Samuel 9:9 is revealing: "Formerly in Israel, anyone who went to in-
quire of God would say, 'Come, let us go to the seer'; for the one who is
now called a prophet was formerly called a seer." The author regards
"seer" as an archaic term that requires explanation; it harkens back to a
time when prophecy was more closely allied to divination and sooth-
saying. It is no accident that the majority of parallels with surrounding
cultures mentioned above are culled from the earlier periods of Israel's
history. That is not to say that later prophets did not borrow from
other traditions; they did, but within the context of an established and
distinctive theological tradition.

Two other points are worth making. First, we should avoid the trap
of thinking that only what is unique is true. Often, the opposite is the
case: beliefs may be shared across cultures precisely because they correspond in some basic way to human experience. If we assume that Judaism or Christianity is true only to the extent that it is different from
other religions, we place ourselves in an untenable position, defending
our little island of uniqueness against the ever-rising floodtide of ar-
cheological discovery. Most humans have two eyes, one nose, two ears,
and one mouth. On that level, there is almost no difference. What sets
us apart is the particular shape of these common features and the particular manner in which they are assembled into a whole. Religions are
distinguished less by their unparalleled elements than by the particular
way that their common elements are shaped and assembled. Genesis 1
shares numerous features with other ancient Near Eastern creation stories, but its theological contours are nonetheless singular and significant. In Genesis, we see the face of God in a new and distinctive way.

Second, we should recognize that all of us think by means of inher-
ited symbols and ideas. Each of us is more restricted by our cultural and
historical environment than we can realize, although our limitations
will be plain enough to later generations. It should not astonish or
worry us if Israelite prophecy, particularly in its earlier stages, looked a
lot like Phoenician or Syrian prophecy. By analogy, we might recall that
many early television shows were transplanted radio programs and
many early computer games were electronic reproductions of board
games. That having been said, it is interesting how little difference can
make a difference. I am told that chimpanzees and humans are 95 percent identical genetically. That fact both heightens my regard for
chimps and elevates my appreciation for each and every percentage

point of difference! For the record, humans beings are at least 99.8 percent identical. Think of all of the diversity found in that two-tenths of one percent.

True and False Prophecy

Not all oracles were created equal. The biblical authors themselves were aware of the difficulty of distinguishing between true and false prophets, the latter being those "who teach lies" (Isa. 9:15), who "see false and deceptive visions" (Lam. 2:14), "who come to you in sheep's clothing but inwardly are ravenous wolves" (Matt. 7:15).[17] Apparently, it was no easier then than it is now to discern who is on the Lord's side. It may be that the great majority of prophets in ancient Israel, all but a few of whom are unknown to us, would not meet a rigorous biblical standard. Certainly that is the impression left by Jeremiah 23:9-40, a scathing denunciation of the host of popular prophets: "Do not listen to the words of the prophets who prophesy to you; they are deluding you. They speak visions of their own minds, not from the mouth of the Lord" (v. 16).

Prophets often acted as moral teachers, speaking to the present sociopolitical reality from the perspective of God's righteousness (Micah 3:7-8). It is only fitting, then, that prophets should be expected to behave morally. Hence, Jeremiah cites, for example, the adulteries of the prophets as evidence of their illegitimacy. "Both prophet and priest are ungodly; even in my house have I found their wickedness, says the Lord" (Jer. 23:11). Of course, such a test is hardly infallible. Not all ethical people are prophets, and not all prophets always behave ethically. Naturally, the same can be said of pastors and other moral leaders.

Without question, the most influential and problematic text on the subject of false prophecy is Deuteronomy 18:20-22:

> But any prophet who speaks in the name of other gods, or who presumes to speak in my name a word that I have not commanded the prophet to speak — that prophet shall die. You may

---

17. See also Micah 3:11; Zeph. 3:4; Ezek. 12:24; 13:7-9; Zech. 10:2; Matt. 24:11; Luke 6:26; and Acts 13:6.

say to yourself, "How can we recognize a word that the Lord has not spoken?" If a prophet speaks in the name of the Lord but the thing does not take place or prove true, it is a word that the Lord has not spoken. The prophet has spoken it presumptuously; do not be frightened by it.

Two criteria are offered: (1) the true prophet speaks only in the name of the one God; and (2) the true prophet's predictions always come to pass. The first point is straightforward enough, although one might make allowance for the possibility that God could speak or work through people outside of Judaism or Christianity (e.g., Balaam in Num. 22 or Cyrus in Isa. 45). It is the second criterion that is the more perplexing since, strictly applied, it would eliminate all but a handful of biblical prophets. It simply is not the case that every prophetic expectation for the future was fulfilled. Some anticipated calamities were only partially fulfilled; e.g., Jeremiah's prediction of Egypt's destruction by King Nebuchadrezzar (Jer. 46; Egypt was attacked but not conquered by Babylon). Other woes were averted entirely; e.g., the destruction of Jerusalem by the Assyrians prophesied in Micah 3:12 and later explained in Jeremiah 26:17-19. Often such reversals were credited to the people's repentance and/or to God's change of mind.[18] In some instances, earlier prophecies were even reversed; for example, compare Isaiah 2:4 and Micah 4:3 with Joel 3:10. In times of national loss, prophets offered exalted visions of future restoration, some of which were approximated in general but few of which were fulfilled in detail in the community's subsequent history.[19]

I was fortunate once to be near Anchorage, Alaska, on an exceptionally clear day. Looking to the horizon, I was amazed to see Denali (Mt. McKinley) and the surrounding mountains, situated over one hundred and fifty miles away. Without question, I was genuinely affected by Denali's grandeur; nevertheless, I would have been hard pressed to map the mountain range, and I knew nothing at all of the vast territory that separated us. Likewise, the prophetic vision appears to have been more impressionistic than cartographic, more a sketch and less a photograph than is usually imagined. With passion and po-

---

18. Jer. 26:17-19; see also Jer. 18:5-11; Exod. 32:14; Amos 5:15; etc.
19. Isa. 2:1-4; 4:2-6; 35; 54; Jer. 31:38-40; Ezek. 39:25-29; Micah 5:7-9; etc.

etry the prophets contested and consoled, hoping to redirect the present and so to recast the future. Therefore, the notion of a fixed, inviolable destiny is actually contrary to much of the prophetic witness.[20]

The other problem is one of timing. Prophets called for an immediate response. Waiting to see whose predictions (for example, on the fate of Jerusalem) came true was a luxury that Israel could ill afford. Practically, decisions must be made about the legitimacy of prophecy far in advance of such evidence — and much to the relief of many a false prophet, no doubt.

So what are we to make of Deuteronomy 18? Overwhelmingly, scholars are convinced that the book of Deuteronomy in its present form comes from the period shortly after the Exile (the deportation of the Jews to Babylon), that is, about the year 500 B.C. The authors made use of earlier traditions, to be sure, but revised them in light of the destruction of Jerusalem and the Babylonian Captivity. Much the same group is thought to be responsible for the so-called Deuteronomistic History, comprised of Joshua–2 Kings. All of these books share a common theme: Israel prospers when it obeys the Law and heeds the prophets, and Israel is punished when it does not. The true prophets were those like Jeremiah who warned the people of coming judgment. The false prophets foretold peace and safety, oracles amply discredited by intervening history. The view of prophecy in Deuteronomy is therefore fairly late, a bit wooden, and more than a little idealized. Its main interest is in showing that God faithfully warned unfaithful Israel through the agency of the prophets. It does not provide a comprehensive account of prophecy, and we would be wise not to view the phenomenon entirely through this one lens. This observation is true equally of NT as of OT prophecy. The hopes of the postexilic community did not materialize quite as they had anticipated, and neither did those of the early church. That does not mean that the expectations of either group were fundamentally misplaced. God was with them, but they had mistaken foothills for mountains.

20. As I noted in footnote 3, there are exceptions. Some oracles of doom extended no hope for repentance and relief.

The Covenant Future

At the heart of Jewish and Christian thinking is the idea of covenant, an agreement between God and humans made at God's gracious initiative. By their nature, covenants are future oriented; they enshrine a mutually beneficial ideal toward which both parties are to direct themselves. Marriage is a good example. A couple is married in a covenant ceremony, a wedding, that might last only half an hour (even less in the state of Nevada), but their marriage will be achieved over a lifetime. Husbands and wives need continually to *become* married, to better approximate the utopian vision that is marriage. Moreover, while the original covenant remains, the day-to-day terms by which it is enacted and the conceptual world in which it is experienced may vary considerably over time. Few couples married in the 1940s or 50s could have anticipated the changes in women's roles realized in subsequent decades, but many have adapted to and flourished because of them. So, too, Israel's covenant with God changed shape over the centuries, but its core ideal did not.

The notion of covenant is essential to biblical thought about the future. God's relationship with humanity has a history, and it is on the basis of that history that prophets evaluated the present and anticipated the future. We might say that the future is a product of the past, and the past, biblically speaking, is covenantal. It is sensible therefore to consider what the Hebrew Bible says about the future within its covenantal context. To this end, let us look briefly at four separate clusters of biblical material, in more or less chronological order.

Abraham/ Sarah	Moses	David	Amos & Isaiah	Jeremiah & Ezekiel	Later prophets (e.g., 3 Isaiah)
	Exodus from Egypt	*Unified Monarchy*	*Fall of Israel*	*Fall of Judah*	*Return from Exile*
2000 B.C.	1300 B.C.	1000 B.C.	722/1 B.C.	587/6 B.C.	400 B.C.

1. *The Covenant with Abraham*

The covenant traditions of Genesis center on the figure of Abraham. You might recall that Abraham and Sarah were well into "retirement age" (he in his eighties and she in her seventies) when they were promised their first child. In Genesis 15:5-6 we read:

> [God] brought him outside and said, "Look toward heaven and count the stars, if you are able to count them." Then he said to him, "So shall your descendants be." And he [Abraham] believed the Lord; and the Lord reckoned it to him as righteousness.

Abraham believed that God would do something that, humanly speaking, was impossible. Actually, it became even more impossible. Abraham was one hundred and Sarah ninety when Isaac at last was born (cf. Gen. 16:16; 17:17; 21:5). Although God's promise was not eschatological — that is, it did not have to do with the ultimate fulfillment of human history — it is the cornerstone for later eschatological belief. Abraham's faith was directed toward the eventual fulfillment of God's purposes. This point is made even clearer in the promises of land (Gen. 15:7, 18-21), prosperity, and blessing (22:18), expectations only partly realized in Abraham's own lifetime. These promises are restated and elaborated in the narratives concerning Abraham's son Isaac (26:2-5), Isaac's son Jacob (Gen. 28:10-17; 35:11-12), and Jacob's twelve sons (Gen. 49).

These materials form a kind of constitution to which later Jewish and Christian authors appealed and a rule against which their place in history was measured. The esteem in which David was held by subsequent generations is due in part to the fact that it was under him and his son Solomon that the promises to Abraham, especially the pledge of land, came nearest to complete fulfillment. Moreover, these texts create a set of standard expectations concerning the character of God and the nature of God's dealings with humanity. The Divine is not seen as impersonal and aloof but as personal and relational. Faith, devotion, and obedience are established as core human responses. The expectation is fostered that God will act in human history on behalf of Abraham, his offspring, and the entire world (Gen. 22:18; 26:4). These ideas are basic to all biblical eschatology.

2. The Covenant at Mount Sinai

The future is also a prominent theme in the biblical texts concerning Moses, the Exodus, the giving of the Law, and the settlement in Canaan. Exodus 3:7-10 and 6:2-8 contain promises of deliverance, land, and divine revelation. The future blessings of Israel are recorded in Exodus 19:3-6:

> Then Moses went up to God; the Lord called to him from the mountain, saying, "Thus you shall say to the house of Jacob, and tell the Israelites: You have seen what I did to the Egyptians, and how I bore you on eagles' wings and brought you to myself. Now therefore, if you obey my voice and keep my covenant, you shall be my treasured possession out of all the peoples. Indeed, the whole earth is mine, but you shall be for me a priestly kingdom and a holy nation. These are the words that you shall speak to the Israelites."

The basic terms of this covenant are laid out in the next chapter (Exod. 20), which contains the Ten Commandments. In Exodus, the promise is more conditional than in Genesis: if Israel obeys, God will bless. Scholars have highlighted the many similarities between the "Mosaic covenant" (mediated by Moses but made with the whole of Israel) and ancient suzerain-vassal treaties by which a king made an alliance with a lesser power. Such "covenants" included, among other things, a historical introduction detailing the relationship between the states, the specific terms of the treaty, a list of blessings if the treaty was kept and curses if it was broken, a public recital of the treaty, and a ceremonial meal. All of these elements are found in the accounts of Exodus 19-24 and Deuteronomy 27-30. The legal and political dimensions of the covenant stress the importance of Israel's obedience to the Law and the exclusivity of its allegiance to God.

A weakness of this model is that it tends to depersonalize the relationship between Israel and God. A legal contract is more easily broken and set aside than is a relationship, say, between parent and child or husband and wife. It is instructive that many later prophets turned to these relational models when speaking of God's forgiveness and reconciling love. This is especially true for those who contemplated the destruction of the kingdoms of Israel and Judah (721 and 587 B.C.). What hope is there for the future if the covenant is broken?[21] Is Israel cut off from God? The contract model allows little room for God's grace or for Israel's repentance, and so it was counterbalanced over time by more personal ideas of covenant, not least in the teaching of Jesus himself (e.g., the parent/child relationship in the parable of the Prodigal Son).

For our purposes, the main point is to see how fundamentally the Mosaic covenant shaped Israel's consciousness of its own history and destiny. We have already seen that blessings or curses were thought to be the direct consequences of covenantal faithfulness or infidelity. This conviction became a handy instrument for judging the past, as in the belief that Israel was conquered by Babylon because it failed to meet its covenant obligations. Just as important, it fueled the expectation that a change in Israel's behavior would lead to a restoration of Israel's fortunes. Such was the hope of the Pharisaic party, which believed that God would recognize and honor the piety of a holy minority within Israel. The call to repentance was a common feature of eschatological proclamation in both Judaism and Christianity, as one finds, for example, in both the preaching of John the Baptist and the teaching of the apostle Paul. The idea that the future kingdom of God would be a kingdom of righteousness owes much to the Mosaic covenant.[22]

Significant as it is, the Abrahamic covenant was (at least in theory) limited to a single family. The Mosaic covenant transformed that family into a people, gathering individuals of disparate backgrounds together under a new and common identity. Scholars now recognize that the "Hebrews" included many persons who were not themselves descendants of Abraham; indeed, Exodus 12:38 specifically mentions that those who departed Egypt were "a mixed crowd." Henceforth, Gentiles who wanted to become Israelites could in principle do so by entering into the covenant. In time, this possibility gave rise to the expectation that many or even all Gentiles would one day be included in Israel, a hope that is presupposed by the early church's acceptance of Gentile converts.

At the same time, the Mosaic covenant increased the distinctiveness of Israel as a separate and holy people. Their strong sense of iden-

21. Isa. 24:5; Jer. 11:1-13; 22:9; Ezek. 16:59; Hos. 8:1; etc.
22. See, for example, Isa. 9:7; Matt. 6:33; and Rom. 14:17.

tity allowed the Jews to survive horrendous calamities and, even more, to resist the temptation to assimilate — and disappear — into the wider world. On the other hand, it led some to regard Gentiles as existing outside the sphere of God's interest. While many Jews looked forward to the eschatological incorporation of Gentiles into Israel, others eagerly anticipated the Gentiles' future destruction.[23]

It would be difficult to overstate the importance of the Mosaic covenant for Israel's self-understanding. It is this people, defined in this way, to whom God made promises and through whom God would work. Few Christians appear to grasp the "givenness" of Israel. Why? Because for them the church now occupies its place. Technically, this perspective is called "supersessionism," because the church is thought to have superseded Israel in God's plan. One can see this idea taking preliminary shape in the late first century as Christianity and Judaism split apart and the church became an increasingly Gentile institution. Nevertheless, it is an idea foreign to the earliest Christians. The most notable opponent of such thinking is Paul, whose wrestling over the fate of the Jews in Romans 9-11 is compelled by his certainty that "the gifts and the calling of God are irrevocable" (11:29). Israel must have a future in God's plan. So Paul declares that at the return of Christ "all Israel will be saved" (11:26). This conclusion defies the logic of Paul's earlier argument, which would have led us to believe that most Jews had failed to meet the terms of the new covenant (that is, they have not believed in Christ) and so would be separated from God. The original covenant is so essential that Paul cannot imagine that it is within God's character to abandon Israel.

3. The Covenant with David

2 Samuel 7 records a remarkable oracle of the prophet Nathan concerning King David:

> I will make for you a great name, like the name of the great ones
> of the earth. And I will appoint a place for my people Israel and
> will plant them, so that they may live in their own place, and be

23. E.g., Jubilees 24:29-30; 1 Enoch 90:19.

disturbed no more; and evildoers shall afflict them no more, as formerly, from the time that I appointed judges over my people Israel; and I will give you rest from all your enemies. Moreover the Lord declares to you that the Lord will make you a house [a dynasty]. When your days are fulfilled and you lie down with your ancestors, I will raise up your offspring after you, who shall come forth from your body, and I will establish his kingdom. He shall build a house for my name, and I will establish the throne of his kingdom forever. . . . I will not take my steadfast love from him, as I took it from Saul, whom I put away from before you. Your house and your kingdom shall be made sure forever before me; your throne shall be established forever. (vv. 9-16)

The "Davidic covenant" is unconditional. It is not clear from the text what if anything David did to deserve such an honor, nor is mention made of the worthiness of David's descendants. No strings are attached at any point. Hence, David's progeny would not suffer the fate of Saul, whose failings cost him his crown. Likewise, the Davidic covenant is eternal. It follows that an eternal throne requires an everlasting kingdom, so the promise of permanence is made not only to David but to all of Israel through him.

The covenant with David became especially meaningful after the Babylonian Exile, which broke the Davidic line. The expectation of a restoration of the Davidic kingship and kingdom is foundational to much eschatological thinking. Isaiah 11:1 promises that "a shoot shall come out from the stump of Jesse," that is, a descendant will arise from the line of David (Jesse's son), who will rule over a glorious kingdom of universal peace. Similarly, Jeremiah 23:5-6:

The days are surely coming, says the Lord, when I will raise up for David a righteous Branch, and he shall reign as king and deal wisely, and shall execute justice and righteousness in the land. In his days Judah will be saved and Israel will live in safety. And this is the name by which he will be called: "The Lord is our righteousness."

These expectations are elaborated in Jeremiah 33:14-26, which ends with the statement, "For I will restore their fortunes, and will have mercy upon them." (Understandably, "restoration" is a key word in Jewish eschatology.) Over time, the Davidic figure was associated by many Jews with the hoped-for Messiah, the agent through whom God would restore Israel (a connection aided by Genesis 49:8-12 and Psalm 2). Characteristically, the Davidic Messiah was imagined as a warrior king who would defeat Israel's enemies.[24] Matthew 12:23 assumes that the title "Son of David" was popularly understood to refer to the Messiah: "All the crowds were amazed and said, 'Can this be the Son of David?'" Compare the people's declaration on Palm Sunday: "Blessed is the coming kingdom of our ancestor David!" (Mark 11:10). As one might expect, the New Testament writers made frequent reference to Jesus' Davidic credentials;[25] nevertheless, they do not portray him as a military conqueror, although the idea is sometimes associated with his return.[26]

4. The Broken and Restored Covenant

Unfortunately for human history, the unthinkable is not the impossible. Despite popular confidence that such misfortunes could not occur, the city of God, the temple of the divine presence, and the throne of David were obliterated in 587 B.C. Jeremiah and other prophets had warned of impending disaster, but the majority of their contemporaries were unconvinced. After all, the inviolability of the city and its institutions was thought to have been guaranteed. Recall, for example, the statement in Psalm 46:4-5 concerning Jerusalem:

> There is a river whose streams make glad the city of God, the holy habitation of the Most High. God is in the midst of the city; it shall not be moved; God will help it when the morning dawns.

The destruction of Jerusalem and subsequent deportations of thousands of Jews to Babylon were a catastrophe of enormous significance. It is the watershed event that divides Old Testament history,

---

24. E.g., in the non-biblical *Psalms of Solomon,* chapter 17, and the *Scroll of Blessings* from Qumran.

25. Matt. 1:1; 9:27; Mark 10:47-48; 12:35-37; Luke 1:32; 2:11; Rom. 1:3; 2 Tim. 2:8; etc.

26. See 2 Thess. 2:8; Rev. 6:2; 17:14; 19:11-16.

much as the Holocaust divides modern Jewish history and September 11, 2001, divides recent American history. Afterward, life could never be quite the same. As we have already seen, for those who compiled the Hebrew Bible and wrote much of its history, the destruction of Jerusalem was the fact above all other facts that informed their perspective. Never again should such a thing be allowed to happen. The severity of postexilic leaders such as Ezra — who, among other things, required Jewish men to divorce their foreign wives (Ezra 10:3) — is understandable in this light. The Pharisees of Jesus' day were the natural-born descendants of this movement. One needs only to review the exhaustive list of curses in Deuteronomy 28:15-68 to get a feel for what was considered to be at stake. "Getting it right this time" was serious business.

The events of 587 B.C. were no less a watershed for biblical prophecy. In the years preceding Jerusalem's destruction, the biblical prophets became increasingly pessimistic about the future. More than a century before, Isaiah had prophesied that Jerusalem would be cleansed and restored to glory (e.g., 2; 4:2-6). Things looked less hopeful two or three generations later. The coming of the "day of the Lord" would mean, not deliverance, but destruction and desolation (Zeph. 1:7, 14-18; cf. Amos 5:18). Israel had broken its covenant with God (Jer. 22:5-9; Zeph. 1:2-6). It is worth remembering that much of Israel had already been lost in the Assyrian conquest of the northern kingdom in 721 B.C. Among others, Amos had prophesied that country's complete annihilation: "Fallen, no more to rise, is maiden Israel" (5:2). The "ten tribes" of the north had not been reconstituted; their cities had not been raised from ash and ruin. Was the fate of Judah to be any different? Was the covenant at an end? Was the religion of God to be forsaken?

After the dreaded cataclysm arrived, the role of the prophets reversed: they became the bearers of good news. God had not rejected Israel. Babylon would be destroyed. A bright future awaited the children of Abraham and Sarah. The prophet Jeremiah is a fascinating bellwether because he prophesied both before and after Jerusalem's destruction. Formerly, he preached a message of doom and gloom, anguish and sorrow. Later, he offered words of profound hope. According to 46:27-28:

But as for you, have no fear, my servant Jacob, and do not be dismayed, O Israel; for I am going to save you from far away, and your offspring from the land of their captivity. Jacob shall return and have quiet and ease, and no one shall make him afraid. As for you, have no fear, my servant Jacob, says the Lord, for I am with you. I will make an end of all the nations among which I have banished you, but I will not make an end of you!

The key passage is Jeremiah 30-31, which may be summarized in a single verse, 31:17: "there is hope for your future, says the Lord." But would not things be just as they were before? Would not Israel again sin and again be punished? No, for God will make a new covenant, one that Israel will be divinely empowered to keep:[27]

The days are surely coming, says the Lord, when I will make a new covenant with the house of Israel and the house of Judah. It will not be like the covenant that I made with their ancestors when I took them by the hand to bring them out of the land of Egypt — a covenant that they broke, though I was their husband, says the Lord. But this is the covenant that I will make with the house of Israel after those days, says the Lord: I will put my law within them, and I will write it on their hearts; and I will be their God, and they shall be my people. (31:31-33)

One sees the same pattern in the prophecies of Jeremiah's contemporary, Ezekiel. In 2:9-10, Ezekiel is commissioned to speak words of "lamentation and mourning and woe." For the next thirty chapters, he pronounces judgment on the people of Israel and surrounding nations:

I will make you a desolation and an object of mocking among the nations around you, in the sight of all that pass by. You shall

---

27. Anyone acquainted with the New Testament will know something of the importance of this passage for Christian theology. Indeed, "New Testament" means "new covenant." The new covenant is referred to explicitly in Luke 22:20; 1 Cor. 11:25; 2 Cor. 3:6; Heb. 8:8, 13; 9:15; and 12:24. The first two citations are from accounts of the Lord's Supper; Mark and Matthew leave out the adjective "new" but also mention the institution of a covenant. The idea was especially important to the apostle Paul, who believed that Christians — that is, those participating in the new covenant — were now empowered by the Spirit to obey the "just requirement of the law" (Rom. 8:4). Paul even refers to the "old covenant" in 2 Cor. 3:14.

be a mockery and a taunt . . . when I execute judgments on you in anger and fury, with furious punishments — I, the Lord, have spoken. . . . (5:14-15)

The fall of Jerusalem is recorded in Ezekiel 33:21-22. Almost immediately the tone shifts. In chapter 34, God is depicted as the good shepherd who will seek out the lost sheep of Israel and return them to their land. The Davidic king will be restored (vv. 23-24) and God will establish "a covenant of peace" (v. 25; cf. 37:26-27). As was the case with Jeremiah's vision of a new covenant, the people will be supplied with moral provision ("a new heart . . . and a new spirit"): "I will put my spirit within you, and make you follow my statutes and be careful to observe my ordinances" (36:26, 27). The most famous of such passages is chapter 37, containing the vision of the Valley of Dry Bones, representing "the whole house of Israel" (v. 11) on which the Spirit will blow and generate new life. Much of the remainder of the book is concerned with the institution of a new and glorious temple, which will be "in the midst of them forevermore" (37:26).

Ezekiel also contains a number of strange visions that anticipate a new age that will be ushered in at God's command. First, however, there must be a titanic battle between the forces of good and evil (Ezek. 38-39). This marks a beginning of apocalyptic thought, a matter that will be discussed at some length in the next chapter.

The book of Isaiah is an invaluable source for Jewish hopes both during and after the Exile. That statement might seem strange, given the fact that the prophet Isaiah lived and died more than a century prior to the destruction of Jerusalem. In fact, there is widespread consensus (but not universal agreement, which is a near impossibility among scholars, who make their living by disagreeing with one another!) that the present book of Isaiah is composed of at least three layers of material representing three distinct historical periods.[28] The first section is comprised of chapters 1-39, which contain the oracles of Isaiah of Jerusalem (though chaps. 36-39 are taken from 2 Kings 18:13–20:19, and chaps. 24-27 and 34-35 might be of later origin). As we have already seen, while these passages contain numerous words of judg-

---

28. In summary: chapters 1-39 are before the Exile, chapters 40-55 are during the Exile, and chapters 56-66 are after the Exile.

ment, they are relatively sanguine compared to some later prophetic writings. A dramatic transition occurs at 40:1:

> Comfort, O comfort my people, says your God. Speak tenderly to Jerusalem, and cry to her, that she has served her term, that her penalty is paid, that she has received from the Lord's hand double for all her sins.

From this point through chapter 55, the text presupposes that Jerusalem has been destroyed and that the Jewish leaders are in exile in Babylon. Twice the Persian ruler Cyrus is mentioned (44:28; 45:1), the very Cyrus who defeated the Babylonians and freed the Jews. The unnamed author (commonly referred to as "Second Isaiah" or "Deutero-Isaiah," that is, "Isaiah, the Sequel") of these oracles appears to have been a distant follower of Isaiah of Jerusalem, adapting many of the prophet's ideas to Israel's new situation. This prophet sounds strong notes of consolation and hope in passages that are among the Bible's most lyrical and inspiring. 49:14-15 is illustrative:

> But Zion said, "The Lord has forsaken me, my Lord has forgotten me." Can a woman forget her nursing child, or show no compassion for the child of her womb? Even these may forget, yet I will not forget you.

Intertwined in these chapters are two ideas that would come to have particular significance for eschatology and the birth of Christianity: Israel's role as a light to the nations and its call to servanthood. Both thoughts are present in 42:1:

> Here is my servant, whom I uphold, my chosen, in whom my soul delights; I have put my spirit upon him; he will bring forth justice to the nations.

Allied with this interest is the author's emphasis on God as Creator:

> Have you not known? Have you not heard? The Lord is the everlasting God, the Creator of the ends of the earth. He does not faint or grow weary; his understanding is unsearchable. (40:28)

I made the earth, and created humankind upon it; it was my hands that stretched out the heavens, and I commanded all their host. (45:12)

It may well be that the experience of living in Babylon opened the prophet's eyes to the scope of God's creation. If so, it is analogous to the way that the Civil War altered popular perception of the United States. The mingling of tens of thousands of soldiers and their movement across the country fostered an unprecedented sense of nationhood. Prior to the war, people said, "The United States are . . . ," but afterward, "The United States is . . ." Americans had become aware as never before that they were part of something larger than their home state. Similarly, the prophet saw that Israel was part of a much bigger world and that it participated in a much greater plan:

Thus says God, the Lord, who created the heavens and stretched them out. . . . I have given you as a covenant to the people, a light to the nations, to open the eyes that are blind, to bring out the prisoners from the dungeon, from the prison those who sit in darkness. (42:5-7)

So, God is concerned with the entire world and is at work through Israel to redeem all of humanity (45:22-23, *KJV*):

Look unto me, and be ye saved, all the ends of the earth; for I am God, and there is none else. By myself have I sworn, the word is gone forth from my mouth in righteousness, and shall not return, that unto me every knee shall bow, every tongue shall swear.

Had it not been for the writings of this "Isaiah," it is quite possible that I, a non-Jew, would not today be worshiping the God of Israel. The expectation that the Gentiles would one day enter Israel (worked out more fully in the last section of Isaiah; see below) was essential to the early church's self-understanding and mission. It is unfortunate that so many Christians think of Judaism as exclusivistic and Christianity as universalistic. Without the universalism of earlier Jewish thinkers there would be no Gentile church today.

There is more. Redemption extends even to the world of nature, which would welcome the returning exiles with easy and abundant harvests.[29] Ezekiel, the William Blake of OT prophets, made much the same point using still more fantastic imagery.[30] These and similar passages are crucial because they witness to the beginning of the expectation of God's universal, even cosmic, victory.

Equally important but trickier by an order of magnitude are the four main passages that concern "the servant of God" (Isa. 42:1-4; 49:1-6; 50:4-9; and 52:13–53:12). A hurricane of controversy swirls endlessly about these passages. The most turbulent winds are stirred by the question of the servant's identity. Is the author referring to Israel itself or to some individual who personifies Israel? The likeliest answer is "both." Some passages refer to the whole of Israel (e.g., 41:8; 49:3), and others to someone who acts on behalf of Israel (49:5-6; 52:13–53:12). Bernhard W. Anderson has noted that such a shift is not unusual:

> Again and again we have seen that an individual may incarnate the whole community of Israel or, vice versa, the community may be addressed as an individual who stands in direct, personal relation to God.[31]

It is not possible to know if the author had a historical person in mind (Moses, Jeremiah, himself), or if he was referring to someone yet to come. What is more important is recognition of the possibility that Jesus himself viewed his ministry from the perspective of the servant passages.[32] It is certain that the early church understood him in that way, e.g., in Acts 8:26-39. As prophets so often do, the author has provided an ideal vision of God's *modus operandi* that transcends any one context or any single interpretation.

Beginning in Isaiah 56, we leave the Exile behind and enter the period shortly following the return of thousands of Jews to Jerusalem

29. Isaiah 41:17-20; 43:18-21; 51:3; the idea is anticipated in 11:6-9.

30. See Ezek. 34:25-31; 36:8-12, 29-30.

31. Bernhard W. Anderson, *Understanding the Old Testament*, 4th ed. (Englewood Cliffs, N.J.: Prentice-Hall, 1986), p. 493. Anderson offers a helpful table on p. 492 that compares the similarities and differences between the texts that speak of a corporate Israel and of an individual.

32. See Mark 8:31; 9:30-32; 10:33-34, 45.

from Babylon. For these pilgrims, there is good news and there is bad news. The good news is that a remnant of the people has returned and is gradually rebuilding the city and temple. The bad news is that their expectations of glory are more than a little premature. The going is rough: there are enemies without and dissension within. Contrary to the exalted expectations of the prophets, nature is not bending over backwards to cooperate. Even worse, some of the people have returned to their bad old ways and are worshiping pagan gods. The righteous remnant is not living up to its billing.

The remaining chapters of Isaiah (56-66) challenge political and economic oppression, attack idolatry, and reassure readers that the hoped-for golden age is yet to come. The disappointed expectations of earlier chapters are not toned down; instead, they are amplified. Jerusalem is about to be restored to great majesty (chapters 60-62, 66):

> Say to daughter Zion, "See, your salvation comes; his reward is with him, and his recompense before him." They shall be called, "The Holy People, The redeemed of the Lord"; and you shall be called, "Sought Out." (62:11b-12)

The dispersed children will return (60:4), and the wealth of the nations will pour into Israel (60:5-17; 61:6; 66:12). The Gentiles will come to Zion and join in worshiping God (60:3; 66:18-20 [echoed by Paul in Rom. 15:16]; cf. 2:3; 11:9-10). Clearly, we are once again in the realm of eschatology. The perspective becomes unmistakable in 60:19-22:

> The sun shall no longer be your light by day, nor for brightness shall the moon give light to you by night; but the Lord will be your everlasting light, and your God will be your glory. . . . Your people shall all be righteous; they shall possess the land forever. (vv. 19, 21)

Even more striking is 65:17-25, which begins with the announcement "I am about to create new heavens and a new earth." This viewpoint is paralleled in other postexilic writings. For example, the prophet Haggai expected God to "shake the nations," overthrowing kingdoms and bringing their treasure into the reconstituted temple (2:6-9; 2:20-23). Haggai also believed that Zerubbabel, then governor of

Judah, would be the Davidic Messiah, a belief shared by the prophet Zechariah (6:9-15). We see in Zechariah's many visions, as in those of Ezekiel several years before, the stirrings of apocalyptic thought; e.g., the lampstand and bowl of 4:2, images used later in Revelation, and the "divine warrior" motif in chapter 9, which (regrettably, I think) is a mainstay of most apocalypses.

The final chapter of the Old Testament, Malachi 4, is thoroughly eschatological. "See, the day is coming . . ." (Mal. 4:1). The last two verses concern the return of the prophet Elijah, whose arrival will proceed "the great and terrible day of the Lord," and whose preaching will "turn the hearts of parents to their children and the hearts of children to their parents" (4:5-6). The Gospels explicitly identify John the Baptist as this Elijah figure, the forerunner of Jesus (combining Mal. 4:5-6 and Mal. 3:1; e.g., Matt. 11:10-14; 17:12), thus forging a link between the conclusion of the first testament and the beginning of the second.

It is commonly said that the Old Testament ends with expectation and the New Testament begins with fulfillment. There is much truth to this statement. In his first-recorded utterance in Mark (probably the earliest Gospel), Jesus declares, "The time is fulfilled" (Mark 1:15). The promise-fulfillment scenario is prominent throughout much of the New Testament.[33] We should recognize, however, that the NT also ends with expectation (Rev. 22:20-21). Jewish hopes were not entirely unfulfilled, nor were Christian hopes completely realized. Rather, both traditions saw God at work in their history and anticipated the perfection of that work at some future day. In neither case did the incomplete realization of prophetic expectations lead to the death of hope. In a sense, hope cannot die so long as Judaism and Christianity survive. Belief in God's righteousness and trust in God's covenant are basic, and both are inextricably bound up with expectation for the future. Nevertheless, the shape of that hope changed over time. After the sixth century B.C., the most important channel for its evolution was apocalyptic speculation, which itself became the seedbed of early Christianity.

---

33. Matt. 1:22; 4:14; 8:17; 12:17; Mark 14:49; Luke 4:21; 22:37; John 12:38; 13:18; Acts 1:16; 3:18; etc.

CHAPTER FOUR

Apocalypse Then

I n high school I was something of an expert on eschatology. Like many of my friends, I consumed tall stacks of Last Days literature. Like swallows to Capistrano, our weekly fellowship group returned habitually to End Times study. Whenever possible, I visited churches to watch guest speakers pilot their maze of Millennium charts. ("And here we have the fifth trumpet. Notice the locusts pictured beneath, which, as you know, represent the troops of the Soviet Union.") I attended the screening of a handful of "rapture" films, which are rather like horror movies for Christians, depicting life before and after Christ snatches believers from the earth. (In case you missed the show, "before" is better.) After a couple years under such tutelage, I could tell you the meaning of every seal and bowl in the book of Revelation, the identity of Gog and Magog, Babylon, and the beast, the likely timing of the Tribulation, and the precise chronology of events leading up to the Great White Throne Judgment. It's funny, isn't it, how often it is the case that the less you know, the more certain you are?

It has been said that the person who knows only one thing knows nothing. That is a pithy but obscure way of saying that it is important to study an object in its context, to compare one thing with other things like it. That point was made most memorably in Walter M. Miller's novel *Canticle for Leibowitz,* which describes a post–nuclear-war era in which a few surviving literary scraps are preserved by monks who sincerely venerate but egregiously misunderstand them. A less dramatic example is my relative unfamiliarity with cookbooks. I know what words like "render," "clarify," and "dress" mean in some other contexts, but I can only guess at their signification in *Betty Crocker*. I do not know the genre, so I am bound to make a hash (at best) of its interpretation.

The maxim about knowing only one thing is especially pertinent in the case of the NT book of Revelation, which represents a type of literature with which few people today are familiar. It was not until I was in graduate school that I learned that a considerable number of other things like Revelation do exist to which it ought to be compared. These are the apocalyptic writings of Judaism, the great majority of which are not found in the Hebrew Bible. (Daniel is the major exception.) These materials are of inestimable value for understanding not only Revelation but Christianity as a whole. It might almost be claimed that the Jewish apocalypses comprise the missing link between the Hebrew Bible and the New Testament. While it is true that Christianity grew up in the company of many counselors (e.g., wisdom literature and Hellenistic culture), none was more persuasive an influence than apocalyptic thought. No one can rightly claim to have come to grips with New Testament eschatology without some knowledge of these texts. They are that basic.

Characteristics of Apocalyptic Literature

"Apocalyptic" is constructed of two Greek words, *apo*, meaning "from," and *kalypsis*, meaning "covering." An *apocalypse* is an uncovering, a revealing of something otherwise unknown.

"Apocalyptic" is a title given to a type of literature that claims to disclose hidden details about the end of history and/or human destiny. Ordinarily, the content of the disclosure is said to have been revealed by an angel to a holy individual, often of the distant past (e.g., Enoch, Ezra, Daniel, or Baruch). "Apocalyptic" is also used to describe a way of viewing the world that is consistent with the apocalyptic writings. Apocalyptic thought presupposes that the natural world of humans interacts with a supernatural world of angels and demons, and that the destiny of the two realms is inextricably intertwined. The true nature of reality is mysterious, unavailable to the senses, and so accessible only by revelation. These revelations most often concern a coming judgment of the ungodly and a subsequent restoration of Israel under the kingship of God or the Messiah. Apocalyptic literature was not the product of any single group, social class, or movement, and apocalypses vary a good deal in their content and purpose. Nevertheless, a number of features are common to apocalypses generally, though not to each and every apocalypse specifically. These include the following:[1]

1. **Division of History into Old and New Ages**
   The old, evil age is about to come to an end. There will be a great crisis, a victory over the forces of evil, often pictured as a military triumph, and a new age of restoration and renewal.

2. **Dualism**
   Good and evil spiritual powers are engaged in unremitting conflict. Knowingly or unknowingly, human beings are aligned with these powers. One might say that the apocalyptic palette is short on grays but copiously supplied with black and white.

3. **Determinism**
   History is moving forward to its inevitable conclusion. Contrary to much prophetic literature, humans are not called upon to repent and so to change the future. It follows that apocalypses are internal documents directed primarily at existing believers.

4. **Exclusivism**
   A clear distinction exists between the few insiders, who will be saved, and the many outsiders, who will not. There is a strong tendency toward sectarianism; the values and norms of wider society are largely rejected.

5. **Portrayals of Judgment**
   Long before Dante's *Divine Comedy,* there were apocalyptic descriptions of the terrors awaiting sinners. More often than not, these involve deep chasms and searing flames. It is not always clear whether an author wishes to portray the destruction or the eternal

---

1. This list is based in part on Stephen L. Harris, *The New Testament: A Student's Guide* (Mountain View, Calif.: Mayfield, 1988), pp. 320-24.

punishment of wrongdoers. The distinction might not have mattered to the author in any case, although it would presumably be of more than technical interest to anyone so destined.

6. Expectation of the End

The great events on which human history turns are about to occur. Typically, a period of great tribulation is imagined as the next step in the unfolding drama. One of the unhappy consequences of modern apocalyptic thinking is the fatalism, even enthusiasm, with which some believers speak of the latest war, famine, earthquake, or flood. To such a mindset, bad news is good news.

7. Code Words, Numerology, and Cryptic Symbols

There is much use of special insider language (e.g., "Babylon" for Rome), numbers (e.g., "666"), and strange symbols (e.g., multiheaded beasts). The oddness and inscrutability of apocalyptic writing are part of its draw. People in the ancient world loved mysteries and savored the possession of special knowledge. Not that we are any different: had Nostradamus written memoranda instead of quatrains, he would have been forgotten long ago.

8. Means of Revelation

Hidden knowledge is communicated by a variety of means, especially in visions and dreams. Most information is related by archangels, whose particular occupation this seems to be.

9. Transportation of the Visionary

The author reports being taken up into heaven and other realms where he (inevitably "he") can see and hear things that would otherwise be unknown. Most important, he gains a heavenly perspective on the current troubles facing believers on earth.

10. The Heavenly Realm

What happens on earth is directly determined by the councils of heaven, to which the author is a privileged witness. Frequent mention is made of the opening, closing, and sealing of heavenly books containing secrets about human destiny.

11. **Exhortations to Endurance**

An apocalypse aims to encourage believers to endure their present trials. If they will hang on just a little longer, salvation will arrive. "Here is a call for the endurance and faith of the saints" (Rev. 13:10).

12. **Demonstration of God's Justice**

Theologically, the point of the apocalypse is that despite all appearances to the contrary, God has everything under control. Ultimately, God's righteousness will prevail.

The last point is crucial. We saw in Chapter One that eschatology is concerned at heart with the question of God's justice (technically called "theodicy"). This observation is nowhere more true than in the case of apocalyptic literature.[2] Apocalyptic thinking flourishes in times of dislocation and crisis. The peak periods of Jewish apocalyptic writing coincided with three great national traumas:

1. the Exile (sixth century B.C.);
2. the attempts by the Seleucid (Syrian) king Antiochus IV to outlaw the observance of Jewish Law (second century B.C.); and
3. the destruction of Jerusalem by the Romans (late first century A.D.).

At such times, it is difficult not to doubt God's justice — or even God's very existence. For all of the strangeness of apocalyptic language, its core expressions are entirely comprehensible, in particular, its cry for justice and its call to endurance. Given these purposes, it is not surprising that Revelation is the canonical ally of present-day liberation theologians, who are among the book's freshest and most vigorous interpreters. Apocalypses might not offer a nuanced view of the world, but they are extraordinarily adept at exposing the evils perpetrated by unrestricted human power and at staking out a place for faith in the

---

2. A word about the distinction between "eschatology" and "apocalyptic" as the terms are used in this book: *Eschatology* is a system of beliefs about God's ultimate victory. An *apocalyptic* eschatology is one such system. We might say that "eschatology" is the species and "apocalyptic" the sub-species. All bears are mammals, but not all mammals are bears; likewise, all (or nearly all, to split hairs) apocalypses are eschatologies, but not all eschatologies are apocalypses.

face of injustice. It is easy for modern readers to disdain the wild and even violent imagery and the expansive and mostly unfulfilled hopes of the apocalyptic writers. A fairer and more charitable attitude compels us to honor their courage, respect their sense of justice, and emulate their trust in God.

From Prophecy to Apocalypse

Professional academics are known to mark out and hold ground with soldierly tenacity, and the clash of scholarly border patrols is an often fearsome sight. One Kashmir-like battleground lies at the boundary between prophetic and apocalyptic writings. In point of fact, the two categories overlap. For example, we have seen that the themes of universal judgment and national restoration are already found in the biblical prophets. Still, some helpful distinctions can be made. The most substantial concerns means and ends. By and large, the prophets expected that God would work through normal historical circumstances (e.g., armies and nations) to produce "ordinary" historical results (e.g., a chastened or renewed Israel). We saw in the previous chapter the beginnings of a shift in expectation among the later prophets. Those nations that would war against Israel will be miraculously defeated (Ezek. 38:17–39:8). The new Israel will be glorious beyond compare (Isa. 60). The people will be equipped by the Spirit to obey the Law wholeheartedly (Jer. 31:33; Ezek. 36:26-27). The Gentiles will be incorporated into the people of God, and the glory of the Lord will spread throughout the earth (Isa. 66:18-23). Nature itself, blighted by sin, will be rejuvenated (Ezek. 34:25-31). To varying degrees, these texts imagine new and better things that will displace present-day existence, changes of a sort that could be instituted only by God. After all, not even Cyrus[3] in all his glory could make Zion's "wilderness like Eden" (Isa. 51:3).

The movement away from human agency is a major step toward an apocalyptic perspective. Nevertheless, the biblical prophets anticipated a future that still looked much like this one. Isaiah 65 describes a "new earth" in which people plant and harvest, beget children and die. The difference is more one of degree than of kind:

3. See Isa. 44:28.

No more shall there be in it an infant that lives but a few days, or an old person who does not live out a lifetime; for one who dies at a hundred years will be considered a youth, and one who falls short of a hundred will be considered accursed. (65:20)

The distinction between prophetic and apocalyptic writing is especially blurry in the case of Isaiah 24–27. Indeed, such is the character of these chapters that they are sometimes called "The Isaiah Apocalypse." The origin of these materials is uncertain, but most commentators date them at least a hundred years after the time of the prophet Isaiah. (As we have already seen, the book of Isaiah is a collection of writings composed over a span of about two centuries.) In the section's opening verse (24:1) we read, "Now the Lord is about to lay waste the earth and make it desolate." The judgment is universal: "On that day the Lord will punish the host of heaven in heaven, and on earth the kings of the earth" (24:21).

Those who survive will live in a kingdom ruled directly by God (24:23), who will host a great banquet for all peoples (25:6). Chapter 27 makes use of a popular image from Canaanite myth: "On that day the Lord with his cruel and great and strong sword will punish Leviathan the fleeing serpent" (27:1), an act that symbolizes the final destruction of the powers of evil and chaos. Most noteworthy is the mention of the destruction of death (25:7: "he will swallow up death forever") and the resurrection of the dead (26:19):

Your dead shall live, their corpses shall rise. O dwellers in the dust, awake and sing for joy! For your dew is a radiant dew, and the earth will give birth to those long dead.

These last two passages are problematic in the minds of many interpreters. It appears that it was not until many years after the Exile that it became common for Jews to believe in resurrection. Prior to that time, biblical authors referred only to an afterlife in Sheol,[4] a shadowy netherworld from which there is no return: "As the cloud fades and vanishes, so those who go down to Sheol do not come up" (Job 7:9). Isaiah 25:7 and 26:19 might be evidence of a comparatively early belief in resurrection, or they might be a later addition to the text. As someone

---

4. E.g., Gen. 37:35; Num. 16:30; Deut. 32:22; 2 Sam. 22:6; 1 Kings 2:6; Ps. 6:5; Isa. 5:14.

whose ideas sometimes run ahead of themselves to natural but unexpected conclusions, I would not want to rule out the first possibility. It
is worth remembering that the creation tradition recorded in Genesis 3
linked sin and death, and the renewal of creation is a major theme of
these chapters. In such a framework, the anticipation of God's universal triumph over evil leads logically to a belief in God's ultimate victory
over death. Either the original author thought the matter through to
this conclusion or others did so later under his influence. For our purposes, the distinction is not important.[5] By the end of the third century B.C., belief in eternal life was well established as a feature of Jewish
eschatological expectation (as in Dan. 12:13).

Another biblical prophet with a foot well inside the door of apocalyptic eschatology is Ezekiel. From his exile in Babylon, Ezekiel foresaw
a glorious future restoration of Israel.[6] Nature itself would be transformed for the benefit of the returning Israelites[7] (no word about the
elimination of ticks and mosquitoes, which would be high on my list).
Especially memorable is Ezekiel's description of a river that would flow
from the threshold of the Temple to the Dead Sea, which, newly fresh-
ened, will teem with life (47:1-12).[8] (Anyone who has seen — and smelled
— the Dead Sea knows what a miracle that would be.) Of particular importance for later writers[9] is the oracle concerning the defeat of the pagan leader Gog, from the land of Magog (Ezek. 38–39).[10] Almost certainly, Ezekiel here is building on Isaiah's promise that God would
protect Zion against its enemies[11] and on Jeremiah's numerous references to an enemy from "the north" (Ezek. 38:15).[12] ("Meshech and

5. It is likely that Jewish belief in resurrection was influenced to a degree by Persian
and Greek ideas. Concern over the dating of these chapters is fueled by the premise that
an idea must be early and/or unique to be true. Both assumptions are faulty.

6. Ezek. 11:17-20; 34-37; 39:21-29; etc.

7. Ezek. 34:25-31; 36:8-12, 29-30.

8. The same idea is found in the later prophets Joel (3:18) and Zechariah (13:1; 14:8).

9. E.g., Dan. 11:40–12:1 and Rev. 20:7-10.

10. There is a link to Genesis 10:2, which lists Magog, Gomer, Tubal, and Meshech
among the descendants of Japheth (cf. Ezek. 38:2, 6). This seems to be the primary
source of the names used in Ezekiel's oracle. No such person as Gog is known to have existed, although the name might be modeled on the powerful seventh-century Lydian
king Gyges (or Gugu).

11. Isa. 4:5-6; 10:12, 24; 14:32; 24:23; 29:1-8; etc.

12. Jer. 1:14-15; 4:6; 6:1, 22; 10:22; 13:20; 15:12; 25:26; etc.

Tubal," mentioned in 38:2, were nations in northeastern Asia Minor.) Note the statement in 38:17:

> Thus says the Lord God: Are you he of whom I spoke in former days by my servants the prophets of Israel, who in those days prophesied for years that I would bring you against them?

Ezekiel weaves together two separate and essentially opposite prophetic traditions — that God would protect Zion against a great enemy (Isaiah) and that a devastatingly powerful adversary would come from the north (Jeremiah) — and sees in the combination a yet unfulfilled prophecy of national rescue. Thus, Gog personifies the long-standing military threat against Israel that must finally and decisively be eliminated. Gog will lead a vast international army in an attack on God's people, recently returned from exile and defenseless (38:8, 11). As a sign to the nations of God's faithfulness to Israel (39:21-29), Gog and all his forces will be miraculously destroyed (38:17-23). The eschatological framing of this rescue is evident in 38:8, "after many days . . . in the latter years," and 38:16, "the latter days."

To be perfectly frank, the lot of the returning exiles was neither so glorious as "Second Isaiah" imagined, nor so perilous as Ezekiel envisaged. The point of such visions is to be found on the level of theological affirmation. Once again, the issue is theodicy, the justice of God. As Israel had been humiliated in defeat, so Israel will be vindicated in triumph. In the latter case, the victory will be God's alone, proving to all the world God's continued election of and care for Israel:

> My holy name I will make known among my people Israel; and I will not let my holy name be profaned any more; and the nations shall know that I am the Lord, the Holy One in Israel. It has come! It has happened, says the Lord God. This is the day of which I have spoken. (Ezek. 39:7-8)

At worst, one could characterize these chapters — and a good deal of later apocalyptic literature with them — as revenge fantasy, a popular genre in our own day, typified by the Hollywood action movie. Anyone who has seen one such film knows the plot: the first half of the movie catalogues the inhumanities of the evildoers, thereby justifying the terrible vengeance that is to be wreaked upon them in the second half. In apocalyptic literature generally, evil is an abstraction, not unlike the one-dimensional villainy of the typical cinema bad guy. A not insignificant difference is that in the movie version the hero is allowed to execute his own brand of "justice" on his adversaries, matching cruelty with cruelty. In these chapters, however, judgment is in the hands of God. Ezekiel 38–39 is not a call to arms but to faith. One is encouraged to trust in God's righteousness, not in human might (Isa. 31:1). Nevertheless, the violent imagery of such oracles is easily twisted, as the sorry history of the interpretation of apocalyptic texts so amply demonstrates. Words meant to give comfort to the powerless become weapons in the hands of the powerful. Make no mistake, Ezekiel 38–39 is a dangerous text, easily abused.

The idea that the restoration of Israel would be preceded by a great battle in which God would intervene is of great importance for subsequent Jewish and Christian apocalyptic thought. The books of Joel (e.g., 2:20), Zechariah (e.g., 12:1-9; 14:1-5), and Daniel (e.g., 11:13, 40-45) all demonstrate its influence. In the New Testament, we find its Christian equivalent in the famous battle of Armageddon (Rev. 16:16). Behind all of these passages lurks the old Jewish question, "What about the neighbors?" How will the fulfillment of God's promises to Israel affect the Gentile world? As we have already seen, there was no single answer. Perhaps the Gentiles would be destroyed, perhaps they would be converted, perhaps some mixture of the two. Practically, the expectation of an eternally safe and secure Israel moved the prophets to imagine a corresponding transformation of international political realities. If the situation of Israel is to change, the surrounding world must change with it. By one means or another, the threat to Israel must be removed. Perhaps, then, the imagined defeat of the great alien hordes was less motivated by a desire for vengeance than by a longing for peace. One can only hope that it was so.

Many characteristic apocalyptic features are to be found in Ezekiel 38–39;[13] nevertheless, some key elements are lacking, such as a mediat-

---

13. E.g., determinism (38:4), a division between old and new ages (38:8), exclusivism (39:21), imminent eschatological expectation (39:8), numerology (the frequent use of the number seven, as in 39:9, 12, 14), and the demonstration of God's justice (39:21). Ezekiel also mentions an earthquake (38:19-20), an eschatological sacrifice and feast (39:17-20, borrowed from ancient Ugaritic myth), and the eschatological gift of the Spirit (39:29; cf. Joel 2:28-29 and Acts 2:16-21), all commonplace ideas in later apocalypses.

ing angel and speculation about heavenly and spiritual realms. Therefore, while Ezekiel 38-39 might not offer a fully formed apocalypse, it
spans most of the gulf between prophetic and apocalyptic literature
and "makes straight the way" of the thoroughgoing apocalypse.

Of the later prophetic books, Joel and Zechariah are the most apocalyptic in their orientation.[14] In Joel 2:30-31 we read the following oracle, echoed centuries later in Mark 13:24-25 par.:

> I will show portents in the heavens and on the earth, blood and
> fire and columns of smoke. The sun shall be turned to darkness,
> and the moon to blood, before the great and terrible day of the
> Lord comes.

Harkening back to Ezekiel, Joel says that the nations will come to
the valley of Jehoshaphat, where they will be defeated ("judged") by
God (3:1-17). So "Jerusalem shall be holy, and strangers shall never again
pass through it" (3:17). Ezekiel's river is also mentioned (3:18, as in Zech.
14:8); additionally, "the mountains shall drip sweet wine, the hills shall
flow with milk, and all the stream beds of Judah shall flow with water."
(A desert-dweller's vision if ever there was one. What's the future going
to be like? It's going to be *wet*.)

The book of Zechariah is even more strikingly apocalyptic. In the
first six chapters, the prophet relates a series of mysterious visions
whose meaning is revealed by an angel. Like a visitor in the Senate gal-
lery, Zechariah is allowed to witness the deliberations of the heavenly
council (chapter 3). It is a timely visit: he is on hand to see Satan (or "a
satan") rebuked by God. The hoped-for restoration of the Davidic kingship is mentioned in 3:8 and 6:12. Numerous other pieces of apocalyptic
furniture appear, including lamps, horns, bowls, olive trees, scrolls, colored horses, and chariots. Chapters 9-14 take a darker turn, perhaps reflecting a greater disillusionment with the situation of postexilic Israel.[15] The author portrays God as a mighty warrior who will defeat Is-

14. The most thoroughly apocalyptic book in the Hebrew Bible is Daniel, which
was not composed until about the year 165 B.C. It will be considered in its proper historical context below.

15. Many scholars believe that these chapters represent the work of a second author.
A number of OT books appear to be composite documents, so the possibility of multiple authorship is not unusual.

rael's enemies (9:1–11:3; 12). A climactic battle is reported (14:1-5, 12-15), which owes much to Ezekiel 38–39. God's victory is supernatural in character:

> On that day there shall not be either cold or frost. And there shall be continuous day (it is known to the Lord), not day and not night, for at evening time there shall be light. . . . And the Lord will become king over all the earth; on that day the Lord will be one and his name one. (Zech. 14:6-7, 9)

In sum, the apocalyptic perspective that dominates so many Jewish writings of the inter-testamental period (the time between the Old and New Testaments, roughly the four centuries before Christ) did not appear suddenly, unpredictably, or out of thin air. Instead, it arrived gradually and naturally, in air thick with prophetic expectation.[16] It is as much the child of what went before as it is the parent of what came after.

Outside Influences

Like the prophets, the authors of the apocalypses were influenced by the cultures of surrounding nations. Many commentators have viewed the apocalypses as foreign contagions that a healthier Jewish body would have rejected, but that is surely a biased and simplistic view. As the prophets did before them, the apocalypticists borrowed ideas and images from a wide variety of sources and built them into a new and distinctly Jewish construction.

The many foreign parallels to Jewish apocalyptic thought make for fascinating study. One example is the Akkadian (northern Babylonian) "dream vision," which purported to contain revelations about future events disclosed to some ancient figure. In reality, the "vision" was a recent literary product and all but a few of the things that it "prophesied" had already occurred. Such an oracle's predictive abilities were predictably faultless. (The technical name for this phenomenon is

---

16. This is the thesis of Paul Hanson's influential book *The Dawn of Apocalyptic* (Philadelphia: Fortress, 1975).

vaticinia ex eventu, prophecy after the fact.) The remaining prophecies concerned matters in which the author had an interest, for example, some institution or course of action that he sought to support. Similar materials have come to us from ancient Persia. The *Bahman Yasht* records a series of cryptic visions given to the prophet Zarathustra, founder of Zoroastrianism:

> He . . . saw a tree with four branches, one of gold, one of silver, one of steel, and one of mixed iron. Ahura Mazda [the deity] explained the vision, saying that the four branches were four kingdoms. . . .[17]

Such writings are called "historical apocalypses" because they contain reviews of past history in the form of prophetic oracles. One purpose is to explain the meaning of history; another is to give credence to prophecies about the near future. The biblical book of Daniel fits the mold perfectly. In chapter 2, Daniel interprets a dream about a great statue:

> The head of that statue was of fine gold, its chest and arms of silver, its middle and thighs of bronze, its legs of iron, its feet partly of iron and partly of clay. . . . You, O king . . . are the head of gold. After you shall arise another kingdom inferior to yours, and yet a third kingdom . . . and there shall be a fourth kingdom. . . . (2:32-33, 37, 38-40)

Five chapters later, we are told a vision of four beasts, which also represent kingdoms:

> As for me, Daniel, my spirit was troubled within me, and the visions of my head terrified me. I approached one of the attendants to ask him the truth concerning all this. So he said . . . "As for these four great beasts, four kings shall arise out of the earth. . . ." (7:15-17)

---

17. John Collins, *The Apocalyptic Imagination: An Introduction to Jewish Apocalyptic Literature,* 2nd ed. (Grand Rapids: Eerdmans, 1998), p. 30. Collins's book is a standard introductory work and is strongly recommended to readers who want to pursue this subject further.

As we shall see in the next chapter, most commentators believe that Daniel was composed by an unknown Jewish author at the time of the Maccabean Revolt. The practice of pseudonymity (or "pseudepigraphy"), writing in the name of someone else, usually a venerated figure from the distant past (e.g., Enoch, Baruch, and Ezra, all famous wise men), was well known in the ancient world. Pseudonymity lent authority to what was written. It also reinforced the determinism so prevalent in the apocalyptic writings: history is seen to be moving according to schedule, just as it always has. Pseudonymity often strikes modern students as fraudulent and dishonest. One certainly could make the case that it was deceptive, however well intentioned it might have been. On the other hand, we are very far removed from the world of these authors, and it is presumptuous of us to pass easy judgment on their practices. Perhaps they felt some spiritual relationship to the one in whose name they wrote. Unfortunately, it is unlikely that we will ever know how these scribes viewed their work.

Persian texts also divided history into periods (millennia), viewed the spiritual world in strongly dualistic terms, and spoke of the resurrection of the dead. They also described eschatological woes that would precede the coming new age. The *Oracle of Hystaspes* mentions both future political unrest and a future destruction of the world by fire.[18] All of this would become familiar territory for both Jewish and Christian apocalyptic writers.

Persian influence was extensive in the Hellenistic age. The *Potter's Oracle,* an Egyptian prophecy written in Greek, follows the Persian model closely. According to John Collins,

> It contains a "prophecy" of Greek domination, followed by cosmic and social chaos and a war with a king from Syria. Finally, Alexandria will be laid waste and a king will come from the sun, sent by the great goddess Isis, to restore Egypt.[19]

The schematization of history into four kingdoms became very widespread, being used, for example, both by Rome and by Rome's enemies. The loss of national identity and the displacement of large popu-

---

18. Collins, *The Apocalyptic Imagination,* p. 32.
19. Collins, *The Apocalyptic Imagination,* p. 36.

lations in the Greco-Roman era undoubtedly contributed to the spread of such apocalyptic ideas both in and beyond Judaism. Jews and Christians were not the only people to feel the need to explain the serpentine twists of destiny.

Alongside the historical apocalypse is a second type, the so-called "heavenly journey apocalypse," in which the oracle is taken up into the heavenly realm to behold sights formerly unseen by human eyes.[20] At least one Persian apocalypse of this sort is known, although its date is uncertain. Many examples of otherworldly journeys exist from the literature of other cultures, e.g., in Homer's *Odyssey,* book 11, and in Virgil's *Aeneid,* book 6. Similar ideas appear in the works of Plato, Cicero, and Lucian. (I recently drove my children from Paris to Euro-Disneyland, which is the closest I myself have come to an otherworldly journey.)

A number of other apocalyptic images appear to have found their way to Judaism via pagan religions. Two in particular are worth singling out. The first is the depiction of the god as a warrior, a commonplace idea in the religions of the ancient Near East.[21] Often the warrior god's coming is associated with storm clouds, fire, lightning, and earthquakes. The god's victory might then be celebrated in a great banquet. Similar descriptions can be found at a number of points in the Hebrew Bible,[22] and they are the stock in trade of later apocalyptic writers. Canaanite influence is felt particularly in the image of the divine "Son of Man [Humanity]" who would come on the clouds to rule the earth (Dan. 7:13-14; see below),[23] an idea that is of particular importance to Christian beliefs about the return of Christ (e.g., Acts 1:9-11). The extent to which Jesus' own use of the term Son of Man is dependent upon apocalyptic tradition is a perennial — and probably unresolvable — issue in NT scholarship (see Chapter Six).

It is worth saying again that such borrowing is normal and occurs in all religions. It is natural for people to articulate their faith in God

20. Collins notes that "only one Jewish apocalypse, the *Apocalypse of Abraham,* combines an otherworldly journey with a review of history, and it is relatively late (end of the first century A.D.)" (*The Apocalyptic Imagination,* p. 6).

21. Frank Moore Cross, *Canaanite Myth and Hebrew Epic* (Cambridge, Mass.: Harvard University Press, 1973), pp. 91-111.

22. E.g., Ps. 24:7-10; 46:6; 68:2; 97:1-5; Isa. 11:4; 13:1-22; 42:13; Ezek. 38:17–39:8; Joel 2:20; Zech. 12:1-9; 14:1-5; Dan. 11:13, 40-45; Nahum 1:2-8; Micah 1:3-4.

23. Cross, *Canaanite Myth,* p. 17.

by means of the symbols available to them. We do it ourselves. Just look at Christian bumper stickers, such as the ever-popular "God is my co-pilot." Another factor was the never-ending "our god is better than your god" competition. As we have seen, the search for absolute uniqueness is misguided and largely futile. Still, the interpenetration, diversity, and fluidity of eschatological ideas ought to give us pause. No single biblical eschatology exists, and the attempt to assemble one inevitably diminishes the multilayered, multidimensional witness of the Bible.

1 Enoch

The earliest and most important of the Jewish apocalypses are contained in 1 Enoch,[24] a collection of materials composed in the name (obviously) of Enoch, one of the Bible's most mysterious figures. R. H. Charles, the dean of apocalypse scholars, went so far as to say that "1 Enoch has had more influence on the New Testament than has any other apocryphal or pseudepigraphic work."[25] To back up that claim, Charles provided an impressive list of more than fifty parallels to the NT.[26] Because of its significance and because it so ably represents apocalyptic thought in general, 1 Enoch will be the primary focus of our short study of the non-biblical Jewish material.

Enoch is described in the terse and cryptic account of Genesis 5:21-24:

> When Enoch had lived sixty-five years, he became the father of Methuselah. Enoch walked with God after the birth of Methuselah three hundred years, and had other sons and daughters. Thus all the days of Enoch were three hundred sixty-five years. Enoch walked with God; then he was no more, because God took him.

24. Perhaps the most widely available source for these materials is R. H. Charles's *The Apocrypha and Pseudepigrapha of the Old Testament* (Oxford University Press, 1913 and numerous reprints). A paperback containing Charles's translation of 1 Enoch is available from SPCK Press: *The Book of Enoch* (London, 1997).

25. Charles, *The Apocrypha*, p. 180.

26. Charles, *The Apocrypha*, pp. 180-81.

Like ants to a picnic, apocalypticists are drawn to Enoch as the quintessential revealer of divine mysteries. No doubt about it, Enoch has the right stuff. His first credential is his unqualified righteousness, inferred from the statement "he walked with God." The author of the New Testament book of Hebrews put it this way:

> By faith Enoch was taken so that he did not experience death; and "he was not found, because God had taken him." For it was attested before he was taken away that "he had pleased God." (Heb. 11:5)

As we see, the phrase "God took him" was interpreted to mean that Enoch was snatched from the earth and taken alive to heaven. Thus Enoch was ideally placed to act as revealer of divine mysteries and to be regarded as a mediating figure between the physical and spiritual realms. It is interesting that the one other OT figure to cheat death, Elijah (2 Kings 2:11), also was given a role in the eschatological consummation (Mal. 4:5; Matt. 11:14; John 1:21; etc.). It is entirely possible that the two End Times prophets envisaged in Revelation 11:3-13 are none other than Enoch and Elijah, who at the end of their service are again taken "up to heaven in a cloud" (v. 12).

Enoch is of the seventh human generation, a not insignificant datum in the world of apocalyptic numerology. This fact is noted in the NT book of Jude (v. 14, which quotes 1 Enoch as Scripture) and in Luke's genealogy of Jesus (3:37). In the *Sumerian King List*, Enmeduranki, the seventh king, was "the founder of a guild of diviners and a recipient of revelations." Likewise, Utuabzu, "the seventh sage . . . was said to have been taken up to heaven."[27] In the Greco-Roman world, added credence was given to ideas thought to be especially ancient; therefore, Enoch's situation in primitive human history was a big plus. Equally important is the length of Enoch's life on earth: 365 years. 1 Enoch defends the solar year against a rival calendar of 360 days (equal to twelve months of thirty days), so it is unlikely that Enoch's age is a coincidence. It is interesting that Enmeduranki, mentioned above, was said to have been appointed king and given divining powers by Shamash, the sun god. Hence, it is likely that the description in

---

27. Collins, *The Apocalyptic Imagination,* p. 45.

Genesis 5:21-24 already reflects speculation about Enoch as the Jewish equivalent of the primordial sage of other cultures.

1 Enoch is a compendium of Enoch materials, some of which go back as far as the third century before Christ. Despite the many parallels with Babylonian and Persian thinking, most scholars locate these texts in postexilic Israel. The same could be said for Daniel, whose story is set in Babylon but whose author almost certainly was a native Judean. 1 Enoch contains at least five separate works:

1. The Book of the Watchers (chapters 1-36)
2. The Similitudes (Parables) (37-71)
3. The Astronomical Book (72-82)
4. The Book of Dreams (83-90), which includes the Animal Apocalypse (85-90)
5. The Epistle of Enoch (91-108), which includes the Apocalypse of Weeks (93:1-10; 91:12-17).

These materials provide a fascinating glimpse into the world of inter-testamental Judaism and emergent Christianity. They are well worth our careful attention.

The Book of Watchers

The Book of Watchers contains some of the earliest Enoch material. It tells the story of the "Watchers," the two hundred angels who, like King David from his balcony, looked down from heaven and lusted after mortal women. Unable to contain their passion, they descended from heaven (conveniently, via Mt. Hermon) and took for themselves wives, with whom they had children. The author gives them no credit for first marrying, which puts them ahead of David at least on that account. Their kids were more spawn of hell than children of heaven. In fact, they were evil giants who ravaged the earth.[28] (Whatever your kids do to the living room is nothing by comparison.) The world was saved from annihilation only because the giants managed first to destroy

---

28. See also Wis. 14:6; Tob. 6:14; Sir. 16:7; 1 Bar. 3:26; 3 Macc. 2:4; and Jub. 7:22-23; Charles, p. 192.

each other. Unfortunately, that was not the end of it: their demonic spirits haunt the earth until the day of judgment.

The angels also sinned by teaching their wives the secrets of herbs, metals, stars, clouds — even jewelry and makeup. (Evidence, if more were needed, that the authors of these texts were men.) For these errors, they were to be bound for seventy generations, after which they would be judged and cast into the abyss of fire. Understandably discontented with this fate, the Watchers implored Enoch to intercede for them with God. Enoch was taken before God's throne, but he was told to inform the Watchers, "You [will] have no peace" (16:4). Their fate was sealed.

Many people are surprised to learn that the core of this story is biblical. In one of the obscure byways of Genesis we come upon the following:

> When people began to multiply on the face of the ground, and daughters were born to them, the sons of God saw that they were fair; and they took wives for themselves of all that they chose. Then the Lord said, "My spirit shall not abide in mortals forever, for they are flesh; their days shall be one hundred twenty years." The Nephilim [literally "fallen ones"; in Numbers 13:33 they are giants] were on the earth in those days — and also afterward — when the sons of God went in to the daughters of humans, who bore children to them. These were the heroes that were of old, warriors of renown. (Gen. 6:1-4)

The New Testament books of 2 Peter (2:4-5) and Jude (v. 6) refer to this story, identifying the "sons of God" explicitly as angels.[29] Moreover, the episode is widely mentioned in non-biblical writings, both

---

29. Modern interpreters fall into three basic camps: (1) those who argue that the "sons of God" really are humans, and "Nephilim" are not giants; (2) those who accept that the passage refers to angels and their titanic offspring and believe in the literal accuracy of the account; and (3) those who see Gen. 6:1-4 as a piece of ancient mythology about the union of gods and humans that has been transposed into a Hebrew key. The first approach is wishful thinking with nothing to support it. Although I would select the last of the remaining options ("3," ancient myth), there is little at stake if we do or do not credit the existence of antediluvian, semi-divine, barbarian giants. There are bigger — or at least more important — things to worry about.

Jewish and Christian, e.g., in the work of Josephus and Philo, Justin and Irenaeus.

Much of the remainder of chapters 1–36 is given to reports of Enoch's journeys to Sheol and the ends of the earth, primarily under the escort of the archangel Uriel. Enoch's itinerary includes the place where the evil angels are bound, the garden containing the tree of wisdom from which Adam and Eve ate, and the repositories where different categories of souls await the day of judgment. Fascinating as they might be, there is more to Enoch's travels than spiritual tourism. The reader is taken behind the scenes to see how the whole cosmic production operates. The message is that the world is under God's active direction; in particular, the reader is assured that it is in God's plan to reward good and punish evil. Like all apocalypses, the bottom line is that God can be trusted with human destiny.

The Similitudes and the Son of Man

The next portion of 1 Enoch, chapters 37–71, is called "The Similitudes," or Parables. (Parables only in the sense that they are analogies; nothing here resembles Jesus' story of the Good Samaritan.) These are among the most recent of the Enoch materials, probably dated to the period immediately preceding the birth of Christianity. The main themes are the future judgment of sinners and the resurrection and final bliss of the righteous, whose eternal abodes Enoch is privileged to visit.

The extraordinary feature of these chapters is their extended and exalted portrayal of the "Son of Man [Humanity]." The origin and identity of the Son of Man in ancient Judaism is an enormously controversial and complex topic that can be addressed only briefly here. What follows is a fairly typical — but no means incontestable — reading of the evidence.

From an early date, "Son of Man" was used to refer to people generally, with emphasis upon human mortality and finitude. So Psalm 8:4: "What are human beings that you are mindful of them, and the Son of Man that you care for them?"[30] Occasionally, the king was singled out

---

30. The NRSV translates "Son of Man" as "mortal" in this and other verses; see also Isa. 51:12; 56:2; Job 16:21; etc.

as a Son of Man,[31] a usage that both relativized the king as mere mortal and exalted him as human representative before God. By far the most frequent occurrence of Son of Man (a dizzying 93 times) is found in Ezekiel, where it serves as the title by which God addresses the prophet: "He said to me: Son of Man, stand up on your feet, and I will speak with you" (2:1). Skip four centuries, and one finds the same usage in Daniel 8:17: "Understand, O Son of man, that the vision is for the time of the end." The surprise comes earlier, in Daniel 7:13-14:

> As I watched in the night visions, I saw one like the Son of Man coming with the clouds of heaven. And he came to the Ancient One and was presented before him. To him was given dominion and glory and kingship, that all peoples, nations, and languages should serve him. His dominion is an everlasting dominion that shall not pass away, and his kingship is one that shall never be destroyed.

It is probable that the author of Daniel has taken over and reinterpreted a piece of Canaanite mythology concerning the enthronement of Baal. The title "Ancient One" ("Ancient of Days") is certainly borrowed from Canaanite descriptions of the god El. (The name El is included in Isra*el*, meaning "may God contend," and in many other names, such as Elohim, Elijah, and Bethel.) Baal was subservient to El but was given authority in a manner reminiscent of Daniel 7:13-14. Of course, this does not mean that the author of Daniel meant to refer to Baal. He certainly did not. Instead, like so many of the biblical authors, he adapted a well-known image to his own theological purpose.[32]

Identifications of Daniel's Son of Man vary widely. Some regard him as a symbol for Israel collectively; others see him as an extraordinary human exalted by God. Christians have long found in these verses a prophecy of Christ's second coming (e.g., Matt. 24:30). Among Bible scholars, the tide has turned in recent years toward identifying this figure with an angelic being, probably Michael, the protector and heavenly counterpart of Israel (cf. Rev. 12:7-9).[33] The argument hinges in

---

31. Ps. 80:17; cf. 146:3, where foreign rulers are called "Sons of Men."
32. See the helpful discussion in Collins, *The Apocalyptic Imagination*, p. 19.
33. John Collins, *Daniel*, Hermeneia (Minneapolis: Fortress, 1993), pp. 304-10.

part on the fact that this figure appears "like" a human, a characteristic description of an angel. Indeed, in Daniel 8:15-16 the archangel Gabriel is described as being "in the appearance of man," having a "human voice." In 9:21 he is referred to as "the man Gabriel, whom I had seen before in a vision." Likewise, 12:5-13 describes a vision in which two angelic figures appear as men (vv. 5-7).[34] The emphasis upon angelic activity is typical of apocalyptic literature and was a regular feature in other contemporary Jewish literature, such as the Dead Sea Scrolls.

It is especially noteworthy that the prophecies of Daniel do not include an eschatological king (i.e., a Davidic Messiah). The only ruler mentioned is Michael, who is referred to in 10:21 as "your prince." 12:1-2 is even more emphatic:

> At that time Michael, the great prince, the protector of your people, shall arise. There shall be a time of anguish, such as has never occurred since nations first came into existence. But at that time your people shall be delivered, everyone who is found written in the book. Many of those who sleep in the dust of the earth shall awake, some to everlasting life, and some to shame and everlasting contempt.

Michael's coming is associated with both judgment and resurrection, a conception that anticipated and quite likely influenced later Christian ideas about the return of Christ. In effect, the roles of Daniel 7:13-14 and 12:1-2 merged, not in the figure of Michael but of Jesus. In the process, there was a good deal of angelic carryover, since Christ's return as Son of Man is usually associated with the coming of angels who assist him in judgment.[35]

While it is true that the original referent of these verses probably was Michael, that fact might not have proved as disturbing to first-century Christians as it is to many modern believers. According to Leslie Allen,

> There is a canonical assumption that, although the prophets spoke for their own times, their words were not exhausted in ear-

34. Collins, *Daniel*, pp. 305-6.
35. See, for example, Matt. 13:41; 16:27; 24:30-31; 25:31 and parallels; 2 Thess. 1:7; cf. John 1:51.

lier fulfillments: there was an overplus of meaning, a typological pattern to be realized at a still later time. One may compare Joel's insistence that Obadiah's "day of Yahweh" was not consummated in the tragedy of 587 B.C. but found a comparable encore in a locust plague that threatened to wipe out the community. In such Old Testament antecedents lie the seeds of the New Testament's treatment of earlier scriptures.[36]

In other words, prophecy, even written prophecy, was not static. Oracles from earlier times were constantly being reinterpreted and even revised in light of new experience. Many contemporary Christians have a hard time getting beyond questions about the literal meaning of a passage. "Is the Bible true?" is for us mainly a question of factual accuracy. By contrast, it was possible for ancient authors (Paul, say) to hold to the truth of a scriptural passage while at the same time rewriting it to suit their own purposes. The New Testament authors may at times appear heavy-handed in their use of the Hebrew Bible, but they were no more so than some of their non-Christian Jewish contemporaries.

The Similitudes of Enoch were written only about a century and a half after Daniel (that is, around the turn of the millennium); nevertheless, their representation of the Son of Man goes far beyond anything found in Daniel. In fact, the Similitudes are so startlingly similar to the New Testament at this point that some scholars have found it impossible not to regard them as a later development, written either by Christians or under the influence of Christianity. Nevertheless, the evidence for a pre-Christian date is quite strong and is favored by most interpreters.[37] The Similitudes are certainly Jewish,[38] and it is unlikely that a Jewish document so sympathetic to Christian interpretation would have been composed after the rise of the church. Internal evidence, such as the mention of the Parthians in 56:5-7, linked by many to the Parthian invasion in 40 B.C., also favors an earlier date. The closest

36. Leslie C. Allen, *Ezekiel 20–48,* Word Biblical Commentary, vol. 29 (Dallas: Word, 1990), p. 206.

37. The case is made convincingly by John Collins in *The Apocalyptic Imagination,* pp. 177-78, 192-93.

38. A second epilogue appended to the book identifies Enoch himself with the Son of Man, an exceedingly unlikely move for a Christian author.

NT parallels (e.g., Matt. 19:28) seem to reflect the Similitudes' influence on the NT and not the reverse. Of course, even if composed at a later date, the Similitudes would evidence a form of Judaism markedly similar to Christianity at several key points.

In the Similitudes, the Son of Man is a human being, albeit one with superhuman or even divine characteristics. This Son of Man is also called "the Elect One," "the Righteous One," and, most important of all, the "Anointed One," the *Messiah* (48:10; 52:4). He will come in power, sit on the throne of glory, and judge humanity:

> And in those days shall the earth also give back that which has been entrusted to it, and Sheol also shall give back that which it has received, and hell shall give back that which it owes. For in those days the Elect One shall arise, and he shall choose the righteous and holy from among them. . . . And the Elect One shall in those days sit on My throne, and his mouth shall pour forth all the secrets of wisdom and counsel: for the Lord of Spirits hath given (them) to him and hath glorified him. (51:1-3)

Another quite amazing description is found in 48:2-6:

> And at that hour that Son of Man was named in the presence of the Lord of Spirits, and his name before the Head of Days. Yea, before the sun and the signs were created, before the stars of the heaven were made, his name was named before the Lord of Spirits. He shall be a staff to the righteous whereon to stay themselves and not fall, and he shall be the light of the Gentiles, and the hope of those who are troubled of heart. All who dwell on the earth shall fall down and worship before him, and will praise and bless and celebrate with song the Lord of Spirits. And for this reason hath he been chosen and hidden before Him, before the creation of the world and for evermore.

It may indeed seem extraordinary that a pre- or non-Christian Jew could have believed in a Messiah who existed prior to creation, who would sit on God's throne as judge, who would be the light of the Gentiles, who would receive worship, and whose coming would be associated with the resurrection of the dead. If, as it appears, this was indeed possible, then we must conclude that the gap between Christianity and at least some forms of Judaism was much smaller initially than most people realize. In the decades following the birth of the church, and especially after the destruction of Jerusalem in A.D. 70, Christianity and Judaism came to define themselves increasingly over against one another. Aspects of Jewish thought that looked suspiciously Christian were discarded; at the same time, Christianity became increasingly anti-Jewish in its orientation. Over time, the two religions became more distinct and hence more separate. Their ultimate divorce looks a good deal more inevitable to us than it would have seemed to the first Christians, all of whom were Jews.

The Astronomical Book

The Astronomical Book contains the further travels of Enoch, mostly to witness the operation of the sun, moon, and stars. Matters of interest include an assertion that the years will be shortened and nature will run amuck in the End Times (chap. 80) and the mention of heavenly books in which all human deeds are recorded (chap. 81). The author's interest in the arrangement of the universe is clearly theological. Earth will one day come to be ordered just as the celestial bodies are now ordered by God's command. I refer to this as the "Mutual of Omaha" argument. You might recall the television show *Wild Kingdom* in which commercial breaks were introduced with lines like, "Just as the mother porpoise cares for her young, so Mutual of Omaha looks out for the interests of its policy holders." This is an "argument from nature," a rule that draws on an analogy from the natural world. Such arguments were commonplace among the ancients. Their fatal flaw is the fact that one can always find a contradictory example. For every swan who mates for life there is a mantis who devours her consort.

The Book of Dreams

This section contains two dream-visions, the first and shorter of which is a prediction of the flood in the time of Noah, Enoch's great-grandson. Enoch prays that all human flesh might not be destroyed in the great deluge. The flood story thus prefigures (and so justifies) the final judgment in which only the righteous will be spared.

The second dream, the "Animal Apocalypse," surveys history from the time of the fallen angels (Gen. 6:4) to the establishment of the Messianic kingdom. All of the human characters are represented by animals. Noah, Abraham, and Isaac are depicted as bulls; Jacob, his brothers, and their descendants are sheep. (How bulls begat sheep is anyone's guess.) The Egyptians are wolves, and other enemies are various sorts of predatory beasts. In Enoch-meets-Aesop fashion, the author recounts the stories of the sinful angels and their elephantine (literally; 86:4) children, the flood, the call of Abraham, the enslavement in Egypt, the Exodus, the monarchy, the building of the temple, and the Babylonian Captivity. This is not exactly George Orwell, but it makes its point.

The Apocalypse concludes with the expectation that Israel will be reconstituted and that Gentiles as well as Jews will become sinless (with "eyes open" to the good) and worship God. The restoration of the "flock" also encompassed the resurrection of the dead (90:33). Finally, another bull, the Messiah, will be born, who will rule over all of the animals of the earth. Enoch then awakes and weeps, "for everything shall come and be fulfilled; and all the deeds of men in their order were shown to me" (90:41).

True to the form of a historical apocalypse, the rehearsal of past events concludes in the author's own time, in this case, on or about the year 164 B.C., following the first successes of the Maccabean revolt. If one believed that this text had been written by Enoch himself, it would have sounded very convincing indeed. The coming of God, the final judgment, and the Messianic kingdom are the very next events on the prophetic calendar.

The author of the Animal Apocalypse appears to have belonged to one of the groups critical of the restored priesthood in Jerusalem. "[T]hey began again to place a table before the tower, but all the bread on it was polluted and not pure. And as touching all this the eyes of those sheep were blinded so that they saw not" (89:73-74). It was just such a controversy that led some years later to the establishment of the sectarian community at Qumran by Jews of a similarly apocalyptic stripe.

Finally, it is worth observing how late the Messiah appears in this scenario. Here, it is God who sits on the throne of judgment and destroys Israel's enemies. It is only when the restoration is complete that the Messiah is introduced. This fact demonstrates that there was no single conception of the Messiah in early Judaism. The Messiah (or even Messiah*s*) played a prominent role in the hopes of some (e.g., the Similitudes) and no role in the expectations of others (e.g., Daniel). Accordingly, there was no absolute standard against which to test claims of messiahship; on a practical level, this meant that such assertions were nearly impossible either to prove or to disprove. For Christians, even the death of Jesus could not invalidate a messiahship vindicated by resurrection. In other words, the nature of messiahship was disputed within Judaism long before it became a matter of Jewish/Christian controversy.

The Epistle of Enoch

> Let not your spirit be troubled on account of the times; for the Holy and Great One has appointed days for all things. And the righteous one shall arise from sleep. . . . And he will give him power so that he shall be (endowed) with goodness and righteousness, and he shall walk in eternal light. And sin shall perish in darkness for ever, and shall no more be seen from that day for evermore. (92:2-5)

The admonitions that begin the Epistle of Enoch make clear the pastoral interest of the "letter." The idea that "the Holy and Great One has appointed days for all things" is worked out more fully in the "Apocalypse of Weeks," an earlier composition imbedded in the epistle. As in the Animal Apocalypse, the author tells the story of human history, this time as a series of ten "weeks" (= seventy "days"). The narrative is fairly predictable, but there are a few unexpected twists and turns. Those in postexilic Israel (week seven) are characterized as an "apostate generation." Only at the close of the week (that is, in the author's own time) would a group of "elect righteous" appear to whom would be given "sevenfold instruction." (Thus the sectarian character of the writing is made plain.) Weeks eight through ten bring judgment to the unrighteous, both human and angel. Finally, "the first heaven shall depart and pass away, and a new heaven shall appear" (91:16). Uncharacteristically, there is no mention at this point of resurrection or eternal life.

Much of the rest of the epistle is given to a catalog of the woes facing the ungodly. The emphasis upon the improper use of riches is quite unusual for an apocalypse but has numerous parallels in the New Testament.[39] Those who have died in righteousness, whose "names are written before the glory of the Great One" (104:1), will "become companions of the hosts of heaven" (104:6). The idea that the righteous would dwell with the angels occurs frequently in apocalyptic writing; cf. Matthew 22:30; Luke 20:36; Hebrews 12:22-23; and Revelation 5:11.

The most unexpected statement in the whole of the epistle occurs in 98:4:

> [S]in has not been sent upon the earth, but man himself has created it, and under a great curse shall they fall who commit it.

This saying appears to counter the idea that sin originated with the Watchers, which is the characteristic view of the rest of the Enoch literature. Almost as surprising is the appearance of the Messiah at the very end of the letter (105:52):

> For I and My Son will be united with them for ever in the paths
> of uprightness in their lives; and ye shall have peace: rejoice, ye
> children of uprightness. Amen.

It should go without saying that this reference to the Messiah as God's Son is amenable to Christian interpretation. Little wonder that so many early Christians appear to have turned to 1 Enoch for inspiration.

Other Ancient Jewish Literature

The apocalyptic worldview of 1 Enoch is echoed in numerous other ancient Jewish writings, including 4 Ezra, 2 Baruch, the Apocalypse of

---

39. In 94:8 we read, "Woe to you, ye rich, for ye have trusted in your riches," a teaching echoed in passages such as Luke 12:21 and 1 Tim. 6:17. The author is concerned that the wicked prosper and even oppress the unrighteous, a reversal of fortune that appears to belie God's justice: "Woe unto you, ye sinners, for your riches make you appear like the righteous" (96:4). His answer is that the sinners face punishment after death: "know that all your oppression . . . is written down every day till the day of your judgment" (98:8).

Abraham, 3 Baruch, 2 Enoch, the Dead Sea Scrolls (from Qumran), the Testament of Levi 2-5, the Sibylline Oracles, Jubilees, and the Testament of Abraham. No two of these writings share identical perspectives, but all overlap at various points. Perhaps the most helpful way of introducing these materials in a very short space is to highlight seven (of course) key predictions and provide a few representative citations for each. From even a cursory scan of these quotations, it is possible to get a feel for the apocalyptic writings and a sense of their importance to the interpretation of Christian origins.

I. A time of severe tribulation will precede the new age.

Normal human bonds will be broken, nature will go haywire, and unrighteousness will abound.

Testament of Issachar 6:1	"Know ye therefore, my children, that in the last times your sons will forsake singleness, and will cleave unto insatiable desire; and leaving guilelessness, will draw near to malice; and forsaking the commandments of the Lord, they will cleave unto Beliar."
2 Baruch 70:8	"And it shall come to pass that whosoever gets safe out of the war shall die in the earthquake, And whosoever gets safe out of the earthquake shall be burned by fire, And whosoever gets safe out of the fire shall be destroyed by famine."
4 Ezra 5:1-2, 4-5	"Concerning the signs, however: Behold the days come when the inhabitants of earth shall be seized with great panic, and the way of truth shall be hidden and the land barren of faith and iniquity shall be increased. . . . Then shall the sun suddenly shine forth by night and the moon by day: and blood shall trickle forth from wood, and the stone utter its voice: the peoples shall be in commotion, the outgoings (of the stars) shall change."
Jubilees 23:18, 25	"Behold the earth shall be destroyed on account of all their works, and there shall be no seed of the vine, and oil; for their works are altogether faithless, and they shall all perish together, beasts and cattle and birds, and all the fish of the sea, on account of the children of men. . . . And the heads of the children shall be white with grey hair, and a child of three weeks shall appear like an old man of one hundred years, and their stature shall be destroyed by tribulation and oppression."

Assumption of Moses 10:5-6	"And the horns of the sun shall be broken and he shall be turned into darkness; and the moon shall not give her light, and be turned wholly into blood. And the circle of stars shall be disrupted And the sea shall retire into the abyss, and the fountains of waters shall fail, and the rivers shall dry up."

2. The time of tribulation will culminate in a great battle against Israel.

God (often through the Messiah) will destroy the ungodly and usher in an era of peace.

Sibylline Oracles 3:63-64, 67-73, 89-91	"But again the kings of the nations shall throw themselves against this land in troops, bringing retribution on themselves. . . . In a ring around the city the accursed kings shall place each one his throne with his infidel people by him. And then with a mighty voice God shall speak unto all the undisciplined empty-minded people, and judgement shall come upon them from the mighty God, and all shall perish at the hand of the Eternal. From heaven shall fall fiery swords down to the earth. . . . And God shall judge all with war and sword, and with fire and cataclysms of rain. And there shall be brimstone from heaven. . . . And then shall they know the Immortal God, who ordains these things."
4 Ezra 13:33-35, 49	"It shall be, when all the nations hear his [the Messiah's] voice, every man shall leave his own land and the warfare which they have one against another; and an innumerable multitude shall be gathered together, as thou didst see, desiring to come and to fight against him . . . he shall destroy the multitude of the nations that are gathered together, he shall defend the people that remain."
2 Baruch 72:2, 6	"My Messiah . . . shall both summon all the nations, and some of them he shall spare, and some of them he shall slay . . . all those who have ruled over you, or have known you, shall be given up to the sword."
Qumran, War Scroll 1:10, 12	"On the day when the Kittim [Romans] fall, there shall be battle and terrible carnage before the God of Israel, for that shall be the day appointed from ancient times for the battle of destruction of the sons of darkness. . . . And it shall be a time of [great] tribulation for the people which God shall redeem; of all its afflictions none shall be as this, from its sudden beginning until its end in eternal redemption."

3. The unrighteous will be judged and punished, the righteous saved.

2 Baruch 24:1   "For behold! the days come and the books shall be opened in which are written the sins of all those who have sinned, and again also the treasuries in which the righteousness of all those who have been righteous in creation is gathered."

4 Ezra 7:33-34   "And the Most High shall be revealed upon the throne of judgment: (and then cometh the End) and compassion shall pass away, (and pity be far off), and longsuffering withdrawn. But judgment alone shall remain, truth shall stand, and faithfulness triumph."

4 Ezra 8:3   "Many have been created, but few shall be saved."

Qumran, 1QpHab 10:5, 13   "He will bring him thence for judgment and will declare him guilty in the midst of them, and will chastise him with fire of brimstone . . . they . . . [will be] punished with fire who vilified and outraged the elect of God."

Jubilees 36:10   "But on the day of turbulence and execration and indignation and anger, with flaming devouring fire as He burnt Sodom, so likewise will He burn his [the sinner's] land and his city and all that is his, and he shall be blotted out of the book of the discipline of the children of men, and not be recorded in the book of life, but in that which is appointed to destruction. . . ."

4. The Messiah will rule
(again, according to many, but not all, apocalyptic writings).

4 Ezra 7:28-30   "For my Son the Messiah shall be revealed, together with those who are with him, and shall rejoice [with] the survivors four hundred years. And it shall be, after these years, that my Son the Messiah shall die, and all in whom there is human breath. Then shall the world be turned into the primaeval silence seven days, like as at the first beginnings; so that no man is left."

4 Ezra 13:25-26, 35, 37-38   "These are the interpretations of the vision: Whereas thou didst see a Man coming up from the heart of the Sea: this is he whom the Most High is keeping many ages (and) through whom he will deliver his creation . . . he shall stand upon the summit of Mount Sion. . . . But he, my Son, shall reprove the nations that are come for their ungodliness . . . and shall reproach them to their face with their evil thoughts and with the tortures with which they are destined to be tortured. . . ."

Psalms of Solomon 17:35-36, 40-41, 42	"And he (shall be) a righteous king, taught of God, over them, and there shall be no unrighteousness in his days in their midst, for all shall be holy and their king the anointed [Messiah] of the Lord. . . . He will bless the people of the Lord with wisdom and gladness, and he himself (will be) pure from sin, so that he may rule a great people. And he will rebuke rulers, and remove sinners by the might of his word. . . . God will make him mighty by means of (His) holy spirit, and wise by means of the spirit of understanding, with strength and righteousness."
Testament of Levi 18:2-3, 8-9	"Then shall the Lord raise up a new priest. And to him all the words of the Lord shall be revealed; and he shall execute a righteous judgement upon the earth for a multitude of days. And his star shall arise in heaven as of a king. Lighting up the light of knowledge as the sun the day. And he shall be magnified in the world. . . . And there shall none succeed him for all generations for ever. And in his priesthood the Gentiles shall be multiplied in knowledge upon the earth, and enlightened through the grace of the Lord: In his priesthood shall sin come to an end, and the lawless shall cease to do evil."

5. God will deal decisively with the Gentiles.

Psalms of Solomon 17:32-34	"And he shall have the heathen nations to serve him under his yoke; and he shall glorify the Lord in a place to be seen of all the earth; and he shall purge Jerusalem, making it holy as of old: So that nations shall come from the ends of the earth to see his glory. . . ."
Qumran, War Scroll 14:8	"Among the poor in spirit [there is power] over the hard of heart, and by the perfect of way all the nations of wickedness have come to an end: not one of their mighty men stands, but we are the remnant [of Thy people]."
2 Baruch 68:5	"Zion will again be builded, and its offerings will again be restored, and the priests will return to their ministry, and also the Gentiles will come to glorify it."
Tobit 13:11 (NRSV)	"A bright light will shine to all the ends of the earth; many nations will come to you from far away, the inhabitants of the remotest parts of the earth to your holy name, bearing gifts in their hands for the King of heaven."

Assumption of Moses 10:7-8, 10	"For the Most High will arise, the Eternal God alone, and He will appear to punish the Gentiles, and He will destroy all their idols. Then thou, O Israel, shalt be happy. . . . And thou shalt look from on high and shalt see thy enemies in Ge(henna) [Hell], . . . and thou shalt give thanks and confess thy Creator."

6. The New Age will commence.

The temple will be restored or replaced, the exiles will return to Israel, God and/or the Messiah will reign, and nature will be revitalized.

Sibylline Oracles 3:702-6	"Then again all the sons of the great God shall live quietly around the temple, rejoicing in those gifts which He shall give. . . . For He by Himself shall shield them, standing beside them alone in His might, encircling them, as it were, with a wall of flaming fire."
2 Baruch 73:1-2, 6	"Joy shall then be revealed, and rest shall appear. And then healing shall descend in dew, and disease shall withdraw, and anxiety and anguish and lamentation pass from amongst men, and gladness proceed through the whole earth. . . . And wild beasts shall come from the forest and minister unto men, and asps and dragons shall come forth from their holes to submit themselves to a little child."
Sibylline Oracles 3:741-46, 749-51	"But when the fated day shall reach this consummation, and there shall come to mortals the judgement of the Eternal God, there shall come upon men a great judgement and empire. For Earth the universal mother shall give to mortals her best fruit in countless store of corn, wine and oil. Yea, from the heaven shall come a sweet draught of luscious honey. . . . He will cause sweet fountains of white milk to burst forth. And the cities shall be full of good things and the fields rich: neither shall there be any sword throughout the land nor battle din."
4 Ezra 6:25-28	"And it shall be that whosoever shall have survived all these things that I have foretold unto thee, he shall be saved and shall see my salvation and the end of the world. And the men [Enoch and Elijah] who have been taken up, who have not tasted death from their birth, shall appear. Then shall the heart of the inhabitants [of the world] be changed, and be converted to a different spirit. For evil shall be blotted out, and deceit extinguished. Faithfulness shall flourish, and corruption be vanquished."

Tobit 13:16 (NRSV)	"The gates of Jerusalem will be built with sapphire and emerald, and all your walls with precious stones. The towers of Jerusalem will be built with gold, and their battlements with pure gold."
Assumption of Moses 10:1	"And then His kingdom shall appear throughout all His creation, and then Satan shall be no more, and sorrow will depart with him."

7. The righteous dead will enjoy eternal life
(with or without specific mention of bodily resurrection).

2 Baruch 30:1-2	"And it shall come to pass after these things, when the time of the advent of the Messiah is fulfilled, that He shall return in glory. Then all who have fallen asleep in hope of Him shall rise again."
4 Ezra 7:32	"And the earth shall restore those that sleep in her, and the dust those that are at rest therein."
Sibylline Oracles 4:179-80, 187-91	"But when at last everything shall have been reduced to dust and ashes and God shall quench the giant fire, even as he kindled it, then God Himself shall fashion again the bones and ashes of men, and shall raise up mortals once more as they were before . . . all who are godly shall live again on earth when God gives breath and life and grace to them, the godly. And then all shall behold themselves, beholding the lovely and pleasant sunlight."
Jubilees 23:30-31	"And the righteous shall see and be thankful, and rejoice with joy for ever and ever, and shall see all their judgments and all their curses on their enemies. And their bones shall rest in the earth, and their spirits shall have much joy. . . ."
Qumran, 4Q521:1-2, 8, 11-12; cf. Isa. 61:1-3; Luke 4:18-19	"[The hea]vens and the earth will listen to His Messiah, and none therein will stray from the commandments of the holy ones. . . . He [God] who liberates the captives, restores sight to the blind, straightens the b[ent]. . . . And the Lord will accomplish glorious things which have never been. . . . For he will heal the wounded, and revive the dead and bring good news to the poor. . . ."

It should be clear from these examples that a lively and widespread apocalyptic tradition existed prior to and at the time of Jesus and the earliest Christians. It is no surprise that scholars who emphasize the Jewishness of Jesus nearly always stress the importance of eschatology, especially apocalyptic eschatology. On the other side of the equation, scholars who de-eschatologize Jesus inevitably fashion a mostly non-Jewish Jesus, which for some, I suppose, is precisely the point.

As we have seen, many core apocalyptic ideas were already present in the later prophets and came into full flower in Jewish writings of the inter-testamental period. Up until now, we have largely set aside the two biblical apocalypses, Daniel and Revelation, for the sake of knowing those "other things" to which they (and much of the New Testament with them) ought to be compared. In the next chapter, we shall take a brief look at the shape of apocalyptic expectation in Daniel and Revelation, the two books that have most influenced two millennia of Christian reflection on the future.

CHAPTER FIVE

All in the Family: Daniel and Revelation

I purchased my first record album in junior high school, a copy of Simon and Garfunkel's immensely popular *Bridge over Troubled Water*. I did not own a proper stereo; instead, I listened to the record on a chunky box phonograph that made up in volume what it lacked in fidelity. Its two-pound (or so it seemed) tonearm lumbered across the black vinyl like a ten-ton diesel rumbling over asphalt. I listened to the album hundreds of times, finding ever-new ways to apply the lyrics to the circumstances of my life (quite a stretch in the case of *Cecilia!*). It was as though Paul Simon had written with me specifically in mind.

Many years later, I bought a good stereo with a compact disc player. Of course, one of my first CD purchases was *Bridge over Troubled Water*. I was surprised to hear all sorts of things that I had missed previously, such as Art Garfunkel drawing breath. The same was true for CDs of other familiar records. In no time at all, I became an audio deconstructionist, disassembling each song and analyzing its sonic bits and pieces. (Good bass line here, sloppy chord there.) It took me a while to get back to listening to *music*. In time, I came to appreciate the fact that my stereo's increased fidelity had ushered me closer to the original performance, whose occasional imperfections were now more audible. At the same time, it made what was good, such as Simon and Garfunkel harmonies, that much better. It also enabled me to understand lyrics that I had been mis-singing for years. (There is a line in Vanity Fare's *Hitchin' a Ride* that I recall with particular mortification.)

The day that I began academic study of the Bible was much like the day that I purchased my first good stereo. Initially, the experience was disorienting and disconcerting. I had already attended countless Bible studies; certainly, I knew the Bible well on one level, much as I seemed to know *Bridge over Troubled Water* inside out as a teenager. For a while, biblical scholarship appeared only to dismantle Scripture and to distance me from it. Once again, it took time to hear the music, to learn that God could speak through a text whose limitations had previously been masked. I came to see that careful biblical study can remove layers of distortion, taking us closer to the original performance, allowing us to hear the notes more clearly, helping us to get the lyrics right.

Few books of the Bible are heard more differently with the instrument of modern scholarship than are Daniel and Revelation. Because the disparity in perception is so great, it is easy to understand why many traditional interpreters have viewed mainstream biblical scholarship with suspicion and even animosity. At first encounter, the academic study of these books can seem a wholly negative enterprise, an exercise in demolition and debunking. For many, it follows that these are not only the effects but also the goals of scholarship. I do not deny that there are scholars at war with Christian faith, but they constitute a relatively small though often vocal minority. In fact, scholars may be found all along the spectrum of belief and religious practice. Moreover, it is important to recognize that biblical scholarship uncovers more difficulties than it manages to create. The complications are already there, and a faithful reading of Scripture must take an honest account of them. The problem with many highly conservative readings of the Bible is not that they are so conservative but that they are so often inaccurate.

The question that divides traditional and modern interpreters is this: Are Daniel and Revelation principally books of historical *foresight* or theological *insight*?[1] The great majority of popular writers assume the former, viewing the biblical apocalypses as End Times road maps that reliably depict the sequence of events leading up to and extending beyond the return of Christ. Invariably, such interpreters recognize in Daniel and Revelation a description of their own historical

---

1. J. A. T. Robinson, *In the End, God* (London: James Clarke & Co., 1950), p. 38.

terrain, meaning that the time of tribulation is at hand, the beast or antichrist is alive in the world, and Armageddon is fast approaching. Needless to say, every such interpretation has been proved wrong historically. Still, one ought never to underestimate the buoyancy of such thinking; it is as unsinkable as Styrofoam. The map itself is perfectly accurate; the fault lies with each and every navigator who has ever used it.

An alternative is to regard Daniel and Revelation as books that should be interpreted within the context of the apocalyptic tradition that so clearly influenced them. To this way of thinking, it is unreasonable if not intellectually dishonest to dismiss the eschatology of 1 Enoch and 4 Ezra while accepting more or less identical material in Daniel and Revelation as literal historical prediction. In such a case, what is decisive is not the book's historical or literary context but the modern reader's own notions about what it must mean. Obviously, it is a great deal easier to avoid reading these books in context if one is ignorant of that context. It does not help matters that so few popular books on eschatology acknowledge the existence of the non-biblical apocalypses, much less consider their influence on the biblical authors. No doubt some fear that Daniel and Revelation will be stripped of significance by such an approach. In fact, the opposite can be true. Read in context, these books provide invaluable biblical testimony to the theological and political insight of the Jewish and Christian apocalypticists. For many interpreters, the place of Daniel and Revelation has been greatly enhanced by such a reading.

The apocalyptic writers were deeply concerned about theology, in particular, about the question of God's presence in human history. It was their insight that theological affirmations necessarily had future consequences, that a righteous and loving God ultimately must "win." Each of the key apocalyptic concepts — for example, the judgment, the revitalization of nature, the New Jerusalem — arose and evolved because it embodied some essential conviction about the character of God. This is closely analogous to the way that the creation accounts of Genesis 1–3 functioned. If Israel's God is such a God, then creation is meaningful and human history purposeful. Creation stories from other cultures were taken over and modified to express core theological convictions. (The cosmos is good; humans are made in God's image.) So, too, in envisioning creation's destiny, Jewish and then Christian believers borrowed ideas from Persian, Babylonian, and other sources and reworked them into a story of God's triumph.[2]

The authors of Daniel and Revelation believed that the end of history was upon them.[3] In any literal sense, they were mistaken, but it is our error to judge them exclusively or primarily on the basis of the historical accuracy of their predictions.[4] As J. A. T. Robinson put it, neither "Genesis nor . . . Revelation set out to be *historical* reconstructions, i.e. literal accounts of what did, or what will, happen. As history they may be entirely imaginary, and yet remain theologically true."[5] Theological accounts of human origins and destiny have been and always will be conditioned by the particular culture in which they are formulated; therefore, the test of their truthfulness cannot be cultural. If it were, every such account would fail. Instead, the test is theological. Does the apocalypse tell us something true about God?

Here as elsewhere, truth is *incarnational* (literally, "in flesh"): it takes shape in human ideas and takes expression in human actions. The ideas and expressions themselves are no less true for being human and no less human for being true. I am a fan of Jane Austen. On one level, her novels are thoroughly time-bound and relevant to me only insofar as I am curious about the society and manners of the early-nineteenth-century English gentry. (I do however feel a certain kinship to Hill, the Bennets' servant in *Pride and Prejudice*.) On another level, Austen's novels are wonderfully timeless, containing enduring insight into human character. I would be foolish to dismiss Jane Austen because I do not live in a manor or dress in a waistcoat. How much greater would be my loss were I to spurn biblical authors whose world is so unlike my own. For all its flamboyance, theology

2. See the discussion about the background to Jewish apocalyptic thinking in Chapter Four.

3. The sentiment is common to many New Testament authors. Compare 1 John 2:18: "Children, it is the last hour! As you have heard that the antichrist is coming, so now many antichrists have come. From this we know that it is the last hour."

4. While it is true that "the Last Days" can be expanded to include all time after Christ (whether fifty years or fifty thousand), it is obvious that many early Christians believed that Christ would return within their lifetime. To claim, as many do, that all such expectations were fulfilled in the church is historically inaccurate and theologically indefensible.

5. *In the End, God,* p. 34. Robinson's analysis is characteristically brilliant.

dressed in the garb of apocalyptic is still theology and should be evaluated as such.

To Christian fundamentalists, the suggestion that the biblical authors could be wrong on one level but right on another seems like a dodge, a pious mask for unbelief. Radical critics may be equally scornful of such distinctions. The apocalypses were wrong, they would say, and there is no point in trying to find meaning in them. Both viewpoints possess a clarity born of absoluteness and both make the same absolute assumption: either the Bible is true or it is false. Things are seldom that simple. In fact, the Bible is neither free of nor full of error. It is the faithful witness of imperfect and finite people to the perfect and infinite God. The testimony of Daniel and Revelation is problematic, to be sure, but it is also important. Read in this light, the authors of the biblical apocalypses become more realistic and understandable figures. They did not have all of the answers; instead, like many of us, they sought to be people of faith in a world that appeared both to confirm and to disconfirm their trust in God. Indeed, those who struggle most with faith may make the firmest connection with apocalyptic literature, not because it answers their questions but because it shares them:

> Then I said in my heart, Are the deeds of those who inhabit Babylon any better? Is that why she has gained dominion over Zion? For when I came here I saw ungodly deeds without number, and my soul has seen many sinners during these thirty years. And my heart failed me, for I have seen how you endure those who sin, and have spared those who act wickedly, and have destroyed your people, and have preserved their enemies, and have not shown to anyone how your way may be comprehended. Are the deeds of Babylon better than those of Zion? (2 Esdras [4 Ezra] 3:28-32, NRSV)

Daniel and Revelation are members of two families: they are both apocalypses and they are both Scripture. These identities must be kept in balance. To read these books as though they are without historical antecedent or context is inevitably to misinterpret them. To read these books as though they are merely ancient curiosities is inevitably to underestimate them.

Daniel

The figure of Daniel makes his first biblical appearance in Ezekiel 14:14:

> [E]ven if Noah, Daniel, and Job, these three, were in it [the land], they would save only their own lives by their righteousness, says the Lord God.

Noah, Daniel, and Job (cf. v. 20) are regarded as venerable models of faithful obedience, and all three have parallels in neighboring cultures. Many commentators refer to the judge Daniel (or Danel), legendary for his wisdom, who appears in the literature of ancient Ugarit about 1500 B.C. Ezekiel makes a second reference to Daniel in 28:3, "You [the prince of Tyre] are indeed wiser than Daniel; no secret is hidden from you." It is important to note that Ezekiel's mention of Daniel occurred prior to the destruction of Jerusalem (see 14:21) and so predated the mid- to late-sixth century B.C. setting of the book of Daniel (Dan. 1:1-4). Centuries later, the Jewish book of Jubilees recounted the marriage of Enoch (of apocalyptic fame) to one "Edni, the daughter of Dânêl" (4:20). As John Collins observed,

> [T]he association with Enoch of a name so similar to Daniel, and possibly identical with it, is intriguing. It is distinctly possible that the same traditional figure underlies the Daniel of Ugarit and Ezekiel, and the Dânêl of *Jubilees*. It is in any case clear from Ezekiel that the name carried traditional associations that could only enhance the authority of the biblical book.[6]

We saw in the last chapter that apocalypses are usually *pseudonymous,* that is, written in the name of some earlier figure. The fact that Ezra and Baruch were historical characters does not require us to believe that they were in any way responsible for the apocalypses composed in their names. Conversely, the existence of a long-standing tradition about a wise and righteous Daniel does not prove that the

---

6. John Collins, *The Apocalyptic Imagination: An Introduction to Jewish Apocalyptic Literature,* 2nd ed. (Grand Rapids: Eerdmans, 1998), p. 87.

biblical book of Daniel is pseudonymous. So, how are we to judge authorship? There are many tests, but the simplest and surest is historical. Pseudonymous apocalyptic writings of this type[7] are typically hazy about the distant past, increasingly accurate about the recent past, accurate about and attentive to the immediate past, and wholly speculative — and often completely wrong — about the future. Just as we would expect, pseudonymous authors knew a good deal more about their own time than they knew about earlier history, and they possessed no knowledge of events yet to come.

Such works are dated to the moment at which they shift from increasingly accurate and detailed recollection of the past to largely inaccurate and stereotypical speculation about the future. This transition typically occurs at about the same point in the apocalyptic drama, at the end of history-as-usual and the beginning of the period of tribulation preceding God's ultimate victory. The result can be visualized in the following way:

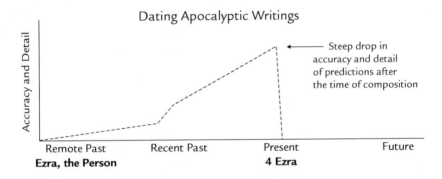

A book's date of composition ("present" time on the above diagram) is reckoned as the point beyond which it ceases to provide accurate information. When this location postdates the lifetime of its reputed author, the book is thought to be pseudonymous. For example, the final historical events accurately "foretold" in 4 Ezra all concern the Roman empire in the first century. The book also refers to the destruction of the temple, which occurred in A.D. 70. For these reasons, the

---

7. That is, a "historical apocalypse." On the distinction between historical and heavenly journey apocalypses, see Chapter Four above.

book is thought to be a product of the late first century. Ezra himself lived hundreds of years earlier, shortly after the time of the Babylonian Captivity; therefore, 4 Ezra is judged to be pseudonymous. (In theory, I suppose, one could believe that Ezra himself was capable of foretelling events, but only to the end of the first century, at which point his tank of inspiration ran dry.) Note that the issue is not whether scholars believe in the possibility of predictive prophecy. Few interpreters of any religious persuasion today believe that Ezra wrote the apocalypse of 4 Ezra. The issue is not the faith of the scholar but the literary genre and historical location of the text.

Does Daniel fit this pattern? Did Rogers and Hammerstein write musicals? Yes, absolutely. Although the story is set in Babylon at the time of the Exile, there are numerous errors in its depiction of the historical events of that period, both in the narrative and the visionary sections of the book. For example, the dating of Nebuchadnezzar's conquest of Jerusalem in 1:1 is incorrect; it was Jehoiakim's son, Jehoiachin, who was defeated and taken captive (2 Kings 24:8-12). Similarly, Belshazzar was neither the son of Nebuchadnezzar nor reigned as king, *contra* Daniel 5:1-2. In general, the author's knowledge of Babylonian and Persian history is both thin and inexact.[8] Once the historical visions take us past the conquests of Alexander (11:3) and the division of his empire (11:4; 2:41), the information increases dramatically both in precision and abundance. The reign of Antiochus IV, a notorious persecutor of the Jews, takes up the whole of 11:21-45. (Think of Antiochus as the Hitler of the second century B.C., and you will get a feel for the literature of this period.) Verses 40-45 relate the story of the destruction of Antiochus and his forces. Unfortunately both for the Jews and for the book of Daniel, although not perhaps for Antiochus himself, it did not happen. Most glaringly, Antiochus did not die in Palestine (11:45); instead, his life ended in Persia a few years later (163 B.C.; 2 Macc. 9). True to apocalyptic form, Daniel sees the eschatological climax as the very next event on the prophetic calendar (e.g., 12:1-4; 2:44-45).

For these and other reasons, scholars, the majority by a long shot,

---

8. A good introduction to the Hebrew Bible (such as Bernhard W. Anderson's *Understanding the Old Testament*, 4th ed. [Englewood Cliffs, N.J.: Prentice-Hall, 1986]) will offer a much more detailed review of the historical problems, such as the presence of the apparently fictional "Darius the Mede" in Daniel.

date the apocalyptic sections of Daniel to about the year 165 B.C., that is, after 167 B.C., when Antiochus erected an altar to Zeus in the Jerusalem temple,[9] but before his death in 163 B.C. This date is passionately challenged by conservative scholars who in principle oppose any claim that Holy Scripture might contain pseudonymous books. Their dedication and resourcefulness are admirable, and I sometimes wish they were right, but they are paddling against a tidal wave of evidence. It is special pleading to argue that Daniel should not be subjected to the same historical analysis that demonstrates that Ezra did not write 4 Ezra and Enoch did not write 1 Enoch. What's good for the goose is good for the gander, and, beyond all reasonable doubt, this particular gander dates from the middle of the second century before Christ.

The Narratives (Daniel 1–6)

The book of Daniel is a tale of two halves. The first six chapters contain stories about Daniel narrated in the third person; the last six chapters contain visions described in the first person. The first half of the book does not mention Antiochus's blasphemy in the temple (the "abomination of desolation"), an event that dominates the second half. For these reasons, it is likely that the stories contained in chapters 1–6 come from a slightly earlier period. The differing attitude toward the state in the two halves also evidences this split. Chapters 1–6 take a relatively optimistic view of foreign rule: Daniel is challenged repeatedly by corrupt officials but always triumphs, eventually becoming a powerful political figure in his own right. In the second half of the book of Daniel, the state is practically demonized; its end is not reform but ruin. The facts that the book is composed in two languages, Hebrew and Aramaic, and that other Daniel stories are known from ancient Jewish sources (see the "Additions to Daniel" in the Apocrypha) make it all the more likely that the present work is a composite of Daniel traditions, much as 1 Enoch is a repository of Enoch materials.

The lively narratives of Daniel 1–6 are justly beloved by both Jews and Christians. There is no need here to recap the familiar stories of the lion's den and the fiery furnace. (A recent experience with my three-

---

9. See 9:27; 11:31; and 12:11; cf. 1 Macc. 1:54.

year-old daughter has endowed the account of the handwriting on the wall in Dan. 5 with particular vividness.) In any case, these narratives are easily and more enjoyably read in full. Moreover, chapters 1-6 add little to our knowledge of Jewish eschatology and so can be dealt with briefly.

In one way or another, each of the stories of Daniel 1-6 touches on the theme of Jewish conduct in the Gentile world. About that subject they are fairly optimistic; Daniel and friends are scrupulously observant Jews who, despite bitter opposition originating in a professional jealousy worthy of Salieri, rise to the top ranks of the Babylonian hierarchy. The clear message is that Jews need not abandon the Law in order to function in Gentile society. By their patient and blameless example, the Jewish heroes silence their critics — permanently, in the case of those eaten by lions (Daniel 6:24) — and win the king's recognition of both themselves and their God. The basic pattern is repeated in each chapter.[10] By contrast, most apocalyptic writings, including the second half of the book of Daniel, take a far more pessimistic view of political power. Which of the two halves of Daniel one finds more realistic says a lot about one's own social and political situation.

There is only one semi-apocalyptic passage in the narrative section: chapter 2, which tells of Nebuchadnezzar's dream and its interpretation. All in all, it is fairly mild stuff. There is no mention of a tribulation and only a passing reference to the destruction of outsiders. We saw in the previous chapter that earlier non-Jewish texts mentioned a mysterious object made of metals of depreciating value (e.g., gold, silver, bronze, and iron), often in conjunction with the widely known four-kingdom scenario.[11] The statue of Daniel 2:31-43 was cast in this mold. The eschatological viewpoint comes to the forefront in verses 44ff.:

> And in the days of those kings [the Ptolemies and Seleucids] the God of heaven will set up a kingdom that shall never be destroyed, nor shall this kingdom be left to another people. It shall

---

10. See 1:20; 2:46-49; 3:28-30; 4:34-37; 5:29; and 6:19-28.

11. Verse 43 slightly complicates the image (iron trying to mix with clay by marriage), but it is useful in dating the story since it refers to the failed attempt to unite the Seleucid and Ptolemaic dynasties by marriage.

crush all these kingdoms and bring them to an end, and it shall stand forever. . . .

A fascinating tension exists between the recognition of the pagan king's God-given authority (vv. 21 & 37-38), on the one hand, and Daniel's pronouncement of the destruction of all pagan kingdoms (v. 44), on the other. It is in keeping with this that the apocalyptic vision was given to King Nebuchadnezzar himself but required the interpretation of Daniel, the Jew.[12] This attitude is both more negative than that of the rest of chapters 1-6 and more positive than that of chapters 7-12. It is reminiscent of the thought of the apostle Paul, who offered a strikingly favorable assessment of the state in Romans 13:1-7, while also believing that "every ruler and every authority and power" would be destroyed by Christ at his return (1 Cor. 15:24-25). One wonders if the viewpoint expressed by Paul would have been moderated had he known that he himself would be slain by the very sword that he commends in Romans 13:4. Likewise, it would be interesting to know how the author of Daniel 1-6 would have dealt with the events portrayed in chapters 7-12.

The Visions (Daniel 7-12)

The remaining chapters were composed in the presence of a much darker reality. Under the rule of the Syrian king Antiochus IV, Jews could be, and many were, killed simply for practicing Judaism. There was no angelic rescue from this fiery furnace. Many sought and eventually won deliverance through a violent uprising, the Maccabean Revolt. The author of Daniel 7-12 preferred nonviolent resistance, believing that present tribulations heralded the coming of God's rule to earth. It would be wrong to generalize from this example that apocalyptic writings always promoted pacifism or even passivity; they could just as easily encourage violence. Unlike many apocalypticists, Daniel did not foresee a great battle in which the armies of Israel would vanquish their foes. Instead, the victory would be God's alone. In the meantime, believers were to batten down the hatches and weather the storm.

---

12. Other stories of this type are known from the ancient world, the most famous of which is Joseph's interpretation of Pharaoh's dream in Genesis 41.

I have heard it said that a leader is one who helps others to conceptualize reality. The success of Abraham Lincoln and Franklin Roosevelt as wartime presidents was due in large part to their ability to articulate a compelling vision of reality, to provide an account of the war's purpose around which their people could rally. The apocalyptic writings served a similar function. Much has been written in recent years about the power of apocalyptic texts to "name" evil, that is, to create literary images, such as the beast of Daniel and Revelation, that help readers to conceptualize the struggle in which they are engaged.[13] Above all, such imaginative constructions worked to subvert the oppressor's own portrayal of reality. The state did not act under God's authority; quite to the contrary, it was a demonic instrument destined for destruction. By "unveiling" the true nature of events, the apocalypse encouraged believers in their stand against the powers of wickedness. Seen in this light, Daniel is a deeply subversive text that decloaks evil and delegitimizes political power. So, Daniel's is anything but a slave religion, requiring submission to the divinely sanctioned authority of one's oppressors.

Like the wardrobe through which one enters C. S. Lewis's Narnia, Daniel 7:1 is the portal by which we again return to the apocalyptic world. Daniel is no longer the interpreter but is instead the dreamer whose visions must be deciphered by an angel. Once again, the revelation concerns four powerful kingdoms, portrayed in Daniel 7 by a series of fantastic animals (cf. 4 Ezra 11), who "came up out of the sea," chaos's mythical abode. The first beast is the Babylonian Empire. (The winged lion was a common image in Babylonian art.) The Median and Persian Empires come second and third. The fourth, "terrifying and dreadful and exceedingly strong," is the empire of Alexander the Great. Following his death, Alexander's vast territories were divided into four kingdoms, one of which was ruled by the Seleucid dynasty, named for Seleucus, the son of Antiochus, one of Alexander's generals. Early Seleucid coins displayed an image of horns, symbolizing power. The Seleucids gained control of Israel in the year 198 B.C. It is they who are symbolized by the ten horns of Daniel 7:7 and 7:24. The "little horn" is undoubtedly Antiochus IV, who eliminated his rivals ("three of the ear-

---

13. E.g., Walter Wink, *Naming the Powers: The Language of Power in the New Testament* (Philadelphia: Fortress, 1984); and Pablo Richard, *Apocalypse: A People's Commentary on the Book of Revelation* (Maryknoll, N.Y.: Orbis, 1995).

lier horns were plucked up by the roots" [7:8; cf. 11:21]). Antiochus, also called *Epiphanes* (a "manifestation" of Zeus), is characterized by his arrogance.[14] Daniel 7:25 describes his rule in this way:

> He shall speak words against the Most High, shall wear out the holy ones of the Most High, and shall attempt to change the sacred seasons and the law; and they shall be given into his power for a time, two times, and half a time.

Antiochus's reign of terror will be limited, symbolized by the figure of three and one half years, half a perfect seven. Immediately after, the heavenly books will be opened, God will judge the earth, and the arrogant horn will be "burned with fire" (v. 11). (For good measure, verse 26 adds "consumed and totally destroyed." No half measures here.) Then comes the Son of Man,[15] who will be given eternal dominion over the earth (v. 14).

The same scenario is repeated with some variation and elaboration in the three visions of the following chapters. The vision of chapter 8 is the most similar. The symbolism is explicitly decoded, for example, in vv. 21-22:

> The male goat is the king of Greece, and the great horn between its eyes is the first king. As for the horn that was broken, in place of which four others arose, four kingdoms shall arise from his nation, but not with his power.

Clearly, the author is again referring to Alexander the Great and the four-part division of the Hellenistic empire upon his death. As in the previous vision, however, Alexander is only a means to an end. The spotlight is on Antiochus IV (vv. 9-14; 23-25), expected to be the last human ruler — and hence the model for the antichrist in Christian thinking. Once more, it is anticipated that Antiochus will be defeated, "but not by human hands" (v. 25).

The prophet Jeremiah had predicted that the Babylonian Exile would last for seventy years (25:11-12; 29:10). Technically, the period was

---

14. V. 8; cf. 2 Macc. 5:21; 7:36; 9:3; etc.
15. Daniel's Son of Man is discussed in the previous chapter.

somewhat shorter: from 587, when Jerusalem fell to the Babylonians, until 538 B.C., when Cyrus issued his edict allowing the return of exiles (see Ezra 1:2-4). Much more worrying is the fact that prophetic expectations of postexilic holiness, prosperity, and security were not fulfilled. These problems form the backdrop to Daniel 9, which begins with explicit mention of Daniel's perplexity over the prophecy of Jeremiah (v. 2). Through the angel Gabriel, God reveals to Daniel the true meaning of the prophecy, namely, that there would be seventy *weeks of years* between the time that "the word went out to restore and rebuild Jerusalem" and the establishment of "everlasting righteousness" (v. 24). The 490 years (seven "days" times seventy "weeks") is a symbolic number that does not correspond to any exact date, much like the seventy generations in 1 Enoch 10. The first seven weeks end with the arrival of an "anointed prince"; the likeliest candidates are Zerubbabel and the high priest Joshua (Ezra 2:2; 3:2; Zech. 6:9-14; Hag. 1:1-14). The next sixty-two weeks zip by with barely a mention. Obviously, the focus is on the final week, which begins with the death of an anointed one. Christians have long been drawn to this passage, which prophesies the killing of a Messiah ("anointed one") followed by the destruction of "the city and the sanctuary" (v. 26). Indeed, Daniel 9:26 might well have influenced Christian interpretation of the destruction of Jerusalem in A.D. 70. It is likely that the original referent was Onias III, an honorable high priest murdered only a few years earlier, in 171 B.C. (2 Macc. 4:30-34). Hence, the final "week" would conclude seven years later, that is, in 164 B.C., a year or two after the text was composed. The prince who conquers Israel makes a pact with some of the Jews (see 1 Macc. 1:11). After three and a half years (i.e., in 167 B.C.), he stops the temple sacrifices and erects "an abomination that desolates," an altar to Zeus, "until the decreed end is poured out upon the desolator" (v. 27; see 2 Macc. 5-6). As in the previous vision, the end of history is on the immediate horizon, at which time Antiochus and his forces will be obliterated by God.

The final revelation is recounted in Daniel 10-12. It is much more detailed but covers essentially the same ground as the previous visions. Chapter 10 tells of the appearance of Gabriel, whose arrival was delayed by a conflict with the "prince of the kingdom of Persia" (v. 13). Behind this odd statement is the very ancient idea that a war between two nations was as much a conflict of gods as of armies (e.g., 2 Kings 18:32-35).

While Israel struggled with Persia, Gabriel (and then Michael, in Gabriel's absence [v. 13]) contended with Persia's supernatural counterparts. Presaging the conflict with Alexander and his successors, Gabriel says, "Now I must return to fight against the prince of Persia, and when I am through with him, the prince of Greece will come" (v. 20). Few passages more vividly illustrate the two-tiered apocalyptic world. The closing verse of chapter 10 is similarly representative of the determinism of such writings: "I am to tell you what is inscribed in the book of truth" (v. 21), namely, the inevitable course of human history, detailed in chapters 11-12.

Chapter 11 is almost exclusively about the Seleucid dynasty, first in its conflicts with the Ptolemies of Egypt and second in its conquest and profanation of Israel. A Bible with good footnotes, such as the *Oxford Annotated Bible* or *HarperCollins Study Bible,* will explain Daniel's many allusions to key events of this period. As we have come to expect, the greatest space (the whole of verses 20-45) is given to a description of the reign of Antiochus IV. Of particular interest are verses 33-35:

> The wise among the people shall give understanding to many; for some days, however, they shall fall by sword and flame, and suffer captivity and plunder. When they fall victim, they shall receive a little help, and many shall join them insincerely. Some of the wise shall fall, so that they may be refined, purified, and cleansed, until the time of the end, for there is still an interval until the time appointed.

Almost certainly, the author of this text was among the "wise" teachers to whom these verses refer. There is no consensus about who helps them ("a little") or what form that assistance takes. Many have interpreted the saying as an early reference to the Maccabees, but that identification is by no means certain. Verse 35 is a call to endurance: they might yet be killed, "for there is still an interval," but their sacrifice will win them eternal life. Such language is echoed in the book of Revelation, e.g., in 13:10:

> If you are to be taken captive, into captivity you go; if you kill with the sword, with the sword you must be killed. Here is a call for the endurance and faith of the saints.

Daniel 12:1-3 spells out the future hope:

> At that time Michael, the great prince, the protector of your peo-
> ple, shall arise. There shall be a time of anguish, such as has
> never occurred since nations first came into existence. But at
> that time your people shall be delivered, everyone who is found
> written in the book. Many of those who sleep in the dust of the
> earth shall awake, some to everlasting life, and some to shame
> and everlasting contempt. Those who are wise shall shine like
> the brightness of the sky, and those who lead many to righteous-
> ness, like the stars forever and ever.

Michael, the chief angelic patron of Israel, has a quasi-messianic
role in Daniel. It is he and not a Davidic heir who is Israel's "prince"
(10:21). It is probably Michael to whom Daniel 7:13-14 ("one like a Son of
Man") refers, a passage that closely parallels Daniel 12:1. Equally surprising is the fact that eternal life, "for better or for worse," appears to
be granted only to the most righteous and most wicked of people. This
exclusivism is quite striking. It is again the author's own group (the
"wise"; "those who lead many to righteousness"; cf. v. 10: "the wise who
understand") that shines — literally, in this case. The association of angels with the stars is commonplace in apocalyptic literature, as is the
expectation that the righteous will enjoy angelic fellowship. 1 Enoch
39:4-5 is typical:

> And there I saw another vision, the dwelling-places of the holy,
> and the resting places of the righteous. Here mine eyes saw their
> dwellings with His righteous angels, and their resting places
> with the holy.

The belief that the righteous themselves would become angels is
derivative of this perspective. (Remember Clarence in *It's a Wonderful
Life*?)

Naturally, the character of Daniel is concerned to know when these
things will take place. He is told, "Go your way, Daniel, for the words
are to remain secret and sealed until the time of the end" (v. 9). This
saying increases the aura of mystery surrounding the text and provides
an explanation for its previous absence. Now (that is, the second cen-

tury B.C.) is the End Time in which Daniel's vision was to be disclosed. Such a statement is troubling for modern readers (I include myself) since it appears to make plain the author's intention to deceive readers into believing in the book's earlier origin. All that I can say in Daniel's defense is that such statements were common in pseudepigraphic works generally. For example, when writing a letter or a speech in the name of a famous teacher, it was considered good form to include mundane details, for example, comments about contemporaries or references to a travel itinerary, that would lend verisimilitude to the work. This literary device strikes us differently than it did many ancients. Frankly, we are in no position to judge the author of Daniel 12 on this matter, about which we should assume he acted with a clear conscience. What is obvious is the gulf that stands between us. Of course, the same will be true as future believers look back in amazement at our glaring deficiencies. "She called herself a Christian, and yet I have read that she ate meat and owned a *car.* Can you imagine?!"

Like other writings of its type, Daniel expresses an intense longing for justice and a profound trust in God's righteousness. The book is a declaration of present faith projected onto the future. To turn to Daniel for literal historical prediction is fundamentally to misunderstand the book. The author(s) of Daniel was convinced that the human future was God's future, that the God who acted in days gone by would act in days to come. From the point of view of Christianity, the most profound of such acts came only a few generations later, in the bat of a chronologist's eye. The manner in which subsequent belief in Jesus shaped and was shaped by the apocalyptic vision is a major concern of the second half of this chapter.

Revelation

Where there is an emperor with divine pretensions, there is need of an apocalypse. As the image of King Antiochus IV darkens the visions of Daniel, so the shadow of Caesar Domitian falls heavily across the pages of Revelation. In both cases, allegiance to the state was tested at its altar, where all counterclaims to ultimacy were sacrificed. To worship Caesar or Zeus, manifest in Antiochus, was to enfranchise oneself in a reality in which God and Christ could have no dominion. That reality might have been illusory, but it was a powerful illusion and full of wrath toward all who would deny it. In the lions' den of the Coliseum, there was no deliverance but death and no vindication but in the world to come. It was in such a context that Revelation was written; it is in similar contexts that it makes the most sense today. Among modern theologians, Dietrich Bonhoeffer stands out as a strong advocate for the apocalyptic faith of Revelation. It was no trivial association: Bonhoeffer himself was put to death for plotting against Hitler, the very image of the beast in modern dress.

Most of us do not live in such a dire political situation; therefore, we are prone to domesticate Revelation in one of two ways. The first is to strip the book of its historical context, decoupling Revelation from the first century and viewing it as a timeless guidebook to the Last Days, which coincidentally happen to be *our* days. Like settlers at the Oklahoma land rush, interpreters race to stake their claim to Revelation's contemporary fulfillments, leaving its author and original audience in their dust.[16] The opposite tack is to limit the book to its Roman context, assuming that to explain Revelation is to be done with Revelation. No enduring insights are met, no ongoing questions entertained. The book is tamed and our world goes happily undisturbed.

A better option is to encounter Revelation as a living text whose strange and uncomfortable images cannot be reduced to a first- or twenty-first-century checklist of events. The symbolism of Revelation is art, not technical description. The power of art is not in its literalness; indeed, art reduced to literalness is no longer art. Great art is born of a particular historical situation which it both exemplifies and transcends. Knowledge of that situation helps us to interpret it, but it is no substitute for personal encounter. There is a certain painting that I see whenever I visit the Art Institute in Chicago. Nothing in my knowledge of the artist, his times, or techniques can account for the power this picture exercises over me. Once there, I find it difficult to go, as though in so doing I should leave some part of myself behind. That might be analogous to the experience of many, like Bonhoeffer, who have had a profound encounter with the book of Revelation. Those of us inclined to pass it by with only a condescending glance at its uncomfortable

---

16. For more on the contemporary interpretation of Revelation, see the Appendix, "Not Left Behind."

subject or rough brushwork might take a cue from the small knot of viewers who stand transfixed before it. Perhaps there is more here than meets our eye.

One of Revelation's many ironies is its title: "The revelation ['apoc- alypse'] of Jesus Christ" (1:1). Revelation is in fact the least "uncovered" (the meaning of *apocalypsis*) book of the entire Bible. It contains a good many familiar apocalyptic ideas, but, unlike Daniel, it provides rela- tively few clues as to the meaning of its symbols. Some of the major im- ages are easy enough to correlate with the world of the late first cen- tury (e.g., Babylon = Rome), but much of the symbolism remains elusive, which may well be deliberate.

Although the book of Daniel exerted considerable influence over the author of Revelation (e.g., in Rev. 1:12-16), there are many differ- ences between the two books. For one thing, Revelation does not ap- pear to be pseudonymous. "John" (1:1), the author, assumes the famil- iarity of his audience, the churches of western Asia Minor. We know very little about him; nothing in the text confirms his traditional iden- tification with John, the disciple of Jesus. His reference in 21:14 to the "twelve apostles" makes it especially improbable that he is one of that group. Literary and theological differences make it equally unlikely that he is the author of the Gospel of John or the letters of 1-3 John. Second, Revelation is not a historical apocalypse; it does not recount the past but instead focuses almost entirely on the present and near fu- ture. Third, Revelation is clearly messianic in orientation; the Christ (Greek for *Messiah*) is the one through whom God triumphs and reigns. These differences are due primarily to the fact that Revelation is a Christian apocalypse. For Christians such as John, the human situa- tion *already* had begun to change because of Christ; history *already* was divided into old and new ages, although the new age was yet to be fully realized. Moreover, the Christian community's history extended back only two or three generations. Hence, there is no interest in the distant past and no need to legitimize the revelation by an appeal to some an- cient figure. The present is the time of spiritual unveiling, and present- day revelations are, if anything, the more valid.

It is interesting to ask what if any experience gave rise to a particu- lar apocalypse. Did the authors of 1 Enoch or 2 Baruch see visions, or did they just make them up? Undoubtedly, the distinction is too clear- cut; the exercise of the imagination is only partly calculated and rational. I can give no account of the origin of my own ideas, nor can I explain the means by which the occasional subconscious insight breaks through to conscious expression. To think apocalyptically is to enter an imaginative world, and it might be that those who did so experienced their thoughts as visions. That such visionary experiences are so frequently associated with dreams points strongly in this direction. The question is most intriguing in the case of Revelation, whose apocalyptic disclosures are attributed to a contemporary author. We cannot know how John's experience compared, for example, to that of the author of 4 Ezra. It is certain that the two books were written at about the same time and contain many of the same ideas. What is debatable is the assumption that the experience of their authors must have been categorically different since Revelation is in the Bible and 4 Ezra is not.

Revelation is likely to have been written about the year A.D. 95, during the reign of the Roman emperor Domitian.[17] The characterization of Rome as "Babylon" (Rev. 14:8; 16:19; 17:5; etc.) reflects Jewish usage following the destruction of the temple by the Romans in A.D. 70. (The first temple was destroyed by the Babylonians, hence the connection.) To what extent Christians were persecuted at that time is much disputed; certainly, Revelation was written against a backdrop of likely if not active persecution.[18] Undoubtedly, this was colored by two experiences from the 60s: the persecutions of the Roman Christians by Nero and the Jewish war, which ended in the destruction of Jerusalem. In some of the later chapters of Revelation, Nero looms large as the archetypal evil emperor. It is easy to see why: Nero's persecutions of Christians in Rome were horrific and must have been widely talked of in the late-first-century church. In Revelation 13:3, one of the heads of the wicked beast "seemed to have received a death-blow, but its mortal wound had been healed," and it again waged war on the saints. This is thought by most scholars to be a reference to Nero, who was expected by many to return to life.[19] It has been frequently noted that the num-

17. The most plausible alternative is that the book was written in (at least two) stages, beginning in the 60s and ending in the 90s.

18. The evidence for persecution was presented convincingly by Raymond Brown in his *An Introduction to the New Testament* (New York: Doubleday, 1997), pp. 805-9.

19. Nero committed suicide in A.D. 68. It was widely believed, especially in the eastern part of the empire where John wrote, either that Nero had not really died or that he would be brought back to life. One popular rumor had it that he would lead the

ber of the beast, 666 (13:18), is equivalent to the numeric value of "Nero Caesar" in Hebrew.[20] It might well have seemed that Domitian (emperor from A.D. 81 to 96) was Nero back from the grave. Revelation 13 also refers to the Beast's "haughty and blasphemous words" and to the requirement that "all the inhabitants of the earth will worship it" (13:5, 8). Even Nero did not go that far, but Domitian did, referring to himself as "Lord and God."

The war with Rome and the sack of Jerusalem in 70 caused a great many Jews to leave Israel. John, the author of Revelation, might well have been among them. The Greek of Revelation is the weakest in the New Testament and seems to have been the author's second language. Choices of vocabulary and phrasing suggest that the author was a native Aramaic speaker. Whether or not John himself was witness to Jerusalem's fall, the event had a profound impact upon his eschatological frame of reference and his view of Rome, which occupies the place of Daniel's fourth beast, a striking example of the elasticity of apocalyptic symbols.

The visions of Revelation are complex to say the least. Fortunately, the pattern of expectation is readily understandable to anyone familiar with apocalyptic writing. In brief: John anticipates a time of dreadful tribulation during which a series of calamities will devastate the earth. His descriptions of impending disaster have a long prehistory in prophetic and apocalyptic texts. For example, the destruction of various thirds of the cosmos (a third of humanity, a third of the stars, etc.) in Revelation 8:6–9:19 echoes Ezekiel 5:12:

> One third of you shall die of pestilence or be consumed by famine among you; one third shall fall by the sword around you; and

---

Parthian armies against Rome. That idea might be linked to Rev. 16:12-16, the anticipated invasion of armies from the east.

20. Letters were used for counting prior to the adoption of arabic numerals; therefore, every name had a numeric value. A charming example is a line of ancient graffiti that reads, "I love her whose number is 545." See G. Adolf Deissmann, *Light from the Ancient East,* trans. Lionel R. M. Strachan, rev. ed. (New York: George H. Doran, 1927), p. 277. Contemporary awareness of this ancient system is owed in no small part to a widely circulated joke that links the children's television character Barney with the beast of Revelation. Using Roman letters (which requires substituting "V" for "U"), Barney is identified as the CVTE PVRPLE DINOSAVR. This yields the Roman numerals CVVLDIV, whose total value (100 + 5 + 5 + 50 + 500 + 1 + 5) is 666.

one third I will scatter to every wind and will unsheathe the sword after them.

Revelation goes on to say that power will be concentrated in the hands of an evil king and his subordinates (*à la* Dan. 11:29-39). A great battle will ensue (from Ezek. 38–39, the progenitor of countless Armageddons), in which the world's forces will be destroyed by Christ. This titanic clash occurs twice, both before and after Christ's millennial rule. Then follow the judgment of the unrighteous, the resurrection of the saints, and the final victory of God. The essential plan is traditional; the apocalyptic landscape is clearly recognizable.

The book of Revelation has been outlined in all sorts of ways, "by scroll and by bowl," often in labyrinthian complexity and detail. Because the chapters do not follow a consistent chronological sequence, it is more helpful to review the book by topic than by chapter. We shall work with five simple divisions, as follows:

1. Introduction and Letters to the Seven Churches (1–3)
2. The Heavenly Court (4–5)
3. Images of Judgment: Seven Seals, Seven Trumpets, Seven Bowls (6–10; 11:15-19; 14–16)
4. The Fate of God's Enemies: The Dragon, the Beast, Babylon, and the Great Whore (11:1-14; 12–13; 14:6-20; 17–18; 19:11-21; 20:1-3, 7-15)
5. The Glories to Come (14:1-5; 19:1-10; 20:4-6; 21–22)

1. Introduction and Letters to the Seven Churches (Chapters 1–3)

Revelation announces itself in 1:1 as an "apocalypse." It is the first known writing to give itself that title; indeed, it is from this verse that the "apocalyptic" genre gets its name. Even without this self-designation, the presence in the same verse of a mediating angel and the mention of upcoming events ("what must soon take place") would be enough to alert us to the book's likely contents. The nearness of John's expectation is worth emphasizing. He did not write for some distant generation; the approach of the end is declared again in 1:3; 3:11; 6:11; 22:6, 7, 12, and 20. In contrast to Daniel 12:4, there is no command to put aside the vision for some future date; on the contrary, "Do not seal up the words of the prophecy of this book, for the time is near" (22:10). The ideas and images of Revelation relate first and foremost to John's own world. Like other apocalyptic writers, John believed that humanity stood at the cliff's edge. History-as-usual had nowhere left to go. One more step, and the world would be plunged into eschatological tribulation. Indeed, its foot was already extended.

The first chapter of Revelation is given mainly to a description of Christ, who appears to John in a vision ("I was in the Spirit" [v. 10]). This portrayal is dependent upon the appearance of the Ancient of Days and the Son of Man in Daniel 7:9-10 and 13-14 and upon the vision of the angel in Daniel 10:5-6. In Revelation 1 the three figures are merged into one; so, for example, the Son of Man has hair like white wool. Further, Christ is said to hold seven stars in his right hand, an imperial symbol of power, "and from his mouth came a sharp, two-edged sword" (v. 16), an image of judgment (as in 2:16; 19:15, 21; see Isa. 49:2). Thus we are introduced to Christ as apocalyptic conqueror, on whose account "all the tribes of the earth will wail" (v. 7). This view of the Messiah is widely known in apocalyptic literature (see the samples at the end of the previous chapter), and so it is not altogether surprising that we should encounter it in Revelation. One of the great questions of New Testament theology concerns the compatibility of this figure with Jesus of Nazareth. To many interpreters, Jesus is the very antithesis of the apocalyptic Messiah. Indeed, it appears that Jesus himself struggled against popular expectations that he should fulfill just such a role. It would be easy to conclude, as many have, that the portrayal found in Revelation is entirely secondary, inferior, and disposable. This conclusion overlooks evidence from the Gospels that Jesus regarded himself as God's eschatological agent, albeit in greatly modified form, that he assumed some of the associated prerogatives, especially the right to judge, and that he anticipated a future eschatological consummation. Seen in this light, Revelation — in places, at least — only extends ideas already present in some form in the ministry and teaching of Jesus.[21] Whether it has extended them in all the right directions can and should be debated in the church.[22]

---

21. To some extent, the same could be said of all of the New Testament authors.

22. Many modern-day interpreters of Revelation insist that the book's images of de-

Chapters 2–3 contain short letters to seven churches in western Asia Minor.[23] Actually, the letters are addressed to the angels of the seven churches (3:1, 7; etc.), which is reminiscent of the representative angels in Daniel. (If Israel has an angel, why not the church at Pergamum?) There probably were more than seven churches in the region; as usual, the number seven signifies completeness. The inclusion of such letters is unusual but not altogether unparalleled in other apocalyptic literature.[24] The letters vary quite a bit in content. For example, to two churches, Smyrna and Philadelphia, the message is wholly supportive; to another two, Sardis and Laodicea, it is wholly corrective; and to the other three it is a mixture of praise and reproof. A chief concern is correct theology and practice. John writes of false apostles (2:2), of "Nicolaitans" (2:6 & 15), a despised sect (associated with the "teaching of Balaam" in 2:14), and of the false prophet "Jezebel" (2:20). Almost nothing is known of the beliefs of those whom John censures. He states only that they eat food sacrificed to idols and practice fornication (2:14, 20); in other words, they have accommodated themselves unacceptably to pagan culture. A similar note is sounded in 3:4: "Yet you have still a few persons in Sardis who have not soiled their clothes." The author's admonitions to purity are paralleled by his repeated calls to diligence. Apparently, the greatest threat was not physical attack but spiritual complacency. The church of Ephesus is chided for abandoning its first love, the church of Sardis is told to awaken "and strengthen what remains and is on the point of death," and the church of Laodicea is condemned for lukewarmness.[25] Endurance of persecution is the other persistent theme. Several of the churches are commended for their patient bearing of past afflictions (2:2-3, 9, 13, 19; 3:8, 10; cf. 1:9),

---

struction are not to be taken literally. Revelation provides moral catharsis, not a program for the elimination of outsiders. See Pablo Richard, *Apocalypse: A People's Commentary on the Book of Revelation* (Maryknoll, N.Y.: Orbis, 1995), pp. 31-32.

23. For readers living this side of the Holocaust, the twin references to the "synagogue of Satan" (2:9 and 3:9) are an especially troubling part of these chapters (cf. John 8:44). Some scholars have interpreted the phrase "those who say that they are Jews and are not" (in both 2:9 and 3:9) to mean that John is referring not to Jews but to Christians who claim to be "true Jews." One can only hope that they are right.

24. The letter that concludes 2 Baruch is the most widely cited example.

25. These are among the few passages in Revelation that are widely quoted in modern pulpits. John's assessment of the well-to-do Laodicean Christians (3:14-22) is especially transferable to the American Church.

and one is warned specifically of impending persecution (2:10; cf. 3:10). All seven letters end with promises to those who conquer, that is, to those who endure faithfully to the end. This is a subject well rehearsed in the apocalyptic tradition.

As one reads Revelation, it is important to bear in mind that John's audience consisted of these seven churches. Many of the points emphasized in the letters will reappear in different guise in the following chapters. For example, the heavenly visions stress the holiness of God (e.g., 4:8), the purity of believers (e.g., 7:13-14), the vindication of the martyrs (e.g., 6:9-11), and the rewards of endurance (e.g., 7:15-17). Much of the imagery of Revelation is otherworldly, but its intended effects are entirely practical.

Finally, it is worth noting that Revelation begins with judgment of the church. This is a necessary counterbalance to the next several chapters, which focus primarily on the judgment of the world. One can hardly accuse John of idealizing the congregations to which he wrote. Repeatedly, they are threatened with judgment and even removal if they fail to reform (2:5, 16, 22-23; 3:3). John's audience might take comfort in the eventual judgment of its enemies, but the moral urgency of the text is directed squarely at them. The beast is not called to repent, but they are.

2. The Heavenly Court (Chapters 4-5)

A key moment in any "heavenly journey" apocalypse comes when the writer is transported into the heavenly realm — most dramatically, into the very throne room of God. So in Revelation 4:1-2:

> After this I looked, and there in heaven a door stood open! And the first voice, which I had heard speaking to me like a trumpet, said, "Come up here, and I will show you what must take place after this." At once I was in the spirit, and there in heaven stood a throne!

John's description is based largely on Ezekiel 1:4-13, 26-28; 10:18-22; and Isaiah 6:3, and so is fairly conventional. Not that such an account could ever be mundane. ("Went to the grocery store, saw Aunt Mary, visited the throne room of God. . . .") The principal theme of chapters 4 and 5 is the worthiness of God and Jesus. Among other things, this vision accentuates the unworthiness of the five churches that John corrects. An even greater contrast exists with those, such as the beast, who assume the prerogatives of divinity. It is God who is worthy "to receive glory and honor and power"; likewise, it is the Lamb (Jesus) alone who is worthy to open the scroll with the seven seals and worthy "to receive power and wealth and wisdom and might and honor and glory and blessing!" The language used of God and of Jesus is nearly identical, and both receive the worship of the company of heaven (5:13-14). What John witnesses in heaven is the true glory and worship, by which standard the cult of Caesar is a shabby counterfeit.

Jesus is called the Lamb twenty-eight times in Revelation. He is not just any lamb, but a "lamb standing as if it had been slaughtered" (v. 6). The death of Christ on the cross was thought to be analogous to the Passover slaughter of a lamb, whose blood protected the Israelites from the angel of death (Exod. 12:21-28; cf. 1 Cor. 5:7). Moreover, Jesus the Lamb is also Jesus the Lion (v. 5), that is, the Davidic Messiah. The tension between these symbols is unresolved; Jesus is at one and the same time the Suffering Servant (the lamb of Isa. 53:7) and the conquering Messiah (the lion of Gen. 49:9-10). The overwhelming predominance of the Lamb image is significant: it is the Lamb, the model of patient endurance, that John and his audience were encouraged to emulate. Like Daniel, Revelation is a call to persistence, not to arms. "Lionhood" remains a divine prerogative.

3. Images of Judgment: Seven Seals, Seven Trumpets, Seven Bowls (6–10; 11:15-19; 14–16)

A consistent feature of apocalypses is the expectation that a period of unparalleled tribulation has begun or is about to begin (Mark 13:19). Among other sources, this tradition draws upon the story of the flood (Gen. 6-9, forever linked in apocalyptic lore to the myth of the Watchers), in which only a tiny remnant of human and animal life was spared from the wrath of God, and the account of the ten plagues (Exod. 7-12; cf. Rev. 16), which preceded and abetted the deliverance of the Hebrews from Egypt. In other words, there existed in Judaism formative paradigms concerning the judgment of the many and the rescue of the few. It is something of a biblical truism that past predicts future, that God will act as God has acted, and so it is understandable that the desire for justice and release should find expression in similar hopes of future judgment. The deluge of calamity anticipated by Revelation is anything but a new idea.

Perfect trouble comes in sevens. John writes of seven seals, trumpets, and bowls, each of which represents a series of woes sent in judgment upon the earth. Like Pharaoh in the time of Moses, humanity responds to these signs by hardening its heart and refusing to repent. The three sets of seven calamities are as follows:

Seals (6:1-17; 8:1-5)	**Trumpets** (8:6–9:21; 11:15-19)	**Bowls** (16:1-21)
1. Rider on white horse = war	Destruction of a third of the land	Sores
2. Rider on red horse = death	Destruction of a third of the sea	Sea turned to blood
3. Rider on black horse = famine	Destruction of a third of the fresh waters	Fresh waters turn to blood
4. Rider on pale (green) horse = pestilence	Destruction of a third of the heavens	Sun scorches the earth
5. Martyrdom	The Locusts from Hell (literally; see 9:2-3)	Darkness
6. Cosmic signs	Destruction of a third of humanity	Armageddon
7. Heavenly signs	Heavenly worship and signs	Great earthquake and hailstones

There is a fair bit of overlap among these catastrophes, especially between those listed in the second and third columns, most of which recall the plagues sent upon Egypt. Other parallels could be enumerated; for example, the four colored horses of 6:2-8 are found in Zechariah 1:8-11; 6:1-7. In sum, John does not lay out a specific chronology of desolation. Instead, various traditional themes (war, cosmic upheaval, death, etc.) are mentioned and several are revisited. Threefold repetition, in this case, three sevens, is a regular feature in Revelation, beginning with the "Holy, holy, holy" of 4:8 (cf. 8:13: "woe, woe, woe" [9:12]).

The silver lining surrounding this desperately dark cloud is the assertion that things really are under control. It is the Lamb who opens the seals. God's angels blow the trumpets and pour out the contents of the bowls. Heaven remains resolute and unthreatened, and earthly events unfold just as they are meant to. Moreover, history's certain conclusion will not be long in coming. Hence, the travails of the believing community are both purposeful and measured. There will be more martyrs, but only a restricted number (6:11).

4. The Fate of God's Enemies: The Dragon, the Beast, Babylon, and the Great Whore (11:1-14; 12–13; 14:6-20; 17–18; 19:11-21; 20:1-3, 7-15)

One of the truly revealing parts of an apocalypse is its description of God's enemies, who happen also to be the author's real or anticipated enemies. In this case, the foe is certainly Rome, whose imperium extended over a quarter of the earth's population. The many parallels between the Greek and Roman empires meant that it was a fairly easy matter to apply the apocalyptic visions of Daniel to the world of the late first century. The fourth beast from the sea in Daniel 7:7 is the model for the "the beast that comes up from the bottomless pit" in Revelation 11:7. The parallel is even clearer in Revelation 13:1-2, which describes a "beast rising out of the sea" that is a composite of the four separate beasts in Daniel 7, right down to the ten horns of Daniel 7:7. The arrogance of Daniel's final beastly incarnation (Antiochus Epiphanes) is paralleled in the beast of Revelation 13, who demands worship and utters blasphemies. Likewise, both Daniel and Revelation predict a period of terrible desolation lasting three and a half years (Dan. 7:25; 9:27; 12:7; Rev. 11:2; 13:5), after which the beast will be destroyed. It is obvious that John was thoroughly schooled in the book of Daniel, whose symbolism is transmuted in the pages of Revelation. It is not so much that John copied Daniel as that John dreamed Daniel's dream. The reality disclosed in Daniel 7-12 would apply almost seamlessly to John's own world, where king and empire again made war on the saints.

The visions of these chapters draw on numerous other sources. For example, the two witnesses, olive trees, and lampstands of 11:3-4 come from Zechariah 4 and referred originally to the priest Joshua and the governor Zerubbabel. The story of the woman, her child, and the Dragon in Revelation 12 evidences a particularly rich mixture of influences. The account is in part an adaptation of a myth concerning the birth of Apollo. According to Eugene Boring,

> Not far from John's island prison is the island of Delos, sacred to the Greeks because, in a story known to all John's hearer-readers from childhood, there the divine Apollo had been born. His mother Leto had fled there to escape the dragon Python, who wanted to kill the newborn son of Zeus. Instead of being killed, Apollo returns to Delphi and kills the dragon.[26]

The myth was used by Augustus and Nero, each of whom cast himself as a modern-day Apollo whose rule would inaugurate a new era of prosperity. "A grateful citizen of the Roman world could readily think of the story as a reflection of his or her own experience . . . the woman is the goddess Roma, the queen of heaven; the son is the emperor, who kills the dragon [the forces of chaos] and founds the new Golden Age."[27] Once again, the politically subversive role of apocalyptic literature is evident. In Revelation, the characterizations are reversed: Rome is allied with the dragon; the woman stands for the people of God (Israel, first and foremost; note the crown of twelve stars in 12:1), whose son is not Caesar but Christ (cf. John 19:15).

Of equal importance is the account of the Fall in Genesis 3, which is followed by the pronouncement of eternal enmity between the serpent and the woman and her offspring. In Revelation 12:9, the archenemy — named the dragon, the Devil and Satan — is explicitly identified as the "ancient serpent" of Genesis 3:1-7, "the deceiver of the whole

---

26. M. Eugene Boring, *Revelation* (Louisville: John Knox, 1989), p. 151.
27. Boring, *Revelation*, p. 151.

world." The story of Satan's downfall existed in Judaism outside the New Testament (e.g., in 2 Enoch 29; cf. Luke 10:18) and is based in part on the description of the ruin of the king of Babylon in Isaiah 14:12-23. For this reason, many scholars regard the core of Revelation 12 as transplanted Jewish myth.[28]

Chapter 12 is especially interesting because it contains the only back story in Revelation, which is otherwise unconcerned with history. The point is both to refute the mythic claims of empire and to put in spiritual context the present conflict with Rome. The dragon, having failed to destroy the woman and her child (God's people and the Christ, the latter of whom was "snatched away" to God, v. 5), made war in heaven against Michael and the angels. Once again, his evil designs were thwarted, and the dragon and his angelic followers were cast down to earth. (The timing is most curious; ordinarily, the devil's fall to earth is regarded as a primordial event. Clearly, we are dealing with mixed myth.) The dragon's fury is insatiable; he now pursues the woman's other children, the faithful believers "who keep the commandments of God and hold the testimony of Jesus" (v. 17).

Here as elsewhere in Revelation, a few lines of liturgy are inserted into the story that help to interpret its meaning. Such "hymns" are the clearest and, thanks in no small part to Handel's *Messiah,* among the most familiar passages in Revelation. In this case, believers are said to conquer (a favorite word) the dragon "by the blood of the lamb and the word of their testimony, for they did not cling to life even in the face of death" (v. 11).

> Rejoice then, you heavens and those who dwell in them! But woe to the earth and the sea, for the devil has come down to you with great wrath, because he knows that his time is short! (v. 12)

Martyrdom itself is victory, since the dragon kills only those whose faith he cannot defeat. Yes, the earth is in thrall to Satan; nevertheless, one can rejoice, for "redemption draweth nigh" (Luke 21:28; *KJV*). To those with eyes to see, the darkening night portends the hastening dawn. Once again, an esoteric passage yields a practicable lesson, "a call for the endurance and faith of the saints" (13:10).

---

28. Collins, *The Apocalyptic Imagination,* p. 275.

The dragon's final ploy is to create a world ruler, the infamous beast, whose brief it is to make war on the faithful and commit blasphemy against God. A second beast, representing the imperial cult,[29] is also mentioned (13:11-17). Elsewhere in Revelation, "Beast II" is described as a false prophet who forces the world to worship the beast (16:13; 19:20; 20:10). He appears as a lamb, that is, he personifies pseudo-religion, mimicking the true Lamb, but speaks only evil, "like a dragon" (13:11).

All those not sealed on the forehead by God (7:3) are sealed by the beast (13:16), that is, they are marked out as his own possession, like cattle branded by ranchers. The control of this unholy trinity, the dragon and the two beasts, is absolute. "No one can buy or sell who does not have the mark" (v. 17). These verses are the Old Faithful of fantastic interpretation; new explanations spout almost hourly. For example, some now claim that John foresaw a day when the government would implant surveillance computer chips in all humans. Theories about the beast's mark are like gulls foraging in the wake of technological advancement. Twenty-five years ago, bar coding was all the apocalyptic rage. What is on the drawing board at Sony and Intel today will no doubt find its way into the pages of tomorrow's End Times bestseller.

It is far more probable that the mark symbolizes the all-embracing economic power of Rome, whose very coinage bore the emperor's image and conveyed his claims to divinity (e.g., by including the sun's rays in the ruler's portrait). It had become increasingly difficult for Christians to function in a world in which public life, including the economic life of the trade guilds, required participation in idolatry. Finally, it is worth noting that most modern authors who insist on a literal interpretation of the beast's seal in 13:16 accept a spiritual interpretation of God's seal in 7:3 and 22:4. So far as I am aware, no one has yet suggested that God will enter the microchip business.

The city of Rome is symbolized both as Babylon and as the Great Whore[30] who sits on seven mountains (17:9, the "seven hills" of Rome).

---

29. Other plausible identities (such as local Roman officials) have been suggested. The important point is that the second beast is the dragon's agent in compelling human subservience to the beast.

30. On the problematic and stereotypical feminine imagery of Revelation, see Susan Garrett, "Revelation," in *The Women's Bible Commentary,* ed. Carol A. Newsom and Sharon H. Ringe (Louisville: Westminster/John Knox, 1992), pp. 377-82.

As we have already seen, Babylon became a code name for Rome following the destruction of Jerusalem in A.D. 70. Prostitution and sexual infidelity were long-established metaphors for spiritual unfaithfulness (cf. Rev. 14:8); hence, the Great Whore, Rome, is the source of universal "fornication," the spiritual debauchery of idolatry (17:2). Those who have resisted are characterized in 14:4 as "virgins." In addition to idolatry, both figures are accused of economic exploitation and violence:

> As she [Babylon] glorified herself and lived luxuriously, so give her a like measure of torment and grief. . . . And in you was found the blood of prophets and of saints, and of all who have been slaughtered on earth. (18:7, 24)

> The woman [the Great Whore] was clothed in purple and scarlet, and adorned with gold and jewels and pearls. . . . And I saw that the woman was drunk with the blood of the saints and the blood of the witnesses of Jesus. (17:4, 6)

The anticipated fall of Babylon/Rome is celebrated at great length in chapter 18 (cf. 14:8), which borrows heavily from the prophets' earlier condemnations of the Babylonian empire (e.g., Isa. 21:9, quoted in v. 2). Similar sentiments are expressed concerning the judgment of the Great Whore in 19:1-3. It is easy for us to take the fall of ancient Rome for granted, but to anyone who saw it in its heyday, it must indeed have appeared an Eternal City. Its magnificence was tremendous and its arrogance terrible. To anticipate its passing required a great leap of imagination; to regard the reign of God as more certain required a great act of faith.

The main passage concerning the demise of the beasts and the dragon is found in 19:11–20:10. Christ appears on a white horse, joined by the armies of heaven. Characteristically, the war that follows is modeled on the description of the decisive battle in Ezekiel 38–39 (as is Rev. 20:7-9).[31] The beast and false prophet are captured and then "thrown alive into the lake of fire that burns with sulphur" (19:20). The concluding drama is unique to Revelation and has generated unremitting con-

---

31. In particular, the gorging of the birds on the flesh of the defeated is reminiscent of Ezek. 39:4, 17-20.

troversy. There is a second battle, two punishments of Satan, two resurrections, and two reigns of Christ. The events, in the order presented in Revelation 20–21, are as follows:

- *An angel casts the dragon into the bottomless pit,* where he is held secure for a thousand years.
- *Christ reigns on earth for a millennium.* Those "who had been beheaded for their testimony to Jesus" "came to life and reigned with Christ. . . . (The rest of the dead did not come to life until the thousand years were ended.) This is the first resurrection" (20:4, 5).
- *Satan is released.* The battle of Gog and Magog (yet again, Ezek. 38–39) occurs. As in Ezekiel 39:6, fire comes from heaven to destroy God's enemies (20:9).
- *Satan is "thrown into the lake of fire* and sulfur, where the beast and the false prophet were, and they will be tormented day and night forever and ever" (20:10).
- *Death and Hades give up their dead,* who are judged before the throne of God. All those not found in the book of life were given over to "the second death" (20:14).
- *A new heaven and a new earth* are created in which God and the Lamb reign.

All of us have been told to "get it right the first time," so it is rather surprising to learn that evil requires a second thrashing (20:7-10). Did the first treatment fail? Did the devil deserve a second chance? "If guesses were horses. . . ." The likeliest explanation is simply that John accommodated two popular but competing scenarios, the first of an earthly and limited messianic reign and the second of a cosmic and eternal kingdom. The great battle with evil is the traditional prelude to either event, so it appears twice. Satan is doubly defeated, and the reign of Christ fulfills all apocalyptic expectation.

5. The Glories to Come (14:1-5; 19:1-10; 20:4-6; 21–22)

In a sense, it is John's destiny to work himself out of a job. The conclusion of Revelation describes a reality in which apocalyptic disclosure is unnecessary. God is no longer distant, in heaven and in secret, but is instead on earth, present and known. There is no more need of reproof, consolation, or encouragement. The "bride of Christ," the people of God, is holy, as is the city in which she dwells. No mediation is required; hence, no temple is included (21:22). There is no injustice and no disparity of possessions. In the place of arrogance is praise, in the place of mourning is joy. In short, it is perfection.

Revelation contains several visualizations of God's final triumph that were derived in large part from earlier Jewish writings. For example, the vision of the Lamb standing on Mount Zion in 14:1-5 has a prehistory in Jewish thought. Originally, the idea of a ruler standing atop Zion was associated with the monarchy, as in Psalm 2:6: "I have set my king on Zion, my holy hill." It was not a big step to imagine God, as the true monarch of Israel, occupying that place. So Isaiah 24:23:

> Then the moon will be abashed, and the sun ashamed: for the Lord of hosts will reign on Mount Zion and in Jerusalem, and before his elders he will manifest his glory.

Finally, the idea came to be associated with the Messiah, the human agent through whom God would rule. According to 4 Ezra 13:35-40, "[M]y Son will be revealed . . . he shall stand on the top of Mount Zion." The same tradition is evident, for example, in the NT books of Hebrews (12:22-24) and Romans (11:26, citing Isa. 59:20-21).

One could assemble a similar list of antecedents and parallels to the eschatological banquet (Rev. 19:7), the throne of God (20:11), the recreated heaven and earth (21:1), the new Jerusalem (21:10), the reign of God (21:22-23), the river and tree of life (22:1), the abolition of night (22:5), the pure garments of the righteous (22:14), and so on. These and other familiar images were woven by John into a magisterial and distinctly Christian tapestry of God's glory. In the end, Revelation offers us the world reborn and Paradise revisited.

Conclusion

Revelation is not a compendium of Christian or even New Testament teaching on eschatology. It contains no description of heaven, no mention of a "rapture" of the saints or of an "antichrist," and no catalog of signs signaling the approaching End.[32] More disappointing for some is the realization that (*contra* Hal Lindsey and his ilk) Revelation provides no information concerning the fate of the United States, the European Common Market, or the World Council of Churches. The eminent NT scholar Raymond Brown put the matter succinctly: "*The author of Rev did not know how or when the world will end, and neither does anyone else.*"[33] If that is so, what good is Revelation — and Daniel with it? Let me offer a few suggestions.

The biblical apocalypses take us into a world in which one's decision for God is immediately pressing and ultimately costly, a world in which everything is at stake and nothing is secure. Daniel and Revelation confront our spiritual laziness and complacency; they challenge our measured alliance with God and our easy association with worldly power. They compel us to reconsider the depth of our commitment and the sincerity of our purpose.

The desire for meaning is basic to humans and drives much of our behavior. We want to know that we matter, that we are somebody, that we are a success. How to construct such meaning is one of the essential issues of life. Daniel and Revelation force us to ask about the permanence and legitimacy of our systems of meaning. Which ultimately matters, the glory bestowed by Rome or the glory bestowed by God? Few of us are forced to choose explicitly between worldly and divine approval, so few of us ever consider the matter seriously. Hence, we are easily deceived, believing ourselves to be living for God while directing our efforts toward worldly advancement and recognition. Daniel and Revelation challenge us to question our deepest motivations and attachments.

The biblical apocalypses reveal the dangers and seductions of power and deconstruct the mythologies that legitimate human exploitation. Those who live under acute political oppression are among the keenest adapters and interpreters of the apocalyptic tradition. They understand firsthand the appearance of human government as demonic beast.

Finally, Daniel and Revelation offer a utopian vision that directs believers toward the future, toward hope, and toward God. A measure

---

32. James M. Efird, *Daniel and Revelation* (Valley Forge, Pa.: Judson, 1978), p. 139.

33. Brown, *An Introduction to the New Testament*, p. 810.

of dissatisfaction with the way things are is necessary to human betterment; a transcendent goal is required for human advancement. Apocalyptic literature tells us that we should, we can, and we will be better than we are.

My seminary preaching professor taught us that it was the job of pastors to "comfort the afflicted and afflict the comfortable." The authors of Daniel and Revelation would doubtless have been at the head of the class.

CHAPTER SIX

Jesus and the Things to Come

I t is a defining question in the study of the New Testament: Did Jesus
see himself as an instrumental figure in the great drama of God's
coming triumph, or was he instead a purveyor of wisdom who cared little about such matters, much less imagined himself as having a central
role in their fulfillment?[1] The former view is favored by a great many
scholars,[2] and that for good reason: the evidence is squarely on their
side. To be sure, it is possible to whittle a non-eschatological Jesus out
of the New Testament block, but only by leaving a great pile of shavings
containing much of the best data.[3] Nevertheless, the latter approach

---

1. The first option is not meant to exclude the possibility (indeed, the probability)
that Jesus was also a wisdom teacher. The question is, was Jesus a sage to the *exclusion* of
being an eschatological prophet? On the subject of Jesus' eschatology, see E. P. Sanders,
Jesus and Judaism (London: SCM, 1985), and *The Historical Figure of Jesus* (London: Allen
Lane, 1993); John P. Meier, *A Marginal Jew: Rethinking the Historical Jesus*, vol. 2: *Mentor, Mes-
sage, and Miracles* (New York: Doubleday, 1994); N. T. Wright, *The New Testament and the
People of God* (Minneapolis: Fortress, 1992); Dale C. Allison, *Jesus of Nazareth: Millenarian
Prophet* (Minneapolis: Fortress, 1998); Bart Ehrman, *Jesus: Apocalyptic Prophet of the New
Millennium* (Oxford: Oxford, 1999); and Marinus de Jonge, *God's Final Envoy: Early Chris-
tology and Jesus' Own View of His Mission* (Grand Rapids: Eerdmans, 1998).

2. By my observation, such persons are in the clear majority. Certainly, they represent the dominant group in leading universities with doctoral programs in the field.

3. The well-publicized "Jesus Seminar," whose work incorporates an anti-eschato-
logical presupposition, makes the claim that 82 percent of the words of Jesus reported in
the Gospels are inauthentic. As many scholars have noted, the group's methodology is
deeply circular and hence deeply flawed. If one begins by assuming the inauthenticity of

has always had its share of adherents and is especially well represented in popular literature. Its appeal is comprehensible, especially among those who feel drawn to Jesus but repulsed by the church. Anyone who has felt intellectually starved or emotionally abused by a narrow or corrupt church can understand the impulse to save Jesus from religion. Many pro-Jesus but anti-Christianity books are in fact composed by self-professed disillusioned ex-fundamentalists. The figure who emerges from their makeover characteristically possesses no eschatological opinions and few if any theological convictions. Frankly, he is as unremarkable as he is acceptable, a person so like us that we have only to wonder what all of the fuss was about.

Those who would drive a wedge between Jesus and Christianity have more than a little trouble accounting for the New Testament, which obviously favors a Christian view of Jesus. The usual strategy, going back at least to the schismatic Marcion in the second century, is to postulate a theory of misunderstanding and/or misrepresentation. The resulting picture is usually drawn, with innumerable variations in detail, along the following lines: Both during and after his life, Jesus was understood by only a few people. This small but happy band enjoyed an Edenic existence until the Fall, the arrival of persons who fundamentally misconstrued Jesus. These usurpers wrested control of Jesus' "movement" and set in his place a Jesus of their own devising. It is these

---

"the eschatological Jesus" (see *The Five Gospels* [New York: HarperCollins, 1997], pp. 3-4, which even speaks of the "tyranny" of the eschatological Jesus), one would of course have no choice but to discredit the various eschatological sayings of Jesus. It could not be otherwise. By way of comparison, imagine that fifty conservative Christian scholars, the majority of whom believe in biblical inerrancy, should assemble and vote on the sayings of Jesus. Doubtless, they would conclude that the historical Jesus actually said the words that he is reported to have spoken in the Gospels. Few outsiders would regard this as an impressive act of scholarship, rightly perceiving that the group's findings were simply a restatement of its presuppositions. See Richard B. Hays, "The Corrected Jesus," in *First Things* 43 (May 1994): 43-48 (presently available at www.firstthings.com); Luke Timothy Johnson, "The Humanity of Jesus: What's at Stake in the Quest for the Historical Jesus?" in *The Jesus Controversy: Perspectives in Conflict* (Harrisburg, Pa.: Trinity Press International, 1999), pp. 48-74, and *The Real Jesus: The Misguided Quest for the Historical Jesus and the Truth of the Traditional Gospels* (New York: HarperCollins, 1996), pp. 20-27; Charlotte Allen, *The Human Christ: The Search for the Historical Jesus* (New York: Free Press, 1998), pp. 275-80; Ben Witherington, *The Jesus Quest: The Third Search for the Jew of Nazareth* (Downers Grove, Ill.: InterVarsity Press, 1995), pp. 42-136; and Raymond Brown, *An Introduction to the New Testament* (New York: Doubleday, 1997), pp. 819-23.

evil, dimwitted, and/or misguided people who are responsible for the invention of Christianity and the creation of the New Testament.[4] Fortunately, the NT contains a few strands of *bona fide* Jesus tradition whose preservation is owed to the little company of Jesus' genuine — and conveniently anonymous — followers. In its extreme form, the assertion of Christian misrepresentation of Jesus snowballs into a fully realized conspiracy theory. Every year a spate of new books allege that the early church propagated a hoax and engaged in a massive coverup of its true origins. So, the plot is uncovered, the culprits unmasked, and Jesus liberated. No doubt about it, this is a sensational, made-for-television story. But is it true?

Most conspiracy theories contain at least a grain of truth, and this one is no exception. It is a fact that the Gospels do not give us the precise words of Jesus. They were written in Greek, and Jesus probably taught in Aramaic. Furthermore, as we saw in Chapter Two, the Gospels do not always agree as to the content and context of Jesus' sayings. This reflects the fact that Jesus' teachings were reshaped to some extent between his death in about A.D. 30 and the writing of the Gospels, beginning with Mark in about A.D. 70. That having been said, it is by no means the case that Mark or Matthew invented Christianity. The Gospels are the product of Christian faith, not the reverse. Nor was Paul, who wrote decades earlier, its creator. According to the eminent NT scholar Wayne Meeks of Yale University,

> Perhaps the most significant discovery about Paul in this century's scholarship has been the recognition of his Christian precedents. Paul cannot be called the "second founder of Christian-

---

4. Compare the following quotation from *The Five Gospels,* which seeks to justify its portrayal of Jesus as a non-eschatological figure: "Jesus' followers did not grasp the subtleties of his position and reverted, once Jesus was not there to remind them, to the view they had learned from John the Baptist" (*The Five Gospels* [New York: HarperCollins, 1997], p. 4). In other words, since we (who, unlike those who actually knew Jesus, "grasp the subtleties of his position") understand that Jesus was not an eschatological figure, we can infer that the eschatological orientation of the Gospels is the result of John the Baptist's pernicious influence and the early Christians' unfortunate incomprehension. Theories of this sort, and they are legion, have the effect of exonerating Jesus of some perceived offense(s) in early Christianity. Whatever the stumbling block, it is the fault of someone other than Jesus.

ity," as Wrede named him less than seventy years ago. Christianity in the "Pauline" form — with sacraments, cultic worship of Jesus as Lord, Gentile members, and the doctrines of pre-existence and atoning death of the Christ — had already been "founded" before Paul became first its persecutor and then its missionary.[5]

Similarly, with specific reference to the issue of eschatology, Helmut Koester of Harvard University writes:

> [W]ere the eschatological schemata of his [Jesus'] early followers subsequently assigned to a Jesus whose original ministry and message did not contain any eschatological elements? That seems very unlikely. Within a year or two of Jesus' death, Paul persecuted the followers of Jesus because of their eschatological proclamation. That leaves precious little time in which the followers of a noneschatological Jesus could have developed an entirely new eschatological perspective without a precedent in the preaching and actions of Jesus.[6]

Christianity did not gestate over decades, during which time Jesus' teachings were almost entirely forgotten. To the contrary, Christianity came to birth almost immediately and spread rapidly throughout the Roman empire. Within about three years of Jesus' death, there were Christian believers in Damascus, Syria, well over a hundred miles from Jerusalem.[7] By the year 49, Christians were a significant presence in Rome, a fact alluded to by the historian Suetonius (*Claudius*, 25.4). When Paul wrote to these same Roman Christians a few years later, he was able to quote Christian sayings that he assumed they would know and accept (e.g., Rom. 1:3-4). In short, the great historical gap between Jesus and Christianity is a myth. Much of what Christians claimed about Jesus they proclaimed from earliest days. This is precisely the way

---

5. Wayne A. Meeks, *The Writings of St. Paul* (New York: Norton, 1972), p. 440. And by most accounts, Paul became a persecutor of the church within about three years of the death of Jesus.

6. Helmut Koester, "Jesus the Victim," *Journal of Biblical Literature* III (1992): 14.

7. That is, based upon a typical chronology of Paul's life. See Robert Jewett, *A Chronology of Paul's Life* (Philadelphia: Fortress, 1979).

that Christian origins are depicted in the Acts of the Apostles, a book that is either ignored or dismissed by a host of Jesus theorists.[8]

If time cannot be blamed for the invention of Christianity, then perhaps the resurrection can. Without a doubt, the disciples' perception of Jesus changed significantly because of Easter. Whether it changed so radically that the historical Jesus was all but forgotten is highly questionable, especially in light of the speed and spread of the supposed amnesia. Attributing to the disciples' Easter experiences such overwhelming power, more than the New Testament itself attests, puts skeptics in a bind: they credit the resurrection with having an utterly extraordinary effect upon its witnesses, and yet they regard it as nothing more than a delusion. In other words, they are forced to attribute a much greater effect to a much lesser cause. But the disciples did not simply experience a phenomenon; they experienced the resurrection of a known person, Jesus. Their perception of Jesus, especially of his suffering and death, changed in important ways, but it was still the Jesus of living memory about whom they thought and in whom they believed. To posit an essential discontinuity between the teaching of Jesus and the religion of his nearest followers is both unwarranted and unpersuasive.

Obviously, it is not possible to look at the subject of Jesus and the future without first dealing seriously with the question of history. On the basis of our review of that subject, we shall examine Jesus' view of the future, focusing on those points about which we can be most confident historically.

The Historical Jesus

Prior to photography, engraving was the principal means of creating and reproducing pictures. Images cut in wood, copper, or steel were inked and transferred to hundreds or even thousands of sheets of paper. Prints, often published with accompanying text, were the popular media of the sixteenth to nineteenth centuries, much as television is today. As with television programming, the quality of printmaking varied enormously. The great majority of prints were churned out quickly and sold cheaply to a mass audience. A smaller but still significant

8. See Johnson, *The Real Jesus,* pp. 93-95.

number were fashioned by accomplished artists who invested weeks or even months in the production of a single image.

Several of the best artists, such as Dürer and Rembrandt, attracted students who learned to engrave in their style. Some of these apprentices were so good that their work is all but indistinguishable from that of their teachers. In some cases, it is impossible to discriminate between, for example, a Rembrandt original and a print originating in the Rembrandt "school." The situation is further complicated by the fact that artists would occasionally compose part of a work themselves and then assign its completion to their students. The better the student, the harder it is to tell where the hand of the master ends and that of the apprentice begins.

If I owned such a print, I would be eager to know to what extent it was an "original." I could take the engraving to a series of experts, but they might well disagree among themselves. What should I do? I could apply Wite-Out® to all of the questionable bits, but the result would hardly be a truer or more appealing picture, and there is a good chance that I would obscure parts of the original in the process. A more sensible course would be to find satisfaction in knowing that, both directly and indirectly, the work reflects the genius of the master.

Now imagine that we possessed no original pictures by a certain master engraver, that his art could be "recovered" only through an analysis of the work of his students. Imagine, too, that the engravings of his students varied somewhat in style and subject matter. Any assessment of the master's work based upon such evidence could be convincing on only a fairly general level. Detailed analyses that attempted to separate the master's work from that of his students would at best be speculative exercises. In all likelihood, such studies would produce widely differing, even contradictory results reflecting the biases of the individual interpreters. One critic might claim that only prints containing horses are genuine; another might believe that only lines of a certain width could have been engraved by the master. The further such studies distanced the teacher from his students — and thus from the only source of possible evidence — the more speculative they would become. A master who exercised negligible influence over his "followers" would simply be unknowable. A modern-day account of such a figure would be almost entirely a product of its author's own imagination.

Such is our situation when we undertake a study of the historical

Jesus. Each of the four Gospels presents us with a portrait of Jesus composed by a later follower but containing traditions that go back to Jesus himself.[9] How much of the resulting picture is owed to Jesus and how much to the Gospel writer and to the church, which passed down and shaped the tradition before him, is impossible to sort out cleanly. There is no consistently reliable way of separating the "original" Jesus from subsequent Christian interpretations. This is especially true with respect to the content of Jesus' teaching. Most scholars would agree that Jesus' words underwent some modification and even expansion in the years prior to the writing of the Gospels, but there is no agreement whatsoever as to the extent and nature of these changes. For that reason, an endless parade of incompatible Jesuses emerge from the workshops of scholars. In the unlikely event that someone did manage successfully to separate Jesus' words from later Christian alterations and amendments, we would have no way of knowing it.

The essential question, therefore, is whether the early Christians were, in effect, good students ("disciples") of Jesus, and thus whether the New Testament authors basically got Jesus right. I see no compelling reason for thinking that they did not. Were I to conclude otherwise, I could say little about Jesus. He would be as unknowable to me as the engraver who left behind no original work and no faithful apprentices. Some scholars start from the position that Jesus' followers almost completely misunderstood and misrepresented him. Contrary to what we might expect, this conclusion does not deter them from writing books about Jesus. Instead, it gives them license to pick and choose

9. It is unlikely that the Gospel writers were themselves eyewitnesses to the ministry of Jesus. The traditional assignment of these texts to Matthew, Mark, Luke, and John dates from the second century and is doubtful. For one thing, it appears almost certain that the primary source of the Gospel of Matthew is the Gospel of Mark, a strange state of affairs if the author himself had been a disciple of Jesus. For the sake of convenience, I refer to these authors by their traditional names, but I do not mean thereby to imply, for example, that the author of the Gospel of Matthew was Matthew, the disciple of Jesus.

The value of the Gospel of John as a historical source is an especially controversial and complex issue. I have not quoted John extensively in this chapter, in part to avoid making a complicated argument where a simpler argument will do. For a thoughtful and balanced reflection on the use of John in historical Jesus studies, see Marianne Meye Thompson, "The Historical Jesus and the Johannine Christ," in *Exploring the Gospel of John: In Honor of D. Moody Smith,* ed. R. Alan Culpepper and C. Clifton Black (Louisville: Westminster, 1996), pp. 21-42.

what suits them, since it is presupposed that the real Jesus lies buried in some deep and heretofore unidentified stratum of Gospel clay. Inevitably, such studies are highly reductionistic, that is, they reduce the whole of Jesus' teaching to a few select elements. The result: "Here are five likable things about Jesus, and, by amazing coincidence, they are the only five things that are historical!" Reductionism takes a few, often partial truths ("Jesus was kind to small children and animals," and so on) and declares them to be the whole truth. Such a process is inevitably circular; it tests the evidence based upon a preconception of what Jesus could and could not have said. For example, if one believes that Jesus could not have thought of himself as a Messiah, then all evidence to the contrary will be disparaged as the product of later Christian misrepresentation. Anyone can play this game; indeed, many interpreters have made good careers of it. The absence of agreement among them is telling. Were there a dependable means for removing the Jesus kernel from the Christian husk, one might expect some uniformity of result. But there is no agreement, because there is no accepted method. Is it any wonder then that most interpreters create a Jesus who is the embodied image of their own ideals? Such a Jesus might well be an attractive character, but his appeal is due more to the desirability of the construct than to its truthfulness or completeness.

Are there no tests by which historical accuracy can be judged? Yes, but they are of limited usefulness. For example, it has been proposed that sayings of Jesus that are found in two or more *independent* sources should be regarded as especially credible. The fact that Matthew, Mark, and Luke are all related to each other in some way means that they do not count as independent evidence.[10] Thus, a saying would have to occur both in Mark and in John (or Paul, or some other source) to count. Unfortunately, relatively few such sayings exist. Vanishingly little of Jesus' teaching could be verified on this basis alone. It is telling that scholars who employ this method still include attractive passages that do not meet the criterion, such as the parables of the Good Samaritan and the Prodigal Son, found only in Luke. By the same token, they may

---

10. Matthew and Luke probably used some form of Mark; see Chapter Two ("First Things First: The Bible"). Some scholars would count material that appears in one form in Mark and a somewhat different form in both Matthew and Luke as being multiply attested; in any event, there are only a few such sayings, so the essential point stands.

dismiss passages that are multiply attested, for example, Jesus' Son of Man sayings and the Lord's Supper story. So, not only is the test itself problematic, but it is often applied selectively.

Another standard favored by several recent Jesus books is the "test of double dissimilarity." This is the criterion of uniqueness. Sayings unparalleled in (that is, dissimilar to both) Judaism and Christianity are deemed the most credible since they could not have been imported from either source. One example is Jesus' rejection of fasting in Mark 2:18-22, which fits the practice of neither Judaism nor Christianity. At best, this net catches only a small school of Jesus' sayings, which is hardly astonishing given the fact that Jesus was Jewish and was revered by Christians. As a method for identifying some of the most trustworthy sayings of Jesus, double dissimilarity is a useful but by no means infallible tool. Like multiple attestation, it is often applied selectively: "love thy neighbor" comes from Leviticus 19:18 (before Jesus) and is quoted in Romans 13:9 (after Jesus), but few doubt that Jesus said it. Moreover, we know too little about first-century Judaism and Christianity to make assured judgments concerning Jesus' uniqueness. As a means of invalidating sayings of Jesus — i.e., nothing in the Gospels is historical *unless* it is unique — the test of dissimilarity is worse than useless. It is no surprise that those scholars who employ it in this way construct for themselves a non-Jewish, non-"Christian" (and on both counts, non-eschatological) Jesus.[11] Such a Jesus is highly attractive to contemporary sensibilities. In particular, he makes no off-putting assertions of special status. He is not God's Messiah or other such eschatological agent: eschatological thinking characterizes much of Judaism and Christianity and so, *by definition, cannot be true of Jesus.* Any smack of self-claim on the part of Jesus can thus be eliminated. By one and the same stroke, the figure of Jesus is emancipated from the shackles of his Jewish past and the confines of his Christian future. So it is that we come to the modern Jesus, from whom seldom is heard an eschatological word.

Most scholars take this for what it is, a nonsensical, upside-down

---

11. Cf. *The Five Gospels,* pp. 22-25. See, for example, how the criterion of dissimilarity is used to discredit Mark 7:17-30 (pp. 69-70). Particularly striking is the claim that since the early Christians spoke about having a mission, we can confidently assert that Jesus himself did not. Despite a mountain of contrary evidence, we are told that "Jesus himself does not claim that he had been assigned a specific mission that he had to carry out" (p. 70).

method, guaranteed to produce a thoroughly skewed result.[12] Cut off from Judaism and Christianity, from both historical context and consequence, "Jesus" becomes a free-floating and timeless abstraction into which one may invest whatever meaning one wishes. Furthermore, at the level of its assumptions, this approach is both anti-Jewish and anti-Christian. In practice, one attributes whatever one dislikes in the Gospels to the baleful influences of religion. The result is a remarkably secular Jesus, unconcerned with Jewish hopes and unconnected to Christian expectations, whose only offense was that of being a liberal. Jews are caricatured as narrow, intolerant bigots who would kill anyone who presumed to teach an ethic of love. Christians are caricatured as dolts and charlatans, concocting a religion wildly out of sync with that of their reputed lord and master. Into this drama steps the modern scholar, a heroic figure who alone succeeds where Peter, James, and John have failed and delivers to the world the unvarnished Jesus. Such chutzpah is as amusing as it is amazing.

I am often called upon to speak to church groups about the historical Jesus. It can be a tough assignment. Often as not, those issuing the invitation have read one or more books of the sort just described. Many hope that I will join them in proclaiming the good news of the revolution in contemporary understanding of Jesus. Needless to say, I am bound to disappoint such expectations. Unfortunately, most of what is written on this subject is neither new nor credible. In fact, the flaws in such arguments were exposed convincingly a century ago in Albert Schweitzer's *Quest of the Historical Jesus,* but the lesson has not sunk in. Evaluating the current state of affairs, Professor Graham Stanton of Cambridge University wrote the following:

> [T]he reading public has not been well served by books published on Jesus and the Gospels. Too many have been written by sensation seekers who have twisted evidence to fit fancy theories. Although their books have been so inept that most scholars have not bothered to take them seriously, they have caught the eye of readers who have sorely needed a winnowing fork to sift the wheat from the chaff.[13]

12. See Hays, "The Corrected Jesus," p. 45.

13. Graham Stanton, *Gospel Truth? New Light on Jesus and the Gospels* (London: HarperCollins, 1995), p. vii.

What is required of a truly credible historical portrait of Jesus? Among other things, it must locate Jesus sensibly in the world of first-century Judaism and provide a reasonable account for the known effects of his life, in particular, for the rise and spread of Christianity in the years immediately following his death.[14] In other words, Jesus must fit within a certain historical space, linked plausibly to what came before and after. A high percentage of historical Jesuses fail on both counts: they are neither sufficiently the product of Judaism nor adequately the cause of Christianity. The great exception is to be found in the contribution of scholars, both Jews and Gentiles, who are knowledgeable in the field of ancient Judaism.[15] Almost without exception, these interpreters take a more favorable view of the Gospel evidence. They conclude that the Jesus of the New Testament fits the context of first-century Judaism, particularly in the context of Jewish eschatology. The Jesus who was baptized by John (an eschatologically oriented figure if ever there was one), who preached about "the dominion ['kingdom'] of God," who gathered twelve disciples, who predicted the destruction of the temple, and who was crucified as "king of the Jews," was thoroughly at home in the world of Jewish eschatology. Accordingly, there is no reason to think that Jesus was essentially misunderstood by his nearest followers. The eschatological perspective of the early church was an understandable development and extension of Jesus' own thinking. Above all, the church regarded Jesus as God's eschatological agent because Jesus himself had done so. If later eschatological sayings were added to the traditions concerning Jesus, it is because Jesus already was known to be an eschatological figure. The same can be said, for example, concerning the accounts of healing in the Gospels. Jesus attracted stories about healing precisely because he already was regarded as a healer. In an important sense, all healing stories and all eschatological sayings tell us something true about Jesus, whether

14. According to Larry W. Hurtado of Edinburgh University, "[I]f we respect fully the chronological indications, then we must recognize that the development of early Christian religion did not take place in a slow process that can easily be charted in linear stages but rather seems to have blossomed quite quickly" (*One God, One Lord: Early Christian Devotion and Ancient Jewish Monotheism* [Edinburgh: T. & T. Clark, 1998], p. 125).

15. For example, E. P. Sanders's *Jesus and Judaism* (London: SCM, 1985); Geza Vermes's *Jesus the Jew* (London: Collins,1973); John P. Meier's *A Marginal Jew* (New York: Doubleday, 1994); and Ben Meyer's *The Aims of Jesus* (London: SCM, 1979).

or not they are all factual. Such development or expansion is different from invention. The early church did not concoct the Jesus of Christianity nor did it contrive his eschatological perspective. The master was not the invention of his students.

One of the finest contemporary scholars writing in the field of historical Jesus studies is Professor John P. Meier of Notre Dame University. I cannot improve upon the following summary, taken from the second volume of his important work *A Marginal Jew*:

> All this stands in stark contrast to one popular portrait of the historical Jesus often found in the literature today: Jesus was a kindhearted rabbi who preached gentleness and love. . . . The advantage and appeal of the domesticated Jesus is obvious: he is instantly relevant to and usable by contemporary ethics, homilies, political programs, and ideologies of various stripes. In contrast, a 1st century Jew who presents himself as the eschatological prophet of the imminent arrival of God's kingdom . . . is not so instantly relevant and usable. Yet, for better or for worse, this strange marginal Jew, this eschatological prophet and miracle-worker, *is* the historical Jesus retrievable by modern historical methods applied soberly to the data.[16]

What can we know about Jesus' view of the future? As is so often the case when talking about the past, it is easier to speak with confidence about the big picture, in this instance about the general tenor of Jesus' teaching, than about individual sayings. It is important to note, however, that there is more to the historical record than Jesus' words. Even if we knew nothing of Jesus' teaching, we would still have to account for a figure who, beyond reasonable doubt, was baptized by John, called twelve disciples, demonstrated in the temple, was crucified by the Romans, and left behind an eschatological movement. The major events and consequences of Jesus' life constitute the framework within which the Gospel sayings can be interpreted and, to an extent, evaluated. For example, it is a fact that Jesus of Nazareth is the historical middle term between John the Baptist and Paul the apostle, both of whom were strongly eschatological in orientation; therefore, it is rea-

---

16. Meier, *A Marginal Jew*, vol. 2, p. 1045.

sonable to believe the Gospel report that Jesus himself taught about the approaching reign of God. If we stick to the broad road of likely facts and general teachings, we should not go far wrong. On even so generic a level, several important points can be made.

I. *Like John, Jesus proclaimed the coming dominion ("kingdom") of God.*[17]

The New Testament authors are united in portraying John the Baptist as an apocalyptic prophet who called for repentance in the face of impending judgment. Both Matthew and Mark also claim that he preached about the coming of God's reign; for example, Matthew 3:2: "Repent, for the kingdom of heaven has come near."[18] Naturally, these ideas belong together. The hope that God's rule would come to earth (either directly or indirectly, through a Messiah) was common in ancient Judaism.[19] Zechariah 14:9 states that "the Lord will become king over all the earth; on that day the Lord will be one and his name one." Under the wide umbrella of this expectation were sheltered numerous other hopes, including the restoration of the twelve tribes of Israel, the renovation of creation, and the judgment of the wicked. The perspective of John the Baptist appears to have had much in common with that of the apocryphal Psalms of Solomon, which preceded him by a century:

---

17. The Greek word *basileia* has traditionally been translated "kingdom." There are two problems with this rendering. First, a "kingdom" is usually thought of as a place, but in the teaching of Jesus, the *basileia* of God is more often an activity than a location (cf. Wisdom 10:10 and Tobit 13:1). For this reason, interpreters often translate the term by the words "rule" and "reign." Another useful translation is "dominion," a term that does justice to both the active and spatial dimensions of God's *basileia*. A second problem is that the word "kingdom" serves to reinforce the longstanding but odd notion that God is male. For further information, see Burton H. Throckmorton Jr.'s fine book *Jesus Christ: The Message of the Gospels, The Hope of the Church* (Louisville: Westminster/John Knox, 1998), pp. 42-43.

18. Matthew's Jewishness is demonstrated by his general reluctance to use the word "God." On all but five occasions, he substitutes "kingdom of heaven" for "kingdom of God." In Matthew's usage, the two phrases are essentially interchangeable.

19. On the portrayal of God as king, see Ps. 5:2; 44:4; 47:6-7; 68:24; 74:12; 84:3; 95:3; 145:1; Isa. 44:6; Jer. 10:10; and Dan. 6:26.

Behold, O Lord, and raise up unto them their king, the son of David, at the time in which Thou seest, O God, that he may reign over Israel Thy servant. And gird him with strength, that he may shatter unrighteous rulers. . . . And he shall gather together a holy people, whom he shall lead in righteousness, and he shall judge the tribes of the people that have been sanctified by the Lord his God. And he shall not suffer unrighteousness to lodge any more in their midst, nor shall there dwell with them any man that knoweth wickedness, for he shall know them, that they are all sons of their God. (Psalms of Solomon 17:23-24, 28-30)

A broad and recognizable hope for the fulfillment of God's purposes is abundantly attested in early Judaism, and there can be no doubt that John himself worked within the context of this expectation. The same can be said of Jesus, who associated with John and who, following the Baptist's arrest, drew to himself a number of John's followers, among whom were members of Jesus' inner circle of disciples (John 1:35-42). That is not to say that Jesus and John agreed on all points (cf. Matt. 11:16-19; Luke 7:31-35) or, for that matter, that Jesus' vision of the future comported precisely with that of any other person. Still, it is vital to recognize that when Jesus preached about the kingdom of God, he did not introduce a new, foreign, or unintelligible concept. Such teaching would surely have met with widespread approval on a general level. Controversy lay in the details, and it is here that Jesus did indeed encounter misunderstanding and disagreement. For example, Jesus might well have regarded himself as Israel's Messiah (see below), but his was not the messiahship of popular expectation, e.g., as represented by the above quotation from the Psalms of Solomon. There is no evidence that Jesus ever intended to muster the armies of Israel and lead them in battle against Rome. Instead, he appears to have thought that God would act directly and decisively to bring the "peaceable kingdom" to earth, a perspective similar to the pacifism of Daniel. So the question is not *if* Jesus proclaimed God's coming rule, which seems certain, but *what sort* of kingdom he proclaimed and *how* and *when* he imagined that it would come. We know less about these matters than we would like, but we do know some things with relative confidence.

All of the Gospels mention Jesus' preaching about the dominion (or "kingdom") of God. In fact, it is the dominant topic in Matthew,

Mark, and Luke, where it is mentioned 118 times altogether. The ubiquity of the theme places its authenticity beyond the doubt of all but the most determined skeptics.[20] The repeated identification of Jesus as "king of the Jews" points in the same direction,[21] as does the frequent mention of a future kingdom in the rest of the NT writings.[22] The summary of Jesus' activity in Matthew 4:23 is typical:

> Jesus went throughout Galilee, teaching in their synagogues and proclaiming the good news of the kingdom and curing every disease and every sickness among the people.

The link between Jesus' proclamation of God's dominion and his healing ministry is significant. It was commonly thought that the time of restoration would include a revitalization of creation, including the elimination of sickness. So Isaiah 65:19-20:

> I will rejoice in Jerusalem, and delight in my people; no more shall the sound of weeping be heard in it, or the cry of distress. No more shall there be in it an infant that lives but a few days, or an old person who does not live out a lifetime; for one who dies at a hundred years will be considered a youth, and one who falls short of a hundred will be considered accursed.

Thus it is fitting that, according to Luke's Gospel, Jesus' first public speech consisted primarily of a reading from Isaiah 61:1-2:

> "The Spirit of the Lord is upon me, because he has anointed me to bring good news to the poor. He has sent me to proclaim release to the captives and recovery of sight to the blind, to let the

---

20. If the "dominion of God" sayings are wholly inauthentic, then we ought to abandon the study of Jesus and focus all of our attention on that early and anonymous genius who invented most of his teaching. In short, we would need to create another Jesus to explain Jesus.

21. See Matt. 2:2; 27:11; 27:29; Mark 15:2, 9, 12, 18, 26; Luke 23:3, 37, 38; John 18:33, 39; 19:3, 12, 14, 19, and 21.

22. It is found twenty-six times outside of the Gospels, e.g., in Rom. 14:17; Eph. 5:5; Heb. 12:28; James 2:5; 2 Peter 1:11; and Rev. 11:15. The occurrence of this idea across so many sources counts as evidence in favor of its origin in the teaching of Jesus.

oppressed go free, to proclaim the year of the Lord's favor."
(Luke 4:18-19)

The passage quoted by Jesus is found in the midst of a series of restoration texts in the latter chapters of Isaiah. When Jesus added, "Today
this Scripture has been fulfilled in your hearing," the implication would
have been as clear as it was staggering. The time of God's eschatological
visitation is at hand. But who was Jesus, known from his childhood to
his audience at Nazareth, to claim such a ministry for himself? In all
three Synoptic Gospels, the story ends in rejection. "'Is this not the car-
penter, the son of Mary? . . .' And they took offense at him" (Mark 6:3).

For Luke, Isaiah 61:1-2 functions as Jesus' job description for the en-
suing narrative. That is one of the reasons Luke moves the story to the
beginning of Jesus' ministry (see Chapter Two). Of course, one could
argue that this portion of the story (Luke 4:16-21) was fabricated by
Luke and tells us nothing about Jesus' own sense of purpose. There is
good evidence, however, that passages like Isaiah 61 were indeed important to Jesus' self-understanding. Recall the story in which the impris-
oned John sends disciples to ask Jesus, "Are you the one who is to come,
or are we to wait for another?" (Matt. 11:2-6; Luke 7:18-23). Evidently, Jesus was providing John with insufficient evidence of Messiah-like behavior (burning human "chaff" with "unquenchable fire," and that
sort of thing; e.g., Luke 3:17).

> Jesus had just then cured many people of diseases, plagues, and
> evil spirits, and had given sight to many who were blind. And he
> answered them, "Go and tell John what you have seen and heard:
> the blind receive their sight, the lame walk, the lepers are
> cleansed, the deaf hear, the dead are raised, the poor have good
> news brought to them." (Luke 7:21-22)

The clear implication is that Jesus is indeed "the one who is coming," and that the great eschatological work of renewal has commenced
in his ministry. In the terms of Luke 4:16-21//Isaiah 61:1-2, Jesus is doing
his job. It is noteworthy that this story also occurs in Matthew, who,
unlike Luke, does not mention Jesus' reading of Isaiah in the synagogue at Nazareth.

Exorcisms are another prominent feature of Jesus' ministry: "And he went throughout Galilee, proclaiming the message in their syna-gogues and casting out demons" (Mark 1:39). Once again, the eschato-logical horizon is clear. The victory of God is *par excellence* a triumph over the powers of evil: "And then His kingdom shall appear through-out all His creation, and then Satan shall be no more, and sorrow shall depart with him" (Assumption of Moses 10:1). Jesus himself is reported to have said, "[I]f it is by the Spirit of God that I cast out demons, then the kingdom of God has come to you" (Matthew 12:28; cf. Luke 11:20). The connection between exorcism and eschatology is made evident in numerous other verses, including Mark 3:23-27; Matthew 10:6-8; 17:17-18; Luke 4:41; 8:28-31 and 13:32. It is also present in the demons' recogni-tion of Jesus' identity (e.g., Matt. 8:29). The point is not that all such ac-counts are historically accurate, although relatively few question the fact that Jesus preached about the dominion of God and performed healings and exorcisms. What matters is that all three activities are said explicitly to serve the same eschatological agenda. It is striking that these same three ministries are mentioned together in connection with Jesus' sending of the Twelve (Mark 6:7-13; Matt. 10:1, 5-15; Luke 9:1-6). The pattern of Jesus' own ministry was assumed to be the template for the ministry of his followers:

> He called the twelve and began to send them out two by two, and gave them authority over the unclean spirits. . . . So they went out and proclaimed that all should repent. They cast out many demons, and anointed with oil many who were sick and cured them. (Mark 6:7, 12-13)

Luke 4:18 and Matthew 11:5, quoted above, mention Jesus' preach-ing to the poor. In both passages, this ministry is given an eschatologi-cal context, which is true to its Jewish heritage. The Exilic prophets en-visioned a time when the dispossessed would return to Israel and be granted lives of (by their standards) material abundance. It was widely thought that the oppressed and afflicted would be the particular ob-ject of God's eschatological mercy and provision. Both ideas are pres-ent in Isaiah 61:

> The spirit of the Lord God is upon me, because the Lord has anointed me; he has sent me to bring good news to the op-

pressed, to bind up the brokenhearted. . . . [Y]ou shall enjoy the wealth of the nations, and in their riches you shall glory. Because their shame was double, and dishonor was proclaimed as their lot, therefore they shall possess a double portion; everlasting joy shall be theirs. (Isa. 61:1, 6b-7)

This eschatological dimension is made plain especially by Luke, for example, in the Magnificat (attributed to Mary in 1:46-55):

He has brought down the powerful from their thrones, and lifted up the lowly; he has filled the hungry with good things, and sent the rich away empty. He has helped his servant Israel, in remembrance of his mercy, according to the promise he made to our ancestors, to Abraham and to his descendants forever. (Luke 1:52-55)

By all accounts, Jesus made a point of preaching to and associating with the poor and the marginalized. It is reasonable to suppose that the Gospels are right in linking this activity to Jesus' own sense of eschatological purpose.

As we have seen, the shape of Jesus' expectation for the future appears in many ways to have been fairly conventional. The first petition of the Lord's Prayer asks, "Your kingdom come, on earth as it is in heaven." The earthliness of Jesus' hope is underscored by descriptions of God's dominion that include such mundane activities as eating and drinking (Matt. 8:11; Mark 14:25; Luke 22:28-30). This makes perfect sense in the context of Jewish thinking, but it is a challenge to those of us who have been raised to think of the reign of God as existing (solely) in heaven.

Another link to Jewish expectation is to be found in the calling of the twelve disciples,[23] which likely has in view the much anticipated restoration of the twelve tribes. (The northern Israelite tribes were decimated, although not wholly annihilated, by the Assyrians over seven hundred years earlier.) According to E. P. Sanders,

---

23. Early corroboration of the existence of the Twelve occurs in Paul's first letter to the Corinthians (15:5). An extended defense of the historicity of the Twelve is provided by Sanders in his *Jesus and Judaism*, pp. 98-106.

[T]he twelve symbolize the inclusion of all Israel in the coming
. . . kingdom. The fact is that the number twelve itself, apart
from the details of any individual saying, points to "all Israel."
All we have to know is the fact that Jesus thought of, and taught
his followers to think of, being "twelve."[24]

The calling of twelve disciples "points towards his [Jesus'] understanding of his own mission. He was engaged in a task that would include the restoration of Israel."[25]

In Matthew 19:28 (paralleled in Luke 22:29-30), Jesus makes the following prediction:

Jesus said to them, "Truly I tell you, at the renewal of all things,
when the Son of Man is seated on the throne of his glory, you
who have followed me will also sit on twelve thrones, judging the
twelve tribes of Israel."

A strong case can be made for the authenticity of this verse, based
in part on the fact that it does not foresee the problem created by Ju-
das's subsequent betrayal. In any case, it demonstrates the natural association of the twelve disciples with the twelve tribes and with the fulfillment of Israel's eschatological expectations.

An indirect piece of evidence suggesting a significant overlap between Jesus' conception of God's rule and that of other Jews is the extent to which common Jewish hopes are affirmed without reservation
or revision by the Gospel writers. For example, the crowds on Palm
Sunday shout, "Hosanna! Blessed is the one who comes in the name of
the Lord! Blessed is the coming kingdom of our ancestor David!" (Mark
11:9-10). Joseph of Arimathea is commended as a faithful Jew "who was
himself waiting expectantly for the kingdom of God" (Mark 15:43). Luke
1-2 in particular is choc-a-bloc with such statements, included in the
testimony of angels (1:31-32; 2:11), of Mary (1:46-55), of Zechariah (1:68-
79), of Simeon (2:29-35), and of Anna (2:38). According to Luke, Jerusalem ultimately will be returned to the Jews: "Jerusalem will be trampled
on by the Gentiles, until the times of the Gentiles are fulfilled" (21:24).

---

24. Sanders, *Jesus and Judaism,* p. 104 (original italics eliminated).
25. Sanders, *Jesus and Judaism,* p. 106.

This view is paralleled in a number of Jewish texts, including the Psalms of Solomon 17:24, which holds that the Messiah will "purge Jerusalem from nations that trample (her) down to destruction."

There is no reason to think that this favorable appraisal of Jewish expectations originated with the early church and is somehow antithetical to the teachings of Jesus himself. Many Christian scholars have been reluctant to admit to the Jewishness of the early church's (much less Jesus' own) hope for the future. A good example concerns the interpretation of Acts 1:6-8, the final conversation between Jesus and his disciples:

> So when they had come together, they asked him, "Lord, is this the time when you will restore the kingdom to Israel?" He replied, "It is not for you to know the times or periods that the Father has set by his own authority. But you will receive power when the Holy Spirit has come upon you; and you will be my witnesses in Jerusalem, in all Judea and Samaria, and to the ends of the earth."

A majority of interpreters have argued that the creation of the church fulfilled this hope for the restoration of Israel.[26] There is nothing in Acts to support this view. To the contrary, the book's only other mention of restoration (Acts 3:20-21) refers unambiguously to the situation following the future return of Christ. As for Paul in Romans 11, Israel's eventual restoration appears to be a given. It is telling that so many modern Christians find it unimaginable that so many early Christians might have hoped for the eschatological salvation of Israel.

Finally, we recall again the Lord's Prayer, where Jesus teaches his disciples to pray, "Your kingdom come" (Matt. 6:10; Luke 11:2). Of course, scholars will never agree about whether Jesus actually spoke these (or any other!) words; nevertheless, I think that we can say confidently that this prayer is true to the message and ministry of Jesus, for whom the coming of God's reign was the controlling idea and the central conviction.

---

26. For further information, see my article "Restoring the Kingdom to Israel" in *Shadow of Glory: Reading the New Testament after the Holocaust* (New York: Routledge, 2002).

2. *Jesus believed that he would play a central role in the realization of God's rule.*

> Now when Jesus had finished saying these things, the crowds
> were astounded at his teaching, for he taught them as one hav-
> ing authority, and not as their scribes. (Matt. 7:28-29)

Jesus was no shrinking violet. It is the unequivocal witness of the
New Testament that he spoke with a remarkable and often unsettling
degree of personal authority. The self-assertion so obvious in the Sermon on the Mount ("You have heard that it was said . . . but *I* say to
you") is evident throughout the Gospel record. Jesus did not simply express opinions; he made definitive pronouncements concerning the
character of God and the nature of God's rule. Such extraordinary confidence in his role as God's agent was bound to provoke a response.
"They were all amazed, and they kept on asking one another, 'What is
this? A new teaching — with authority!'" (Mark 1:27). Jesus' actions also
demonstrated a remarkable sense of command. His healings and exorcisms, his activities on the Sabbath and his acceptance of sinners,
raised serious questions in the minds of his contemporaries.

> As he was walking in the temple, the chief priests, the scribes,
> and the elders came to him and said, "By what authority are you
> doing these things? Who gave you this authority to do them?"
> (Mark 11:27-28)

In short, Jesus spoke and acted with authority of the sort that can
be sanctioned only by God. The nearest parallel is to be found in the
prophets, whose sense of legitimacy was located in their call from God.
Figures such as Jeremiah and Hosea worked outside of and frequently
over against the political and religious establishment; hence, their authority was always subject to question. The encounter between the
prophet Amos and Amaziah, the priest of Bethel and crony of King Jer-
oboam, is revealing. Amos admitted that he possessed no official position or authority; instead,

> I am a herdsman, and a dresser of sycamore trees, and the Lord
> took me from following the flock, and the Lord said to me, "Go,
> prophesy to my people Israel." (Amos 7:14b-15)

The Gospels are surely right in reporting that many of Jesus' contemporaries regarded him as a prophet.[27] Jesus himself is said to have claimed the title in a handful of passages (e.g., Mark 6:4; Luke 13:33; John 4:44). Of particular interest is Jesus' statement that prophets such as himself are not honored by their own people. It is one of the relatively few sayings that appears in all four Gospels.[28] Jesus is not identified as a prophet outside of the Gospels and Acts, so the statement is both multiply attested and, to a large extent, dissimilar to later Christian proclamation. Even more convincing is the simple fact that Jesus behaved like a prophet. One of many examples is the incident in the temple, related in all four Gospels.[29] The meaning of the "temple cleansing" is hotly debated. Taking into consideration Jesus' statements about the temple's destruction ("Do you see these great buildings? Not one stone will be left upon another that will not be destroyed"; Mark 13:2),[30] it seems most likely that his action was meant to signal God's judgment of the current temple. Such symbolic acts were frequently performed by prophets; for example, Jeremiah wore a yoke to represent Babylon's God-given authority over Judah (Jer. 27), and Isaiah went naked for three years as a sign of God's judgment (Isa. 20). (Better Isaiah than me!) Whatever the precise interpretation of Jesus' action in the temple, it is reasonable to think that he acted with prophetic self-consciousness. After all, if someone looks like a prophet, speaks like a prophet, and acts like a prophet, he probably is, at least in his own mind, a prophet.

That is not to say that Jesus regarded himself as *simply* a prophet. The authority he assumed exceeded that traditionally credited to the prophetic office. Jesus claimed to know who was in and who was outside of God's dominion.[31] What is more, he taught that following him was more important than observing the Law,[32] and that one's eschato-

27. See Matt. 14:5; 21:11, 46; Mark 6:15; Luke 7:16; 24:19; John 4:19; 9:17; Acts 2:30; 3:22-23; 7:37.

28. Matt. 13:57; Mark 6:4; Luke 4:24; John 4:44.

29. Matt. 21:12-16; Mark 11:11, 15-19; Luke 19:45-48; John 2:13-22.

30. See Matt. 26:61; 27:40; Mark 14:58; 15:29; John 2:19; Acts 6:14.

31. E.g., Matt. 9:9-13; 19:25; Matt. 8:10-13//Luke 13:28-30; Mark 2:5-12; 10:29-31 par.; 12:34; Luke 7:44-50; 10:22; 13:23-29; and numerous verses in John, such as 3:1-15; 5:22-23; 9:35-41.

32. E.g., Mark 2:18-22 par., Matt. 8:21-22; Luke 9:59-60.

logical destiny would be based upon one's response to him.[33] Jesus' table fellowship "with sinners and tax collectors" (Mark 2:16) is attested throughout the Gospels, and is solid evidence for his remarkable sense of authority. According to E. P. Sanders,

> Jesus offered companionship to the wicked of Israel as a sign that God would save them, and he did not make his association dependent upon their conversion to the law. He may very well have thought that they had no time to create new lives for themselves, but that if they accepted his message they could be saved. If Jesus added to this such statements as that the tax collectors and prostitutes would enter the kingdom before the righteous (Matt. 21.31), the offence would be increased. The implied self-claim, to know whom God would include and not, and the equally implied downgrading of the normal machinery of righteousness, would push Jesus' stance close to, or over, the border which separates individual charisma from impiety.[34]

Let us return for a moment to Jesus' statement in Matthew 19:28 and Luke 22:29-30 concerning the future role of the disciples ("you . . . will also sit on twelve thrones, judging the twelve tribes of Israel"). The Gospels report with surprising candor the disciples' continual jostling over rank. Much more was perceived to be at stake than the best place at dinner or the softest cushion at bed. Note, for example, Mark 10:35-37:

> James and John, the sons of Zebedee, came forward to him and said to him, "Teacher, we want you to do for us whatever we ask of you." And he said to them, "What is it you want me to do for you?" And they said to him, "Grant us to sit, one at your right hand and one at your left, in your glory."

---

33. Mark 8:35-38 par.; Matt. 10:37//Luke 14:26-27; Matt. 7:21-23//Luke 6:46; Matt. 7:24-27//Luke 6:47-49; Matt. 11:6//Luke 7:23; Matt. 11:20-24//Luke 10:13-15; Luke 7:44-50; Matt. 12:30//Luke 11:23; Mark 9:42//Matt. 18:6; Matt. 10:40//Luke 10:16; Matt. 10:32//Luke 12:8-9; Matt. 23:37-39//Luke 13:34-35; and numerous verses in John, such as 3:16; 6:47; and 10:9. Again, the issue is not the authenticity of each and every one of these passages. The point is that sayings at every level of tradition demonstrate that Jesus regarded individuals' response to him as decisive to their status in God's dominion.

34. Sanders, *Jesus and Judaism,* pp. 207-8.

In Matthew's version, the request is made by the mother of James and John, who asks that her sons might sit at Jesus' side "in his *kingdom*" (Matt. 20:20-22). (Anyone who has coached a children's sports team has met this parent.) It is not likely that the later church invented these squabbles, which show the disciples in so bad a light. The prominent position given to Simon, including his nickname Cephas/Petros (in Aramaic and Greek, meaning "Rock," the basis for the English "Peter"), is likely to have originated in this same context. The point is this: If Jesus imagined that his followers would enjoy prominent positions in the administration of God's future reign, we can expect that he anticipated an even more exalted role for himself. This is certainly the way that the Gospel writers portray matters, although their account has been questioned by legions of scholars on the ground that such an elevated view of Jesus must be the product of later Christian speculation. Furthermore, it is asserted that Jesus could not have imagined a *future* role for himself in the realization of God's purposes. Both assumptions are open to serious question.

The heart of the debate concerns Jesus' numerous "Son of Man" sayings. These fall broadly into three camps. The first includes statements in which Jesus refers to himself and his current ministry, as in Matthew 8:20//Luke 9:58: "Foxes have holes, and birds of the air have nests; but the Son of Man has nowhere to lay his head." Some of these bear a resemblance to sayings of the prophet Ezekiel, e.g., "Son of Man, I have made you a sentinel for the house of Israel; whenever you hear a word from my mouth, you shall give them warning from me" (Ezek. 3:17).[35]

The second group includes numerous statements concerning Jesus' impending rejection and death:

"How then is it written about the Son of Man, that he is to go through many sufferings and be treated with contempt?" (Mark 9:12)

"For the Son of Man came not to be served but to serve, and to give his life a ransom for many." (Mark 10:45)

---

35. The *NRSV* translates "Son of Man" as "mortal" in this and other verses.

Last are the sayings of Jesus concerning a heavenly figure who will come to judge the earth (a usage originating in Daniel 7:13-14):[36]

> "Then they will see 'the Son of Man coming in clouds' with great power and glory. Then he will send out the angels, and gather his elect from the four winds, from the ends of the earth to the ends of heaven." (Mark 13:26-27)

> "Those who are ashamed of me and of my words in this adulterous and sinful generation, of them the Son of Man will also be ashamed when he comes in the glory of his Father with the holy angels." (Mark 8:38)

Predictably, scholars have dealt with these passages in conflicting ways. Some have argued that only one of the above categories of sayings is authentic, e.g., those that refer to Jesus' present ministry. One difficulty with this approach is the overlap that exists among the three groups. For example, it is by no means the case that all of Jesus' references to himself as a present-day Son of Man are as self-deprecating as Matthew 8:20. For example:

> "But so that you may know that the Son of Man has authority on earth to forgive sins" — he said to the paralytic — "I say to you, stand up, take your mat and go to your home." (Mark 2:10-11)

> "[T]he Son of Man is lord even of the sabbath." (Mark 2:28)

Here the earthly Son of Man's authority is the near equal to that of the future Son of Man. Matthew 13:36-43 refers both to the Son of Man who sows good seed (the earthly Jesus) and to the Son of Man who sends his angels in judgment (cf. Matt. 25:31-46). Likewise, many sayings that predict the Son of Man's suffering also refer to his resurrection and glorification. Luke 17:24-25 includes statements about both the immediate suffering and the future coming of the Son of Man:

> "For as the lightning flashes and lights up the sky from one side to the other, so will the Son of Man be in his day. But first he must endure much suffering and be rejected by this generation."

36. See the discussion in Chapters Four and Five.

The number and range of Son of Man sayings in all four Gospels make it highly improbable that the motif was simply invented by the church. In one sense or another (or, most likely, in multiple senses) the phrase was surely used by Jesus. One especially important piece of corroborating evidence is found in Paul's first letter to the Thessalonians, by most estimates the earliest NT writing:

> For this we declare to you by the word of the Lord, that we who are alive, who are left until the coming of the Lord, will by no means precede those who have died. For the Lord himself, with a cry of command, with the archangel's call and with the sound of God's trumpet, will descend from heaven, and the dead in Christ will rise first. Then we who are alive, who are left, will be caught up in the clouds together with them to meet the Lord in the air; and so we will be with the Lord forever. Therefore encourage one another with these words. (1 Thess. 4:15-18)

The "word of the Lord" quoted by Paul closely resembles the Son of Man saying in Matthew 24:30-31. The simplest explanation is that both Paul and Matthew are referring to something actually said by Jesus, hence the force of Paul's "encourage one another with these words."

As we saw in Chapter Four, the idea of an apocalyptic Son of Man was widely known in ancient Judaism. In the Similitudes of Enoch, the figure is even referred to as a Messiah and his coming linked to the resurrection of the dead. It is not likely that Jesus operated within the framework of Jewish eschatology and yet referred to himself as Son of Man in an exclusively non-eschatological sense. Moreover, the link to eschatology is required to make sense of those verses that refer to the Son of Man's extraordinary authority on earth.

Clearly, the Gospel writers believed that Jesus was the Son of Man who would come again to judge and rule the world. Many critics are unconvinced. A hearty perennial in the scholarly garden is the idea that Jesus did anticipate the coming of the Danielic Son of Man but that he did not identify himself with that figure.[37] Jesus' role was merely that of a prophet, encouraging the people of Israel to prepare for the immi-

---

37. The best recent book of this variety is Bart Ehrman's *Jesus: Apocalyptic Prophet of the New Millennium.*

nent arrival of their heavenly visitor. In effect, Jesus takes over the role of John the Baptist, making straight the way for someone greater yet to come. It follows that all other "Son of Man" sayings must be discredited, since it would be both confusing and inelegant of Jesus to proclaim himself the Son of Man who is not the Son of Man. It is further argued that Jesus' hope for the advent of the Son of Man was disappointed and that the church solved the problem by morphing Jesus himself into that figure, generating dozens of useful Son of Man sayings in the process.

It is a neat theory, but it leaves out too much. For one thing, Jesus did not act like John the Baptist. God's dominion was not only anticipated, it was already being realized in Jesus' own ministry. Jesus' remarkable sense of authority, exhibited both in word and deed, makes a good deal more sense if he did in fact identify himself as the Son of Man. Recall Matthew 19:28, mentioned above:

> "Truly I tell you, at the renewal of all things, when the Son of Man is seated on the throne of his glory, you who have followed me will also sit on twelve thrones, judging the tribes of Israel."

As we have seen, it appears that the disciples expected to play an important role in the eschatological administration, a belief that they appear to have gotten from Jesus himself. We should not be surprised, then, by the many verses that attribute to Jesus even greater expectations concerning his future role. It is overwhelmingly likely that Jesus anticipated his own death, best evidenced in the Lord's Supper tradition, found in 1 Corinthians 11:20-34 as well as the Gospels. It is also likely that Jesus believed that he would be vindicated beyond the grave (see below). But the only future role on offer that is greater than that of the disciples is that of the Son of Man. Note, for example, Mark 14:60-64, the earliest account of Jesus' trial:

> Then the high priest stood up before them and asked Jesus, "Have you no answer? What is it that they testify against you?" But he was silent and did not answer. Again the high priest asked him, "Are you the Messiah, the Son of the Blessed One?" Jesus said, "I am; and 'you will see the Son of Man seated at the right hand of the Power,' and 'coming with the clouds of heaven.'"

Then the high priest tore his clothes and said, "Why do we still need witnesses? You have heard his blasphemy! What is your decision?" All of them condemned him as deserving death.

We should also note the overlap between the assignment of judgment to the disciples and Jesus and to the Son of Man. In short, a great many things come together if we accept that the Gospels are correct in assigning to Jesus the self-ascription "Son of Man."

At the end of the day, "you pays your money and you takes your choice." For some people, it will always seem incredible that Jesus could have held such an extraordinary view of himself.[38] They therefore conclude that the memory of Jesus must have been thoroughly distorted by his followers. The matter can never be proved, so the argument will go on. Of course, the same is true with respect to the other great eschatological title, *Messiah*. Did Jesus think of himself as the "anointed one"?

It is important in thinking about this issue to avoid a common mistake, that of assuming a set definition of Messiah and a fixed canon of messianic predictions. Like other eschatological ideas, messiahship was a fluid concept that meant different things to different people. No one person could possibly have met the contradictory expectations of every interpretive school. It is quite possible that Jesus could have understood himself as Messiah without taking on board all of the title's many and varied associations. Still, some features were typical of most messianic expectation, and it would be rather surprising if a Messiah-to-be did not share them. Chief among these is the expectation of the re-establishment of the Davidic kingship.

One piece of evidence that strongly favors Jesus' self-identification

---

38. With reference to Luke 21:27, *The Five Gospels* reports, "The Fellows doubt that Jesus spoke about the coming of the son of Adam as a future, cataclysmic event" (p. 385; the claim in the next sentence to know that Luke himself did not think that Jesus spoke these words is quite extraordinary). This same doubt is applied to Jesus' other statements concerning the coming of a future Son of Man. See, for example, the discussion of Matt. 10:23 (p. 170), Mark 2:10 (p. 44), Mark 13:26 (p. 112), and Mark 8:38 (p. 80: "'The son of Adam' figure is here an apocalyptic figure. . . . The identification of Jesus with the son of Adam almost certainly excludes the possibility of tracing this saying back to Jesus."). Once again, we enter the labyrinth of circular reasoning. Since we already know that Jesus did not identify himself with the apocalyptic Son of Man, all evidence to the contrary is dismissed.

as Messiah is the charge fixed above his head on the cross, "The King of the Jews" (Mark 15:26; compare Jesus' examination before Pilate in John 18:28–19:16). It should be obvious that a claim to kingship, even a kingship "not from this world" (John 18:36), to be inaugurated by an act of God, would go a long way toward explaining Jesus' crucifixion by the Romans. Related to this is the story of the triumphal entry into Jerusalem, in which Jesus is portrayed as deliberately and publicly fulfilling Zechariah 9:9:

> Rejoice greatly, O daughter Zion! Shout aloud, O daughter Jerusalem! Lo, your king comes to you; triumphant and victorious is he, humble and riding on a donkey, on a colt, the foal of a donkey.

Three times in the Gospels Jesus identifies himself as the Messiah: in response to Peter's confession at Caesarea Philippi (Mark 8:27-33 par.), in the context of his examination by the high priest Caiaphas (Mark 14:62), and in response to the statement of the "woman at the well" (John 4:25-26). Many scholars doubt the authenticity of these accounts, and it is most unlikely that the issue will ever be settled. Again, what matters most is the consistency and plausibility of the big picture. Jesus was regarded as a king by the early church, he was crucified by the Romans as a would-be king, he entered Jerusalem as a king, his disciples quarreled over their place in his kingdom, and so on. It should hardly be surprising to learn that Jesus regarded himself as God's anointed, the viceroy of God's future dominion. Finally, we have already seen that the figures of the Son of Man and the Messiah were fused in the Similitudes of Enoch (1 Enoch 48:10; 52:4). If Jesus thought of himself as one, he could well have thought of himself as the other.

In short, the Gospel accounts seem broadly plausible. Jesus not only preached about the dominion of God, he believed that he would play a central role in its realization. There is no reason to posit a theory of misunderstanding in order to make sense of the evidence. Again, I quote E. P. Sanders:

> I think, then, that we must grant an element of continuity between what Jesus expected and what the disciples expected after the crucifixion and resurrection. It appears that the latter origi-

nally expected something which was *transformed* by the resurrection appearances, but which was not as completely different as is often thought. The resurrection did not change political, military and nationalistic hopes (based on misunderstanding) into spiritual, heavenly ones, but otherworldly-earthly hopes into otherworldly-heavenly.[39]

The early church was an eschatologically oriented community because of, not in spite of, Jesus.

3. God's dominion is characterized by reversal.

The remaining points are simpler and so can be dealt with more briefly. The first is even downright uncontroversial: Jesus offered God's reign primarily to the marginalized of society, including the poor, the lame, and the wicked. In fact, Jesus was notorious for accepting the company of the unacceptable. He touched lepers and healed demoniacs, welcomed prostitutes and ate with tax collectors, approached women with respect and treated the poor with dignity. Little wonder that this aspect of Jesus' story has attracted such favorable attention in recent years. In our age of multiculturalism, Jesus is an icon of tolerance and inclusiveness. Of course, there is more to Jesus' message than openness to outsiders; nevertheless, the recovery of this dimension of his character is much to be welcomed by the church.

Eschatological reversal is one of the key themes of Jesus' teaching. The tables will be turned; those who are on the inside now will be on the outside then, and vice versa. "Many who are first will be last and the last first" (Mark 10:31). This view is exemplified in the Beatitudes:

Blessed are the poor in spirit, for theirs is the kingdom of heaven.
Blessed are those who mourn, for they will be comforted.
Blessed are the meek, for they will inherit the earth. . . .

(Matt. 5:3-5)

Luke's version rounds out the picture with a series of corresponding woes:

39. Sanders, *Jesus and Judaism*, pp. 231-32.

But woe to you who are rich, for you have received
    your consolation.
Woe to you who are full now, for you will be hungry.
Woe to you who are laughing now, for you will mourn and weep.
Woe to you when all speak well of you, for that is what
    their ancestors did to the false prophets.

(Luke 6:24-26)

Several of Jesus' parables serve to reverse expectations concerning who is acceptable and who is unacceptable to God. It is the Prodigal Son and not the obedient but unforgiving elder brother who enjoys the father's banquet (Luke 15:11-32); it is the compassionate-acting Samaritan and not the religiously-correct priest and Levite who fulfills the law (Luke 10:29-37); it is the repentant tax collector and not the righteous Pharisee who leaves the temple justified (Luke 18:9-14). God's dominion demands a reversal of conventional priorities. It is the hidden treasure or pearl for which one would willingly sacrifice everything (Matt. 13:44-46); it is the lost coin or lost sheep whose recovery is all-important (Luke 15:1-10). Other parables reverse common expectations about the arrival of God's rule. The dominion of God is like a tiny mustard seed that grows slowly (Mark 4:30-32 par.); or a seed that grows secretly (Mark 4:26-29); or grains of wheat that grow up among and are presently indistinguishable from weeds (Matt. 13:24-30).

Jesus' eschatological perspective gives his teaching a radical and extraordinarily challenging edge. This is most evident in his instruction about money and possessions. Jesus would require the "rich young ruler" to sell his belongings and give the money to the poor (Mark 10:17-31 par.). In so doing, the young man would gain "treasure in heaven" (v. 21). The saying is paralleled in Luke 12:32-34:

"Do not be afraid, little flock, for it is your Father's good pleasure to give you the kingdom. Sell your possessions, and give alms. Make purses for yourselves that do not wear out, an unfailing treasure in heaven, where no thief comes near and no moth destroys. For where your treasure is, there your heart will be also."

In effect, Jesus offered an alternative reality that required an alternative set of values and priorities. It would take great faith to stake all of one's life and property on the truthfulness of God's coming dominion, but that is what Jesus asked. All of this talk about eschatological reversal sounds desirable until we begin to consider how it might apply to us personally. The Gospel may be "good news to the poor" (Luke 4:18), but relatively few of us in the western church are poor. To live lightly to possessions and reputation in this world and to invest instead in God's dominion is an extraordinarily difficult calling — unless, that is, one lives within the eschatological reality in which Jesus himself lived. It is only there that Jesus' words make sense and his demands seem reasonable.

4. God's dominion is both present and future.

In his preaching, healings, and exorcisms, Jesus saw a fulfillment of God's eschatological promise. This perspective is evident particularly in the answer given by Jesus to the disciples of John the Baptist (Matt. 11:2-6), discussed above. It stands behind Jesus' attitude toward fasting, which he deems unnecessary in the unique, present moment of his ministry (Mark 2:18-20 par.). It is also assumed in the saying about the binding of the strong man (Mark 3:27 par.) and in statements such as Luke 10:23-24 (Matt. 13:16-17):

> "Blessed are the eyes that see what you see! For I tell you that many prophets and kings desired to see what you see, but did not see it, and to hear what you hear, but did not hear it."

On two occasions the Gospels report that Jesus referred explicitly to the arrival or presence of God's dominion in his ministry. The first is found in Matthew 12:28//Luke 11:20: "But if it is by the Spirit [Luke: 'finger'] of God that I cast out demons, then the kingdom of God has come to you." The second is in Luke 17:21: "[T]he kingdom of God is among you." Some interpreters have taken these verses as evidence that Jesus thought *only* in terms of a present-day realization of God's dominion. That puts a very great weight on a very few verses. In fact, the clear majority of Jesus' statements have in view a still-future coming of God's reign. The prayer "Your kingdom come" (Matt. 6:10) asks for something not yet fully present. The statement "I will never again drink of the fruit of the vine until that day when I drink it new in the kingdom of God" (Mark 14:25; Matt. 26:29) has clearly to do with a yet un-realized future state.

What are we to make of this "already but not yet" aspect of Jesus' teaching? One could argue that Jesus was simply confused or self-contradictory, or perhaps that he was being deliberately mysterious. A far more likely explanation is that the already/not yet tension is inherent in the symbol itself, since the *basileia* ("dominion") of God refers both to God's active reign (already present in Jesus) and to God's universal rule (yet to come). As Meier notes,

> [T]he kingdom of God is not primarily a state or place but rather the entire dynamic event of God coming in power to rule his people Israel in the end time. It is a tensive symbol, a multi-faceted reality, a whole mythic story in miniature that cannot be adequately grasped in a single formula or definition. That is why Jesus can speak of kingdom as both imminent and yet present.[40]

Thus it is possible, even likely, that Jesus regarded God's dominion as being both present and future. The tension between what God already has done and what God has yet to do is even more pronounced in the theology of the early church, whose view of the eschatological work of Jesus included both his crucifixion and resurrection. This dynamic is essential to Christianity and will be the principal topic in our examination of NT eschatology in the next chapter.

5. With God's dominion will come judgment.

Let me be honest. I do not like judgment. The mere mention of the word recalls the most unpleasant memories from my childhood, such as the famous incident in which I managed to break almost an entire cabinet-ful of my mother's china. I can well imagine appearing before the throne of God and being told, "Craig, I have a bone to pick with you. . . ." No, judgment is not my idea of a good time, and I sympathize with those kindhearted pastors who eliminate the topic from their preaching. Grace is an altogether easier sell, at least in my little corner of Christendom. We like to emphasize those bits of Scripture that

40. Meier, *A Marginal Jew,* vol. 2, p. 452.

speak of God's extraordinary forgiveness and mercy. The parable of the Prodigal Son plays well, as does the Lost Sheep. Over the years, I must have heard two dozen sermons about Jesus' uncondemning attitude toward the woman caught in adultery.

All the same, one has to face the fact that a substantial portion of Jesus' teaching concerned judgment. One group of parables speaks of the eschatological division of the human race; we are either sheep or goats, good fish or bad fish, wheat or tares.[41] Other parables speak of different outcomes based on different responses, e.g., the Sower, the Ten Bridesmaids, the Talents.[42] Add to the mix the many sayings about the coming judgment by the Son of Man,[43] and the resultant picture may appear more than a little foreboding.

It is not always clear on what basis Jesus imagined that judgment would occur. Frequently, it correlates with a person's or group's response to his message and ministry. For example,

> "Woe to you, Chorazin! Woe to you, Bethsaida! For if the deeds of power done in you had been done in Tyre and Sidon, they would have repented long ago in sackcloth and ashes. But I tell you, on the day of judgment it will be more tolerable for Tyre and Sidon than for you." (Matt. 11:21-22//Luke 10:13-14)

At other points, judgment is rendered because of the unfulfillment of a command or expectation:

> "Then he will say to those at his left hand, 'You that are accursed, depart from me into the eternal fire prepared for the devil and his angels; for I was hungry and you gave me no food, I was thirsty and you gave me nothing to drink, I was a stranger and you did not welcome me, naked and you did not give me clothing, sick and in prison and you did not visit me.' Then they also will answer, 'Lord, when was it that we saw you hungry or thirsty or a stranger or naked or sick or in prison, and did not

41. Matt. 25:31-33; 13:47-50; 13:24-30.
42. Mark 4:1-12 par.; Matt. 25:1-13; Matt. 25:14-30 ("pounds" in Luke 19:11-27).
43. E.g., Mark 8:38; 13:26-27; Matt. 13:36-43; 16:27; 24:30-31, 36-44; 25:31-46; Luke 18:8; 21:36; John 5:27.

take care of you?' Then he will answer them, 'Truly I tell you, just
as you did not do it to one of the least of these, you did not do it
to me.' And these will go away into eternal punishment, but the
righteous into eternal life." (Matt. 25:41-45)

"Not everyone who says to me, 'Lord, Lord,' will enter the kingdom of heaven, but only the one who does the will of my Father
in heaven." (Matt. 7:21)

Judgment might come in the shape of historical events. The evidence strongly supports the view that, like Jeremiah centuries before,
Jesus predicted the destruction of Jerusalem and its temple, which indeed occurred about forty years later.[44] What is far less certain is what
Jesus expected to happen next. The key text is Mark 13 par., which begins with Jesus' prediction of the temple's ruin (vv. 1-2):

As he came out of the temple, one of his disciples said to him,
"Look, Teacher, what large stones and what large buildings!"
Then Jesus asked him, "Do you see these great buildings? Not
one stone will be left here upon another; all will be thrown
down."

Jesus' statement concerning the temple's destruction correlates
with a number of other sayings and is highly probable. The difficulty
comes in the next two verses:

When he was sitting on the Mount of Olives opposite the temple, Peter, James, John, and Andrew asked him privately, "Tell us,
when will this be, and what will be the sign that all these things
are about to be accomplished?"

What follows is a catalog of so-called "messianic woes," events such
as the persecution of the saints and the appearance of dread cosmic
portents ("the sun will be darkened, and the moon will not give its
light" [v. 24]) that precede the time of messianic blessing. It is not clear

---

44. See Matt. 23:37-39//Luke 13:34-35; Mark 13:1-4 par.; 14:58 par.; 15:29 par.; Luke
23:27-31; John 2:19.

how Jesus' response answers the disciples' question. It is possible that Jesus believed that the dominion of God would arrive soon after the temple's destruction, but other verses point to a more distant expectation; for example, Mark 13:5-8:

> Then Jesus began to say to them, "Beware that no one leads you astray. Many will come in my name and say, 'I am he!' and they will lead many astray. When you hear of wars and rumors of wars, do not be alarmed; this must take place, but the end is still to come. For nation will rise against nation, and kingdom against kingdom; there will be earthquakes in various places; there will be famines. This is but the beginning of the birth pangs."

We are also told that "the good news must first be proclaimed to all nations" (v. 10; cf. Matt. 24:14). Even more striking is Jesus' statement in v. 32 ("But about that day or hour no one knows, neither the angels in heaven, nor the Son, but only the Father"), which stands in tension with most of the preceding section, particularly verse 30 ("Truly I tell you, this generation will not pass away until all these things have taken place").

Many scholars suspect that Mark 13 has been shaped significantly by the perspectives and concerns of the mid to late first-century church. This is one of several instances in which I am inclined to accept such a conclusion. Mark 13 deals with the time inhabited by the NT writers, that is, the period during and after the sack of Jerusalem in A.D. 70. (Note the "As for yourselves . . ." in v. 9.) Moreover, many of the apocalyptic elements of this chapter are unparalleled elsewhere in the Gospels. It is possible that Jesus said these things, but it seems just as likely (if not more so) that these verses reflect primarily the hopes, experiences, and concerns of believers a generation removed from Jesus. This can be seen most clearly in Luke 21:20-24, which jettisons the "desolating sacrilege" of Daniel 9:27 and Mark 13:14 and appears to rewrite the remaining prediction to correspond to the events of A.D. 70.

Despite these difficulties, the big picture is fairly clear: Jesus spoke of the destruction of Jerusalem, and he anticipated the coming of the Son of Man and the reign of God. How these elements fit together, if at all, and when and how he imagined these things would occur is almost wholly uncertain. We should honestly face the possibility that Jesus expected a fairly immediate and traditionally apocalyptic climax to history. For me, the problem comes not in factoring such a conclusion into my theology. Any viable Christology (doctrine of Christ) must take seriously Jesus' human limitations, which, after all, he himself is said to have admitted (Mark 13:32). The difficulty lies in our inability to be sure that this is, in fact, the right conclusion. It is equally possible that Jesus held fairly indefinite expectations that were filled out by the church in response to its own experiences of hardship and persecution. Such is certainly the case in the book of Revelation, which borrows heavily from earlier apocalyptic tradition, allowing, among other things, for a depiction of Christ as a warrior (Rev. 19:11-21).

In summary, Jesus believed both in the mercy of God and in future judgment. This is nothing unusual; a great many Jews and Christians have believed the same. Nevertheless, this affirmation compels us to take seriously dimensions of Jesus' teaching that we might prefer to overlook. The Jesus of the Gospels is not so comfortable a figure as we might imagine or like him to be.

6. *Jesus will be vindicated.*

[T]here is no reason why Jesus should not have made such a forecast [of his death]; only . . . as a reasonable man (to say no more) he cannot have left the matter, and the forecast, there. We cannot imagine that he would say, "It is clear that, if I pursue my present course, my adversaries will attempt to put me out of the way. Indeed, I fear they will succeed in doing this, and so my proclamation of the kingdom will come to an end, and we shall all be back where we were when I began my ministry." If Jesus had nothing better to say than this he would presumably have withdrawn, recognizing the argument of *force majeure*. This conclusion he must have drawn, however, *unless he was able not only to foretell his death but also to interpret it in the same eschatological context in which he interpreted his ministry as a whole.* We thus reach the conclusion that if Jesus predicted his death (and there is no reason why he should not have done so), he also interpreted it.[45]

45. C. K. Barrett, *Jesus and the Gospel Tradition* (London: SPCK, 1967), pp. 37-38 (italics mine).

Jesus understood his immediate messianic task to be the division of Israel between faith and unfaith; and he understood his messianic destiny (formally, enthronement and rule) to be scheduled for fulfillment only as the outcome and reversal of repudiation, suffering, and death.[46]

In other words, Jesus expected to be put to death and yet continued to believe that his purpose would succeed, that he would be vindicated by God, even if such vindication came only beyond the grave. Had Jesus imagined that his ministry could be thwarted by death, he could have taken steps to avoid it. Instead, he stayed the course, wishing that some other path were available (Mark 14:32-42), but resolute in his conviction that he was doing God's work and fulfilling God's will. Believing that he would die, he interpreted the meaning of his death to his followers at the Last Supper. It is of no small significance that the Synoptic account of the Last Supper tradition includes the expectation of eschatological vindication:

> "Truly I tell you, I will never again drink of the fruit of the vine until that day when I drink it new in the kingdom of God." (Mark 14:25 par.)

Jesus' acceptance of Calvary was made possible by his belief in resurrection and by his identification with the Son of Man, who must suffer before glorification. Many commentators believe that Daniel's Son of Man came to be seen (or was even meant to be seen originally) as a corporate symbol for the suffering people of Israel, who would rise again and rule. Thus, the themes of suffering, resurrection, and vindication may already have been associated with the Son of Man. In identifying himself with that figure, Jesus might even have thought that he acted on behalf and in the place of Israel.

If Jesus expected to die, and if he believed that his death would be both meaningful and necessary, what are we to make of the cry of dereliction, "My God, my God, why have you forsaken me?" (Mark 15:34)? Did Jesus die a broken and disappointed man, having expected God to rescue him from the cross? That conclusion runs counter to the many

---

46. Ben Meyer, *The Aims of Jesus*, p. 216.

passages that show Jesus both anticipating and accepting his death. It is no more likely that the early church invented Jesus' prayer in Gethsemane than that it fabricated his cry upon the cross, since both show Jesus in a decidedly human light. In his anguished struggle in the Garden, Jesus chooses to accept his fate. If that fate is deliverance, why the anguish?

Many interpreters have pointed to the fact that Jesus' words were taken from the opening verse of Psalm 22, which affirms trust in God despite the author's obvious distress. The description of suffering in Psalm 22 is especially applicable to crucifixion and so became a lens through which the early church thought about Jesus' death. In quoting its first verse, Jesus might well have had the entirety of the psalm in mind. Indeed, some have seen in the Psalm's closing "he has done it" a parallel to Jesus' final words in John, "It is finished" (John 19:30). Many interpreters dismiss such explanations, not wanting to diminish the agony they hear in Jesus' voice. By all accounts, Jesus felt himself in close communion with God, shown most clearly by his use of the familiar title *abba* (rather like the intimate "Daddy" in English). Perhaps Jesus felt the loss of that communion in the extremity of his crucifixion. His cry may therefore — especially in light of its context in Psalm 22 — also have been a prayer that he would not be abandoned in the hour of his death. Of course, we cannot read Jesus' mind, and so the matter will have to be left unresolved. The surest course is to read Mark 15:34 in light of all of the available evidence, which overwhelmingly supports the conclusion that Jesus expected to die and yet still to be vindicated by God. Certainly that is the view of Mark himself, who was assured of Jesus' victory and yet acutely mindful of its cost.

Conclusion

For some, the conclusion that Jesus fits within the world of first-century Jewish eschatology comes as bad news. One reason is anti-Semitism, often manifest in the belief that Jesus is true and important only to the extent he overcomes and overthrows Jewish belief. Another reason is the seeming irrelevance and inaccessibility of the eschatological Jesus. That is a problem for interpreters representing a very wide range of perspectives, all of whom would claim Jesus as their own. In truth, Jesus was not a secularist nor a Christian fundamentalist nor even a liberal Protestant. The desire to make Jesus relevant is understandable and, I think, commendable; nevertheless, true relevance is not achieved by re-creating Jesus in the image of his modern admirers.

Our brief study of Jesus' eschatological perspective presses us to take seriously his humanity. To a degree that we might find difficult to acknowledge, Jesus saw his world in his world's terms. To think of Jesus realistically as modern Christians is to think of Jesus incarnationally. Jesus lived and thought within the setting and limitations of his time. That does not mean that his hopes were misplaced. It does however require us to understand that Jesus' expectations for the future were shaped by and expressed in the symbols of his time, as, for example, in Mark 13:24-26:

> "But in those days, after that suffering, the sun will be darkened, and the moon will not give its light, and the stars will be falling from heaven, and the powers in the heavens will be shaken. Then they will see 'the Son of man coming in clouds' with great power and glory."

It is not incumbent upon modern Christians to believe that stars will fall or that the Son of Man will ride on the clouds. As we saw earlier, eschatological beliefs are at heart theological affirmations, claims about the nature and purpose of God. If anything is certain about Jesus, it is his conviction that God would one day be victorious over the powers of evil and death. It was the judgment of the early church that Jesus was right. It is to their testimony that we now turn.

CHAPTER SEVEN

The Once and Future Kingdom

M y brother, sister, and I were decent, law-abiding children, usually. Now and again, however, one of us would overstep the parental line, and, more often than not, we would get caught. (See previous section on "judgment.") I say "we" because it was not always clear which of the three of us was the transgressor. "Who's been drinking from the milk carton?" "Not me," we would each plead innocently. Once again, it appeared, our sacred hearth had been invaded by gremlins, no doubt the same troublesome sprites known for depositing crumbs on the carpet and switching on lights in rooms vacated by children hours before. My parents were unimpressed by our denials; unfortunately for us, they were after cause and effect, not gnomes in the Frigidaire.

Each link in the historical chain is connected to the one before it. The prophets make sense in light of Israel's covenantal history. Early apocalyptic literature makes sense in light of the prophetic writings. Jesus makes sense in light of Jewish apocalyptic expectation. The first-century church makes sense in light of Jesus. Each new development builds on and modifies what came before. Change happens, but in ways that seem sensible, even predictable, at least with historical hindsight.

The first-century church makes sense in light of Jesus. It is not necessary to interpose a poltergeist (the Gnostic inner circle, the "Q community") between Jesus and Christianity to explain either. The ways in which Jesus' ideas were expanded, altered, and developed by his subsequent followers are readily understandable. Christianity is a new link, to be sure, but in an existing chain. Christianity is not discontinuous with Jesus any more than Jesus is discontinuous with Judaism.

In many important ways, the early church's expectations for the future mirrored those of Jesus himself. Both expected the coming of God's great eschatological victory. Both anticipated the arrival of one who would fulfill the role of Daniel's (and Enoch's) Son of Man. The early church unambiguously identified Jesus with this figure, now vindicated and enthroned in power. So the prediction of the coming of the Son of Man in Matthew (24:30-31) becomes a promise of the Lord's return in Paul (1 Thess. 4:15-18). The picture is essentially the same, although it is now viewed from a different vantage point.

The change in perspective between Jesus and his followers came principally as the result of the crucifixion and resurrection. These were End Times events on which the church looked *back;* they were eschatological work already done. In the crucifixion, Christians saw the climactic battle between the powers of good and evil. Wrote Paul, "None of the rulers of this age understood this; for if they had, they would not have crucified the Lord of glory" (1 Cor. 2:8). Sin was judged on the cross and its dominion broken. Paul himself held a strongly "participationist" view of the crucifixion; in effect, what happened to Christ, happened to all believers: "I have been crucified with Christ; and it is no longer I who live, but it is Christ who lives in me" (Gal. 2:19b-20a).

Jesus' death was thought (universally, it appears) by Christians to have made a decisive difference in the relationship between humanity and God. So widespread and so early is the appearance of this belief that it seems likely to have originated with Jesus himself, as indeed the Lord's Supper tradition attests. The position of 1 Peter is typical:

> He himself bore our sins in his body on the cross, so that, free from sins, we might live for righteousness; by his wounds you have been healed. For you were going astray like sheep, but now you have returned to the shepherd and guardian of your souls. (1 Peter 2:24-25; note the allusion to Isa. 53:6)

The cross was perceived as an eschatological event, albeit an eschatological event that lies in the past. This is all the more true of the resurrection of Jesus, without which the cross itself would be a symbol of defeat. As we saw in Chapter One, the resurrection was the engine that drove the early church. Christianity could not have come into existence apart from the firm conviction that Jesus was risen and vindicated by God. A dead Messiah is no Messiah at all. Of course, the expectation of Jesus' return is grounded in the belief in his resurrection, as is the hope of the resurrection of believers in the last day:

> [F]or as all die in Adam, so all will be made alive in Christ. But each in his own order: Christ the first fruits, then at his coming those who belong to Christ. (1 Cor. 15:22-23)

Note that resurrection is still future for everyone but Jesus. That does not mean that the benefits of the resurrection were thought to be entirely unavailable in the present moment. The NT speaks of the resurrection as an act of God's power (e.g., Mark 12:24; 1 Cor. 6:14; 15:43; Col. 2:12). Participation in Christ's resurrection was thought to confer present-day spiritual power on believers, as in Ephesians 1:18-20:

> [W]ith the eyes of your heart enlightened, you may know what is the hope to which he has called you . . . and what is the immeasurable greatness of his power for us who believe, according to the working of his great power. God put this power to work in Christ when he raised him from the dead and seated him at his right hand in the heavenly places. . . .

The degree to which it was thought that believers already lived in the state of resurrection power varied widely (see below). Obviously, it is an attractive idea. Who among us would not like to possess power against evil, sickness, and the like? Its allure was not lost on the early Christians, some of whom embraced the idea a bit too enthusiastically. That seems to have been the problem at Corinth, where, it appears, believers had become so convinced of their present-day spirituality, evidenced by gifts of the Spirit, that they saw no need for a future resurrection. They had it all, here and now (1 Cor. 15:12). Paul lets them know in no uncertain terms that they were a great deal less spiritual than they supposed and that a future resurrection was still required: "If for this life only we have hoped in Christ, we are of all people most to be pitied" (1 Cor. 15:19). Similarly, the book of 2 Timothy records a dispute caused by "Hymenaeus and Philetus," who asserted that the resurrection had already taken place (2:17-18).

The greatness of Christ's achievement led many Christians to believe that they were living in the Last Days, on the very cusp of the New Age. According to Hebrews,

> Long ago God spoke to our ancestors in many and various ways by the prophets, but *in these last days he has spoken to us by a Son,* whom he appointed heir of all things, through whom he also created the worlds. (Heb. 1:1-2)

Likewise, 1 Peter 1:20: "He was destined before the foundation of the world, but was revealed *at the end of the ages* for your sake." Such expressions illustrate the already/not-yet eschatological tension that is at the heart of Christianity. We are in a new age, *almost.* Things have already changed because of Christ, but not everything has changed. Theologians often characterize this as a tension between "realized" and "future" eschatologies. A realized eschatology emphasizes what Christ has already accomplished (or realized). A future eschatology emphasizes the victory that is yet to come. In practice, few if any Christians hold entirely to one or the other view. An exclusively future perspective would mean that Christ has yet to achieve anything. A wholly realized eschatology would put us in the doubly disprovable position of claiming both perfection and immortality. Instead, Christians have always maintained both perspectives simultaneously, just as Jesus himself did before them. To a significant extent, Christians are defined by how they effect the balance between these two viewpoints.

As the decades went by, the church (or at least some parts of the church) tended toward an increasingly realized eschatology. A kind of perspectival Doppler shift is evident already in the Gospels: Mark is generally — but not exclusively — on the side of a more future eschatology; Matthew takes a few steps in the opposite direction, followed by Luke and finally by John, who stands furthest to the side of realized eschatology. (We shall return to this point below.) The same shift is evident between the Pauline writings and some of the "deutero-Pauline" epistles (letters written in Paul's name by a later follower). In the undisputed letters of Paul, salvation and resurrection are always future categories. In Ephesians,[1] however, we are told that God

---

1. Scholars have good reason for doubting Paul's authorship of Ephesians. The let-

made us alive together with Christ — by grace you have been saved — and *raised us up with him,* and *seated us with him in the heavenly places* in Christ Jesus. (Eph. 2:5-6)

Similarly, in 1 Corinthians 15:20-28, the subjection of the powers of evil to Christ is spoken of as a future event, but according to Ephesians 1:20-23,

[God] seated him at his right hand in the heavenly places, far above all rule and authority and power and dominion, and above every name that is named, not only in this age but also in the age to come. And *he has put all things under his feet and has made him the head over all things* for the church, which is his body, the fullness of him who fills all in all.

This change in perspective is nowhere explained, but it is not difficult to imagine what might have caused it. The years passed, Christ did not return, and it became increasingly evident that the church might be in it for the long haul. One way of compensating for a more distant eschatological future is by assuming a more realized eschatological present. Hence, ideas that once belonged entirely under the "not yet" heading, such as salvation, resurrection, and eternal life, shifted in time, at least for some, into the "already" column.

Associated with this move came the tendency to exalt the church and depreciate Israel in Christian thinking. In the A.D. 50s, Paul could assume that Israel was still the main player in the eschatological drama. Gentile Christians had been grafted into Israel (Rom. 11:17-24), and some Jews were presently cut off, but the expectation remained that "all Israel" would someday be saved (v. 26). The Gentile church was something of an expedient, necessitated by the fact that Israel had not repented and so Christ had not returned. It is perfectly clear in Romans 11 that the action is centered on Israel. That is no longer the case in most of the NT writings of the late first-century. There the move toward Christian supersessionism, that is, the belief that the church has

---

ter's style is significantly different from that of Paul's undisputed epistles, as is its theology. See Raymond Brown, *An Introduction to the New Testament* (New York: Doubleday, 1997), pp. 627-30.

superseded Israel in God's plan, is well and truly under way. Among the Synoptic Gospels, this change is most evident in Matthew. Compare Matthew with Luke and Mark in the following two passages:

Luke 13:28-29

"There will be weeping and gnashing of teeth when you [evildoers] see Abraham and Isaac and Jacob and all the prophets in the kingdom of God, and you yourselves thrown out. Then people will come from east and west, from north and south, and will eat in the kingdom of God."

Matthew 8:11-12

"I tell you, many will come from east and west and will eat with Abraham and Isaac and Jacob in the kingdom of heaven, *while the heirs of the kingdom will be thrown into the outer darkness,* where there will be weeping and gnashing of teeth."

Mark 12:10-11

"Have you not read this scripture: 'The stone that the builders rejected has become the cornerstone; this was the Lord's doing, and it is amazing in our eyes'?"

Matthew 21:42-43

Jesus said to them, "Have you never read in the scriptures: 'The stone that the builders rejected has become the cornerstone; this was the Lord's doing, and it is amazing in our eyes'? Therefore I tell you, *the kingdom of God will be taken away from you* and given to a people that produces the fruits of the kingdom."

Similar sentiments are found in Matthew's version of the parable of the wedding banquet, which makes this chilling statement about God's attitude toward the Jews:

> "The king was enraged. He sent his troops, destroyed those murderers, and burned their city. Then he said to his slaves, 'The wedding is ready, but those invited were not worthy.'" (Matt. 22:7-8)

Post-Holocaust, it has become increasingly difficult for Christian theologians to affirm these and similar NT statements about the Jews and Judaism. One of the most helpful and refreshing trends in New Testament studies is the reclamation of Romans 11 as a starting point for Christian reflection about Israel. When push came to shove, Paul could not write off the Jews, and neither should we.

The church's diminishing regard for Israel finds a corollary in its increasing estimate of itself. It is the church toward which God's purposes were always directed; it is the church that succeeds where Israel had failed. The exaltation of the church is an especially noteworthy feature of Ephesians, probably written in the late first century. For example, Ephesians 3:9-11 speaks of

> the plan of the mystery hidden for ages in God who created all things; so that through the church the wisdom of God in its rich variety might now be made known to the rulers and authorities in the heavenly places. This was in accordance with the eternal purpose that he has carried out in Christ Jesus our Lord. . . .

Of course, the rancorous divorce between Judaism and Christianity was a major factor in the move toward Christian supersessionism and "triumphalism." It might well have encouraged the church to think in terms of a more realized eschatology, thereby accentuating the perceived differences between Jewish hope and Christian reality. In other words, the more Christ can be said to have accomplished, the more superior the position of Christians to Jews. That is the tactic employed by the author of Hebrews, who, for example, contrasts the perpetually unfinished work of the Jewish priesthood with the completed work of Christ (Heb. 10:1-18). Unlike Jews, Christians may now enter God's presence in the eternal Holy of Holies "by the blood of Jesus, by the new and living way he opened for us through the curtain (that is, through his flesh)" (10:19-20).

The move away from Israel, especially understandable in an increasingly Gentile church, fits hand in glove with a move toward a more heavenly and less earthly eschatological expectation. The "restoration of Israel" was less concrete expectation and more spiritual metaphor as time went by. The recovery of the twelve tribes became a non-issue, as did the repossession of the land. Altogether, there was more talk of heavenly and less talk of earthly paradise, although the latter did not disappear entirely (as in Rev. 21).[2] This change in perspective is so in-

---

2. Note that "heaven" itself was a Jewish idea, as we saw in our study of 1 Enoch. It was not the dominant eschatological theme in Judaism, however, nor (as far as we can tell) was it often held to the exclusion of belief in an earthly restoration.

grained that many of my students find it hard to accept that Christians ever believed in a literal, earthly dominion of God. They did, and some still do.

In one form or another, eschatology may be found on almost every page of the New Testament. We could catalog and analyze it until the end of time itself. In the pages that follow, I want to concentrate instead on what I consider to be of greater importance, a deeper look at the dynamic tension inherent in Christian eschatology. Getting a handle on this issue is essential to understanding not only the New Testament but one's own faith and the faith of others. Our brief study will focus primarily on Paul, since he is the NT author about whom we know most and because his theology so perfectly embodies the already-but-not-yet character of Christian thinking.

Which Reality When?

As children of the Enlightenment, we are acutely aware of the tension between religious and scientific accounts of reality. The history of modern theology is to a large extent the chronicle of our attempt to accommodate the logic of divine initiative to the logic of cause and effect. William Dyrness put it this way in his *Learning about Theology from the Third World:*

> Above, God rules and is concerned with the eternal destiny of people; below, matter operates according to scientific laws. . . . I have participated in theological arguments . . . where we have tried to determine how far down the scale God's interest goes before the reign of natural law takes over. Clearly we should pray for a job if we are unemployed, but should we pray for a parking place when we are late to a meeting?[3]

Contemporary Christians are caught in this dilemma. When pastors visit the sick, do they say "be comforted" or "rise up and walk"? If modern believers operate out of two logical systems, one material and

---

3. William Dyrness, *Learning about Theology from the Third World* (Grand Rapids: Zondervan, 1990), p. 187.

the other spiritual, when is which employed? When it thunders, do we conclude that God is angry, or do we look for a naturalistic explanation? How many coincidences does it take to make Providence? In short, where, when, how, and to what extent does God act in the world? All Christians (and many others besides) operate with unwritten rules that guide them in such matters. Where those rules differ, significant theological disagreements are inevitable.

It is important to note that religious accounts of reality have always been subject to competition and question, not least from the side of material explanation. It is a modern prejudice to assume that natural causation was only recently discovered. It was a standard polemic in ancient Judaism that idols are *only* objects of wood and stone.[4] Similarly, the Hebrew Bible warns repeatedly of false prophets who give oracles of their own devising.[5] In the NT, one frequently encounters the argument that Christianity was divinely initiated and so is not "merely human."[6] The tension between religious and material explanations is more pronounced today because the explanatory power of science is so much more evident, but the tension has always been there. Which leads to the next point.

When the NT talks about God acting in this world, it characteristically employs the language of eschatology. Why? Because, from the point of view of first-century Judaism, the coming of the Messiah is an eschatological hope. As we have seen, in Jesus' own ministry, one hears strong notes of both future and realized eschatologies. Post-resurrection, the church can say that it exists in a new era and that the last hour is at hand. At heart, all Christian language is eschatological language.

The distinction between realized and future eschatologies is vital and needs to be clarified. If I say, for example, that the Gospel of John evidences a strongly (but not fully) realized eschatology, I am not saying that Johannine Christians did not believe in Christ's future return. What I mean is that, for them, the benefits of God's great eschatological work in Christ are largely available here and now. How much has changed because of Christ? *A lot.* Such Christians perceive themselves

---

4. Deut. 4:28; 2 Chron. 32:19; Ps. 135:15; Isa. 40:19; etc.

5. Deut. 18:20-22; Jer. 5:12-13; 23:31-32; Lam. 2:14; etc.

6. Matt. 21:25; Mark 7:8; Rom. 9:16; 1 Cor. 9:8; 2 Cor. 5:16; Gal. 1:11-12; Col. 2:8, 22; 1 Thess. 2:13; 2 Peter 1:21; etc.

to be quite different from other people, living in a quite different reality. At the extreme end, think of modern groups that teach that no believer should be sick since Christ has borne our infirmities on the cross and conquered the powers of evil in the resurrection. (All such believers still die, a fact that does seem to faze them.)

Groups with a strongly realized eschatology typically look to the resurrection as the event that defines Christian reality. Of course: it is the example *par excellence* of God's intervening in the material order, overturning the ultimate natural effect, death. So in John there is little emphasis on the cross and much emphasis on the resurrection. Eternal life is a present as well as future category, something already experienced by believers.[7] In John, the crucifixion merges with the resurrection as "the hour" of Jesus' "glorification" (e.g., John 12:23-24); there is no agony in the garden, no cry of dereliction from the cross. Throughout the narrative, Jesus appears to walk six inches off the ground. There is a profound sense of God's presence, control, and immediate activity.

The counterexample is Mark, which tends toward a more future eschatology. To the extent that one holds to a future eschatology, one regards God's eschatological victory as something yet to be experienced. For example, Christians may be forgiven, but they are still sinners like other people. Essential change is yet to come. In Mark, the paradigm for Christian reality is unquestionably the cross of Christ: discipleship is defined as taking up one's cross and following Jesus (Mark 8:34). By contrast, the resurrection fades almost entirely from view. If the resurrection may be employed as a symbol of God's presence in and power over materiality, the cross may be used as a symbol of natural causality's triumph and God's apparent absence: "My God, my God, why have you forsaken me?" (Mark 15:34). A perception of present life grounded in the cross is going to look very different from one grounded in the resurrection.

Note that the cross is used in two fundamentally different ways. With respect to the work of Christ, it is past and refers to work already accomplished; hence, it fits under the heading of realized eschatology. With respect to the life of discipleship, however, the cross stands for a work in progress, the believer's present experience of suffering, weak-

---

7. E.g., John 3:36; 4:14; 5:24; 6:47; 10:10, 28; 11:25.

ness, and foolishness (I Cor. 1:18-31). Here, it is not a symbol of power or rescue but of self-emptying and self-denial. An expectation of final victory remains, but it lies primarily in the future. It is in this sense that the cross is a paradigm for future eschatology.

It may help us to get a handle on the tension between future and realized eschatologies if we see it as a Christian expression of the larger tension between material and spiritual, "scientific" and "religious" accounts of reality, as in the following diagram:

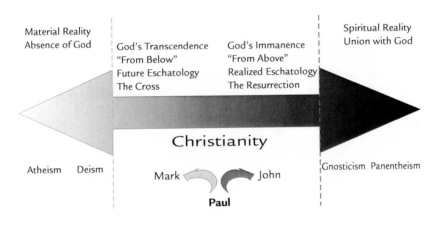

On this spectrum, future eschatologies tend by degrees toward increasingly material versions of reality and thus toward more human depictions of Jesus, as in Mark, and realized eschatologies toward more spiritual understandings of reality and thus toward more divine depictions of Jesus, as in John. It is no surprise therefore that, with notable exceptions, Mark has gained and John lost popularity among modern, critically educated Christians. Mark simply is more like us. Similarly, we should not wonder that rationalist scholars can scarcely resist the temptation to de-eschatologize Jesus, that is, to pull him over to their spot on the left side of the diagram.

I have placed Christianity between two dashed lines. The larger spectrum extends from the left extreme, a fully materialist view of reality, to the right extreme, in which only spirit is real. At these ends of the spectrum God is either fully absent (left) or fully present (right; that is, the individual in some essential way *is* God). Correspondingly, as one moves out from Christianity to the left, one might go from Deism

(God exists but is not present) to Atheism (God is so absent as to not exist). On the right, one moves beyond Christianity into Gnosticism (matter is real but only spirit is good) into a viewpoint like that of Pantheism or Panentheism (everything is spirit and is united in God).

Within the space occupied by Christianity, there is tension between God's transcendence, on the left side, and God's immanence, on the right. This is theological language for God's absence and presence. Those with a more material viewpoint will gravitate toward a more transcendent view of God, and so on. Likewise, those edging toward the left side of the line are likely to think about theological issues inductively, that is, "from below," beginning with material evidence. Those on the right side of the divide will tend to think about theology deductively, "from above," based on spiritual truths. This distinction is especially evident in Christology, the study of Christ. Is the proper starting point the dirt of Galilee or the creed of Nicea? The loss of favor of the second option goes with the shift among modern theologians toward a more material view of reality. For some, if it cannot be demonstrated archaeologically, it cannot be true theologically.

As I have said, future eschatology makes fewer claims about the present and so is more appealing to those who do not see Christians as being all that different from other people and who do not believe that God delivers them from unfortunate or even tragic circumstances. Pastors who think this way will probably preach a lot about the human example of Christ and the need for personal sacrifice. In other words, they will preach the cross. Realized eschatology fits the worldview of those who consider Christians to be of a fundamentally different character from other people and who think that God is actively intervening both to protect and direct their lives. Preachers of this stripe are likely to talk a good deal about God's power and presence, in other words, about the resurrection.

I have placed Mark and John on this chart somewhat left and right of center respectively. The point is not to locate them precisely but to show that while they represent different perspectives, neither is an extreme view, representing an entirely future or realized eschatology. But what of Paul? His is an especially interesting and complicated case. On the one hand, for example, Paul regards spiritual gifts as mere seal or foretaste of the future reality. Such things are of limited usefulness; "when the perfect comes," they will pass away (1 Cor. 13:8-

13). On the other hand, Christians are said now to possess (or to be possessed by) the Spirit to such an extent that they are set free from the power of sin and so do the will of God in a manner impossible for others, including Jews (Rom. 8:4). The duality of Paul's perspective is jarring: it is like Mark with large Johannine interpolations, like a brain surgeon with a weekend exorcism ministry. Granted that nearly all Christians have a foot in each camp, how far can one spread one's feet and still stand?

Paul in Two Minds

Two essential convictions appear to underlie most of what is distinctive in Pauline theology. Both may have arisen directly out of Paul's "conversion" experience, and both affected deeply his perception of reality, his conception of what life now is and means, of what has changed because of Christ and what remains the same. The first of these convictions is this: *Jesus, the crucified, is the Christ (the Messiah)*. In other words, it is the paradigm of the cross.

It is likely that the pre-Christian Paul regarded it as impossible that a crucified man could be God's Messiah. The Pauline phrase "Christ crucified" (1 Cor. 1:23) would, for the younger Paul, have been an oxymoron. A "crucified Christ" is, like "dried water," a contradiction in terms.

When, as a Christian, Paul takes up the matter of unbelief, he has this to say:

> For the message about the cross is foolishness to those who are perishing, but to us who are being saved it is the power of God. . . . For Jews demand signs and Greeks desire wisdom, but we proclaim Christ crucified, a stumbling block to Jews and foolishness to Gentiles, but to those who are the called, both Jews and Greeks, Christ the power of God and the wisdom of God. For God's foolishness is wiser than human wisdom, and God's weakness is stronger than human strength. (1 Cor. 1:18, 22-25)

Christian proclamation is specifically proclamation of the cross. Compare Paul's statement in 1 Corinthians 2:1-2:

When I came to you, brothers and sisters, I did not come proclaiming the mystery of God to you in lofty words or wisdom. For I decided to know nothing among you except Jesus Christ, and him crucified.

2 Corinthians 13:4 speaks of the weakness of Jesus on the cross: "He was crucified in weakness, but lives by the power of God. For we are weak in him. . . ." It is precisely the weakness of Christ that most distinguishes him in Paul's mind. Consider the famous description of Philippians 2:5-8:

Let the same mind be in you that was in Christ Jesus, who, though he was in the form of God, did not regard equality with God as something to be exploited, but emptied himself, taking the form of a slave, being born in human likeness. And being found in human form, he humbled himself and became obedient to the point of death — even death on a cross.

Note that the whole ministry of Jesus is characterized by emptying, humbling, and serving. This is the way Paul *came* to view Jesus.

Not only is the cross an instance of human weakness; it even can be considered a sign of God's curse, which is the ultimate weakness; one cannot go any lower than to be cursed by God. As Paul writes in Galatians 3:13:

Christ redeemed us from the curse of the law by becoming a curse for us — for it is written, "Cursed is everyone who hangs on a tree." (citing Deut. 21:23)

That the cross is central to Paul's own self-conception is evidenced, for example, by Galatians 6:14:

May I never boast of anything except the cross of our Lord Jesus Christ, by which the world has been crucified to me, and I to the world.

Within an extended argument in 2 Corinthians about boasting in human appearances, Paul makes the following statement:

From now on, therefore, we regard no one from a human point
of view; even though we once knew Christ from a human point
of view, we know him no longer in that way. (2 Cor. 5:16)

It is evident that the "human point of view" from which Paul once
regarded Jesus concerned his outward appearance, which was evaluated
superficially, "humanly," and thus wrongly. There was more to Jesus
the crucified than met the eye. It seems reasonable to suppose that the
cross had been the stumbling-block over which Paul the Pharisee had
himself tripped. Specifically, Paul could not understand how a weak,
powerless, rejected-by-Jewish-leaders, crucified-by-Roman-authorities,
and cursed-by-God man could be Messiah. The cross is weakness, foolishness, humiliation, suffering — even cursing. That is not how God
works, is it? God is present in the world in signs, acts of power, deliverance, and wisdom. The Messiah is the victor, not the victim, right?

Somewhere in the environs of Damascus Paul's perspective
changed — radically, forever. Thus, Paul's conversion was a conversion
to a new way of thinking about reality. In effect, what had been the dynamic center of Paul's unbelief became the dynamic center of his belief.
The Gospel is "the word of the cross" and Paul's ministry "the preaching of the cross."

The resurrection, like salvation, is a future category in the undisputed Pauline epistles; therefore, it is not a dominant paradigm for
contemporary Christian life. What is our present situation? In this
world we groan, we are downtrodden, we know in part, we live the cross.
Apostleship is not evidenced so much in the multiplication of spiritual
gifts as in the endurance of multiple sufferings. From the cross, Paul
derives a tough, gritty realism. Here, Paul tips the balance decidedly in
favor of the "not yet"; here, Paul sees shades of gray; here, Paul speaks
of uncertainty and finitude. God works by the agency of human weakness; claims to strength, knowledge, wisdom, and power may be signals
of human self-assertion and lostness, not divine favor and presence.
Here, to my mind, is Paul at his best and most persuasive.

This line of reasoning, however, was not most persuasive to Paul's
churches. For example, almost all of Paul's problems at Corinth arose
from the fact that the Corinthians still looked at persons — Jesus, Paul,
each other — in the old way, based on outward appearance, status,
strength, wisdom, gifts. They certainly viewed religion in the old way,

expecting immediate salvation, instant gratification and rewards. In the classic tension between the already and the not yet, the Corinthians had gone over almost entirely to the side of the already. They already experienced resurrection life (1 Cor. 15); they already were "mature," "wise," and "knowledgeable" (1 Cor. 2:6; 3:1-3; 8:1-13). Paul wrote scathingly of their pretension:

> Already you have all you want! Already you have become rich! Quite apart from us you have become kings! Indeed, I wish that you had become kings, so that we might be kings with you! For I think that God has exhibited us apostles as last of all, as though sentenced to death, because we have become a spectacle to the world, to angels and to mortals. We are fools for the sake of Christ, but you are wise in Christ. We are weak, but you are strong. You are held in honor, but we in disrepute. To the present hour we are hungry and thirsty, we are poorly clothed and beaten and homeless, and we grow weary from the work of our own hands. When reviled, we bless; when persecuted, we endure; when slandered, we speak kindly. We have become like the rubbish of the world, the dregs of all things, to this very day. (1 Cor. 4:8-13)

We could ask for no better summary of the two differing ways of viewing reality, of the two differing models of spirituality. But there is another side to Paul, one that thinks out of the logic of a realized eschatological order, one that sees things in straightforwardly black-or-white terms. This stream of Pauline thought appears to issue from another bedrock conviction: *already there is one people of God without distinction.* The inclusion of Gentiles is profoundly important (perhaps uniquely important) to Paul. A justified Gentile affects Paul in much the same way as does a crucified Messiah: it fundamentally challenges, even reverses, his perception of reality.

The inclusion of Gentiles is a realized eschatological expectation (e.g., Isa. 66 below), and as such it has the potential to shift one's notion of where one stands in the eschatological timetable. In other words, where Paul's thinking is grounded in the reality of full Gentile inclusion, it tends strongly toward a realized eschatology; these are the places where Paul's epistles are most reminiscent of John's Gospel. Elsewhere, Paul tends toward a more future eschatology, especially as

Two Trajectories in Paul's Thought

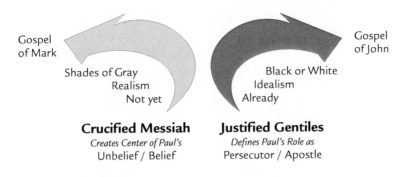

Gospel
of Mark

Shades of Gray
Realism
Not yet

Crucified Messiah
Creates Center of Paul's
Unbelief / Belief

Black or White
Idealism
Already

Justified Gentiles
Defines Paul's Role as
Persecutor / Apostle

Gospel
of John

he draws on the cross to counter what he perceives to be the excesses of his converts. This is Paul at his most Markan.

The shift in the way Paul thinks is so striking that I am led to wonder whether the inclusion of Gentiles was one of Paul's reasons, perhaps *the* reason, for his persecution of Christians (at Damascus, let us not forget). Evidence for this view might be found in Galatians 5:11 and 6:12, in which the circumcision-free gospel to the Gentiles is linked directly to persecution. Note the association of the cross, persecution, and the circumcision-free gospel in each verse:

> Why am I still being persecuted if I am still preaching circumcision? In that case the offense of the cross has been removed.

> It is those who want to make a good showing in the flesh that try to compel you to be circumcised — only that they may not be persecuted for the cross of Christ.

Why would the admission of Gentiles be grounds for persecuting the church? The inclusion of non-Jews *as non-Jews* could have been seen to threaten the existence of Israel. To redefine a group's boundaries is to redefine that group. One can imagine that Jewish leaders would have objections to Christianity as a purely Jewish phenomenon. For someone like Paul, "being . . . exceedingly zealous for the traditions of my ancestors" (Gal. 1:14), the inclusion of uncircumcised Gentiles might well have been the last straw.

According to Galatians 1:16, the risen Christ was revealed to Paul, "that I might proclaim him among the Gentiles." What Galatians implies is said explicitly in Acts (e.g., 9:15): Paul was from the first an apostle to the Gentiles. Why are the Gentiles now so important to Paul? Probably because, like the cross, they already were. The generative, motivating, central questions had not changed, but the answers had — and that, in a way, changed everything. So, Paul made the ultimate career move: he changed worlds as well as jobs. Paul the apostle preached the cross to Gentiles.

What is so interesting is that this second conviction drives Paul in a direction opposite to that to which he is driven by his belief about the cross. Already there is one unified people of God. Acceptance of the Gentiles is no expedient, no half solution awaiting resolution at the return of Christ. The eschatological intentions of, for example, Isaiah 66, already are being fulfilled:

> I am coming to gather all nations and tongues; and they shall come and shall see my glory, and I will set a sign among them. From them I will send survivors to the nations . . . that have not heard of my fame or seen my glory; and they shall declare my glory among the nations. They shall bring all your kindred from all the nations as an offering to the Lord . . . to my holy mountain Jerusalem, says the Lord, just as the Israelites bring a grain offering in a clean vessel to the house of the Lord. And I will also take some of them as priests and Levites, says the Lord. (Isaiah 66:18b-21)

Paul as the apostle to the Gentiles is the one above all others through whom these expectations are being realized (Gal. 2:7-9); see for example Paul's discussion in Romans 15 of the offering of the Gentiles (that is, the offering that is the Gentiles themselves, not just the Gentiles' money) that he is take to Jerusalem (cf. Isa. 2:1-4; 42:1-9; 49; 55:4-5; 60:1-7; 66:18-23). Paul refers to his ministry both here and in Philippians 4:18 in priestly language that reflects the usage of Isaiah.

This is realized eschatology. The promised inclusion of Gentiles is a present reality. *Therefore, when the issue of Gentile admission is at the forefront, Paul's way of talking about reality alters perceptibly.* One might say that he shifts his weight to the foot planted in realized eschatology. Now views are clear-cut, sharply focused, and starkly drawn. Theological concerns that are logically derivative of The Gentile Question are worked out from that same perspective and with that same root logic. One example is Paul's "Christian anthropology," that is, his notion of how Christians are different from other people. The starting point for his thinking is the new, unified people of God; therefore, Paul's anthropology is grounded in a realized eschatology similar to that of John, containing an amazingly optimistic view of insiders and a surprisingly negative view of outsiders. Christians are "in the Spirit"; all others are "in the flesh." Christians are equipped to do the will of God; all others are not (Rom. 8:1-9). Paul is pushed in this direction by his need to justify the inclusion of Gentiles as equal covenant partners with Jews. The present state of believers must be substantially different from that of unbelievers (read "Jews") if obedience to the law, and conversion to Judaism with it, is no longer necessary. But for the law not to be necessary, Christians must be a quite different sort of people, in fact, an entirely "new creation" (2 Cor. 5:17).

Paul's perception of non-Christian Judaism is also derivative of the Gentile question and so is viewed primarily from the perspective of a realized eschatology. The more and greater the immediate effects of Christ's ministry for Christians, the greater is the perceived theological distance between Christians and Jews. The more the haves have, the more the have nots have not. There is a strong tendency in such thinking to strip everything positive from Judaism and transfer it to Christianity. Think of John 1:17: "The law came through Moses; grace and truth came through Jesus Christ." Do any of us really believe that there was neither grace nor truth in Judaism? It is no accident that Galatians and Romans fail to inform us that Judaism ever knew God's love, mercy, atonement, or forgiveness. Judaism as a religion of faith and grace is an obstacle for Paul, as it has been for many Christians. I regard this as an especially problematic streak in Paul, one that effectively forces him into "zero-sum" thinking in which Judaism becomes the problem that Christianity solves.

The approach to Paul that I have outlined above sheds light on numerous matters, not least the issue of continuity and discontinuity within Paul's theology. It also helps to explain why Paul came to conclusions about Judaism and the law so different from those reached by other Jewish-Christian leaders who also accepted Gentiles into the church. The defining issue was not so much Gentile admission as the present *meaning* of Gentile admission. Again, it is at this point that Paul crosses over to the side of the already, and it is at precisely this point that his arguments become most absolutist. The present reality requires an opposite former reality, *even for Jewish believers.*

Two Patterns of Theological Orientation

I have said that Paul appears to think, to draw warrants and analogies, out of a pair of fundamental convictions about reality that correspond to the categories of future and realized eschatologies. As a modern, scientifically oriented person who also prays, I can well understand what it is like to stand with a foot on each side, shifting my weight between them. This situation is endemic to Christian (as to much other religious) thinking, and has always been the source of a good deal of confusion and disagreement. Obviously, two groups with different conceptions of reality are unlikely to see eye to eye theologically.

In the diagram on page 190, I have laid out several characteristics that typify future and realized eschatologies. Most Christians do not fit entirely on one side or the other, which, I believe, is a sign of theological health. It is those who pursue absolute consistency, those who would collapse the eschatological tension, who are in real danger.

As we have seen, future eschatology emphasizes Jesus' humanity and realized eschatology his divinity. Future eschatology tends toward a less prominent view of the Holy Spirit, which is far more important to realized eschatologies. Churches with a future eschatological orientation tend to be more stable and institutionalized. They often have considerable structure and locate authority in recognized offices and traditions. Such things are much more fluid in a church with a strongly realized eschatology. Authority is more charismatic, and structure tends to be flatter, with fewer levels and intermediaries. A seminary education might not be required of pastors, but gifts of the Spirit certainly will be. A serious problem can occur when pastor and congregation are on opposite sides of the line. In that situation, the pastor's formal authority can be undermined by the charismatic authority exercised by others in the church. In fact, the structural authority of the pastorate in most American denominations has been declining for decades. Pastors cannot rely on rank to lead people who are more impressed with spirituality than with office.

Those with a future eschatological orientation tend toward a more

Two Patterns of Theological Orientation

Future Orientation	Present Orientation
Eschatology: Future	Eschatology: Realized
Theological Paradigm: The Cross	Theological Paradigm: The Resurrection
Examples: Synoptics (Mark); Hebrews	Examples: John; Paul's Corinthian opponents; Ephesians
Many "mainline" Protestants and Catholics	Pentecostals and Charismatics

Characteristic Elements:	*Characteristic Elements:*
Jesus' humanity, suffering, example stressed	Jesus' divinity, triumph, empowering stressed
Spiritual gifts as "foretaste" and "seal"	Possession of the fullness of the Spirit/Jesus' presence
Considerable/stable church structure	Little/fluid church structure
Institutionalized authority, e.g., in office (apostle, pope) and tradition (Bible, councils)	Charismatic authority (prophets, gifts)
Sacramental orientation (e.g., "real presence")	Non-sacramental orientation (spiritual presence)
Can allow shades of gray, degrees of truth	Tendency toward sectarianism, absolute truth
Indefinite/flexible group boundaries (weak cohesion)	High, clear group boundaries (strong cohesion)
Social ethic	Inward looking
Imperfect obedience; realistic "anthropology"	Perfect obedience; idealistic "anthropology"
Social distinctions may be accepted/ reinforced	Social distinctions irrelevant/ overthrown

sacramental theology, putting greater store in God's presence in baptism and communion. This suits a worldview in which God is primarily transcendent. In the sacraments, God throws us a line across the great dividing chasm. To the extent that one is on the side of a realized eschatology, one denies the existence of any such chasm. For that reason, Pentecostals have no more idea what to do with the Eucharist than mainline Protestants do the Baptism of the Holy Spirit (Mark 1:8). Both run against the grain of their theology.

Those with a future eschatology tend to be a bit fuzzy on matters of absolute truth. "We know only in part . . ." (1 Cor. 13:9). Realized eschatology is a good deal more confident about what it knows. Indeed, the boundary between insiders and outsiders is often defined by who knows and who does not know the truth. John 8:31-32:

> Then Jesus said to the Jews who had believed in him, "If you continue in my word, you are truly my disciples; and you will know the truth, and the truth will make you free."

And, more notoriously, John 8:44-47:

> "You are from your father the devil, and you choose to do your father's desires. He was a murderer from the beginning and does not stand in the truth, because there is no truth in him. When he lies, he speaks according to his own nature, for he is a liar and the father of lies. But because I tell the truth, you do not believe me. Which of you convicts me of sin? If I tell the truth, why do you not believe me? Whoever is from God hears the words of God. The reason you do not hear them is that you are not from God."

Group boundaries in general are much better defined by those on the right side of the diagram. Being inside makes one different from other people; consequently, there is a strong sense of group identification. In short, being in matters, and one knows who is in and who is out. On the left side, the insider/outsider distinction is a lot more vague, much like Matthew's parable of the Wheat and the Tares (Matt. 13:24-30), which grow up together and are indistinguishable to everyone but God. Speaking from experience, I know of few groups with a less clearly defined membership than the average Methodist church. Who is in? Who knows?

Groups that are more tightly knit often are more inwardly directed. One of the most interesting contrasts between the Synoptic Gospels and John concerns the commandment to love. In the Synoptics, Jesus orders his followers to love their enemies (e.g., Matt. 5:44). In John, they are told to "love one another" (John 13:34-35). It follows that the left side of the chart (future orientation) is more characteristically associated with social ministries (health care, education, etc.), although that is by no means always true, nor is it the case that all groups with a strongly realized eschatology ignore the physical needs of outsiders.

Realized eschatologies, with their emphasis on the present power of the Holy Spirit and their tendency toward absolutism, are more prone to speak of moral perfection and personal holiness. If Christians are all that well equipped, there simply is no reason to sin. Paul is in this camp,[8] as is John Wesley. As you might expect, future eschatologists see things rather differently. Like Luther, they tend to think of salvation from sin as a forensic category. We are pronounced legally righteous, but remain, for the time being, sinners like everyone else. This is the more realistic view (I myself have yet to know a perfect Christian) but it lacks the dynamism that characterizes the more idealistic perspective of realized eschatology.

Finally, realized eschatologies tend to break down existing social hierarchies and status structures. What matters is who you are in the Spirit, and the Spirit is a great leveler. Recall the story of Peter and Cornelius in Acts 10. The Holy Spirit fell on Cornelius and family, Gentiles all, and Peter had no choice but to baptize them. "[W]ho was I that I could hinder God?" explained Peter to his critics (Acts 11:17). Likewise, many of America's earliest women preachers worked in Pentecostal churches, and modern-day Charismatic gatherings are often a denominational cornucopia. Future eschatologies have the unfortunate tendency of reinforcing present-day systems of status and order. Again, this does not have to be the case, but it all too often is.

---

8. Rom. 7:14-25 ("I do not do the good that I want," etc.) is often incorrectly interpreted as a description of the Christian state. For Paul, nothing could be further from the truth, as is seen in the next chapter (Rom. 8). See my essay on Romans in *The Oxford Bible Commentary* (Oxford: Oxford University Press, 2001).

Both future and present orientations have inherent strengths and weaknesses. It is a strength of future eschatology that it does not offer pie-in-the-sky spirituality. It corresponds to reality as most people know it. Life can be difficult, and being a Christian does not necessarily make it any easier. In fact, it can make life a good deal more challenging. Cross bearing is not fun. There is not something wrong with your faith just because you are suffering. In fact, suffering can be a place of revelation and grace.

Second, future eschatology promotes tolerance. It recognizes the present as a place of incomplete knowledge and imperfect answers. Who are we to say who is and who is not a Christian? Believe and let believe.

Negatively, future eschatology can make the world look unnecessarily bleak. Not much is offered to help us face the present. Future eschatology tells us to endure the cross when what we want is to experience the resurrection. It can even put us on a trajectory toward atheism. If God is so distant as all that, why bother believing?

Some forms of future eschatology also promote passivity, most dangerously, passivity in the face of injustice. The old order is not fundamentally challenged. At worst, this is slave religion. Things will change in the great by and by; in the meantime, get back to your chores. Are prejudice and unrighteousness simply crosses that one must bear? Surely not.

Realized eschatology also has its pluses and minuses. Positively, it can be wonderfully egalitarian and liberating. We are living in a new order. We are not defined by social status or family connections. The family of God transcends all that nonsense: "There is no longer Jew or Greek, there is no longer slave or free, there is no longer male and female; for all of you are one in Christ Jesus" (Gal. 3:28).

Similarly, it is encouraging to think that being a Christian makes a practical difference. God gives us power to overcome. Our circumstances do not imprison us. It is not all "somewhere, over the rainbow"; resurrection life can be experienced here and now.

On the other hand, realized eschatology easily leads to an overestimation of the innocence of insiders and the culpability of outsiders. It does not promote tolerance and empathy and may well encourage sectarianism. It creates an us-vs.-them mindset and cuts believers off from others. I know someone who joined a Christian group with a very advanced case of realized eschatology. He was told that the members of his church were now his only true family, and so he broke off contact with all his relations. Sadly, he will not even allow his parents to visit their grandchildren.

Unchecked, realized eschatology can lead to dangerous forms of hyper-spirituality. Think of snake handlers or faith healers who teach parents to shun medical treatment for their critically ill children. Such thinking is unfettered by reason and leaves chaos in its wake. It has been the cause of innumerable church divisions and Christian excesses over the centuries.

These two perspectives correct one another and need to be held in balance. As I said, Paul takes neither approach to the exclusion of the other, and this may be one of his most valuable legacies. I take encouragement from the fact that Paul himself seemed to live on two different levels, in two different realities, not fully to have understood, but always to have been in the process of understanding.

> For now we see in a mirror, dimly, but then we will see face to face. Now I know only in part; then I will know fully, even as I have been fully known. And now faith, hope, and love abide, these three; and the greatest of these is love. (1 Cor. 13:12-13)

Conclusion

The relationship between Jesus and the early church is marked both by continuity and discontinuity. The same holds true of the relationship between ancient and modern Christians. We are separate links in the same chain. Our job is not to reproduce the New Testament church, which is both impossible and, to a certain extent, undesirable. We live in a different time and must think through our faith for ourselves, albeit with their constant guidance and under their watchful gaze.

The tension between science and religion that has dominated and divided Christian theology in the past century was, in different guise, already present in the thinking of the NT authors. It lies just beneath the surface of eschatology, which to no small degree is about the nature of reality. It is manifest particularly in our attempts to effect a proper balance between realized and future eschatological perspectives. Here as elsewhere, the NT provides us with useful guides and helpful examples. The race is ours to run, but it is a relay, not a marathon. It is up to us to pass on to our descendants a faith that is both coherent and cogent, that is rooted in the past and oriented toward the future.

> Wherefore seeing we also are compassed about with so great a cloud of witnesses, let us lay aside every weight, and the sin which doth so easily beset us, and let us run with patience the race that is set before us, looking unto Jesus the author and finisher of our faith, who for the joy that was set before him endured the cross, despising the shame, and is set down at the right hand of the throne of God. (Heb. 12:1-2, *KJV*)

CONCLUSION

Hope Unseen

We know that the whole creation has been groaning in labor pains un-til now; and not only the creation, but we ourselves, who have the first fruits of the Spirit, groan inwardly while we wait for adoption, the re-demption of our bodies. For in hope we were saved. Now hope that is seen is not hope. For who hopes for what is seen? But if we hope for what we do not see, we wait for it with patience.

(ROM. 8:22-25)

"Hope that is seen is not hope." We do not know what the future holds. We do not know if God's reign will commence in one week or in one billion years. We do not know how earthly history fits in the monumental scheme of cosmic history. We do not even know the hour of our own death, much less the day of our resurrection. But we live in hope. Hope, because we believe that the God who has acted in the past, pre-eminently in Jesus, will act again. God is not done with creation, with Israel, with the church, or with us.

One of the sharpest debates I witnessed as a divinity student con-cerned the resurrection of Jesus. One bloc of seminarians asserted pas-sionately that the resurrection was a now-dispensable encumbrance, an antiquated metaphor that modern believers ought either to reinterpret or discard. Their opponents in turn argued vigorously for the necessity and centrality of Christ's victory over death. This "can't live with it/ can't live without it" exchange epitomizes the contradictory attitudes

196

toward eschatology in the church today. I would locate myself squarely in Group Two; nevertheless, I think that I can understand the others' position. The eschatological dimension of Christianity is burden as well as blessing. Its burden is the requirement of faith. Peter, James, John, and Paul had the benefit of seeing the resurrected Jesus, in whom they witnessed the eschatological future. We have their testimony and example to go on, but we cannot duplicate their experience. Our hope is more unseen. For some, it is a light load. For others, the weight of belief seems unbearable.

"Blessed are those who have not seen and yet have come to believe" (John 20:29). Indeed, the blessings of such faith are many. By such faith believers may live without grasping and may die without fearing. By such faith the church may fulfill its vocation as counter-cultural community, challenging the claims of Caesar and resisting the values of the marketplace. By such faith Christians may honor the election of Israel and may anticipate the redemption of creation.

The Bible provides us with numerous models of hopeful expectation. The dreams, visions, and predictions it records are consistent on some levels and inconsistent on others. The latter fact cautions us against holding too-certain ideas about what lies ahead. We should remember that certainty about God's plan rendered some — including, for a time, the disciples themselves — incapable of recognizing Jesus. Faithfulness does not require such certainty, and easy certainty is a poor substitute for true faith. At its core, eschatology is about the character of God. If God can be trusted, then the future can be trusted with God.

That does not mean that eschatological faith excuses passivity. To the contrary, the believer's vocation, insofar as possible, is to bring the eschatological future into the present. If we anticipate justice, then let us live justly. If we anticipate the end of creation's groaning, then let us live today as healers of creation. This is opposite to the attitude famously displayed by James Watt, Secretary of the Interior under Ronald Reagan, who advocated the wholesale exploitation of natural resources in view of the nearness of Christ's return. Against this view, I invoke the words of Paul in Romans 6:1-4:

> What then are we to say? Should we continue in sin in order that grace may abound? By no means! How can we who died to sin go on living in it? Do you not know that all of us who have been

baptized into Christ Jesus were baptized into his death? Therefore we have been buried with him by baptism into death, so
that, just as Christ was raised from the dead by the glory of the
Father, so we too might walk in newness of life.

We are called to newness of life *now*. The values and priorities of
God's dominion are believed only so far as they are enacted. Eschatological faith demands more, not less, of us. The radical call that Jesus
issued his followers is in perfect proportion to the radicalism of his expectation. Jesus is hard to follow to the very extent that he is hard to
believe. Those who would reject Jesus' eschatology while upholding his
ethic have no idea what they are up against. Eschatological demands require eschatological commitments and eschatological resources.

To live Christianly is to live hopefully. On first glance, Revelation,
that most eschatological of biblical writings, appears dark, dismal, and
foreboding. Its view of the immediate future is thoroughly pessimistic:
the world itself appears to be at war with Christ and his people. Nevertheless, when the book shifts focus to the distant horizon, it radiates
light. It offers a luminous vision for which we may yet hope.

> Then I saw a new heaven and a new earth; for the first heaven
> and the first earth had passed away, and the sea was no more.
> And I saw the holy city, the new Jerusalem, coming down out of
> heaven from God, prepared as a bride adorned for her husband.
> And I heard a loud voice from the throne saying, "See, the home
> of God is among mortals. He will dwell with them as their God;
> they will be his peoples, and God himself will be with them; he
> will wipe every tear from their eyes. Death will be no more;
> mourning and crying and pain will be no more, for the first
> things have passed away." (Rev. 21:1-4)

Not Left Behind

Twenty years ago, it was common knowledge that duodenal ulcers were caused by stress, smoking, diet, and other lifestyle factors. "You'll give yourself an ulcer!" the anxious and overworked were warned. It seemed perfectly obvious. As it turns out, common knowledge was wrong. Spurred by the pioneering work of Dr. Barry J. Marshall of Perth, Australia, scientists now believe that as many as 90 percent of these ulcers are caused by the bacterium *Helicobacter pylori,* which also has been linked to some forms of stomach cancer. As is so often the case, the obstacle that stood between us and the truth was the very thing we thought we already knew.

Millions of Christians today are convinced that Jesus will return secretly to snatch (or "rapture," from the Latin *raptus*) them from the earth. Those "left behind" will endure the horrors of a seven-year "tribulation," after which Christ will return a second time to inaugurate his millennial kingdom. To such persons, it is perfectly obvious. The message is reinforced by most popular Bible teachers and "prophecy scholars," including Tim LaHaye, Hal Lindsey, Kenneth Copeland, Rex Humbard, John Hagee, Jerry Falwell, and John Walvoord. Their message holds sway over vast tracts of the American Evangelical landscape, across which only an occasional dissenting wind blows.[1] For those liv-

---

1. That is not to say that all Evangelicals (or even all Christian fundamentalists) accept this view. The timing of the rapture (before or after the tribulation?) is an especially hot topic in conservative Christian circles. For a balanced presentation of the history of

ing within the territory of this perspective, it is easy to assume that the Bible supports this belief and that Christians have always thought in this way. In fact, both assumptions are wrong.

Background

The idea that Christ will return twice, initially in secret and later in glory, is a central tenet of the interpretive school called "premillennial dispensationalism," which originated in the 1820s and 30s in Ireland and England.[2] Its principal author was the magnetic, autocratic Evangelical clergyman John Nelson Darby.[3] Darby argued that human history spans several ages or "dispensations."[4] In each dispensation, God tests humanity in some new and distinct way. Darby's dispensational-

---

Christian eschatology written from an Evangelical perspective, see Robert G. Clouse, Robert N. Hosack, and Richard V. Pierard, *The New Millennium Manual: A Once and Future Guide* (Grand Rapids: Baker, 1999); and Richard Kyle, *The Last Days Are Here Again: A History of the End Times* (Grand Rapids: Baker, 1998).

2. Like many such movements, dispensationalism has split and evolved into a number of different camps (see Kyle, *Last Days*, p. 117). This short essay focuses on the more traditional forms of premillennial dispensationalism represented in the work of LaHaye and most other popular End Times writers. A particularly interesting development in dispensationalist thinking is the emergence in the past decade of the "progressives," led by, among others, Craig A. Blaising, Darrell L. Bock, and Robert Saucy. While still fundamentalist in orientation, "progressive dispensationalism" has taken greater account of biblical scholarship and has avoided many (although by no means all) of the pitfalls of traditional dispensationalism. Of particular importance is its rejection of the "parenthesis" theory of Darby and its acceptance of a much higher degree of continuity between Israel and the church. See Craig A. Blaising and Darrell L. Bock, *Progressive Dispensationalism* (Wheaton, Ill.: Bridgepoint, 1993), and Robert Saucy, *The Case for Progressive Dispensationalism* (Grand Rapids: Zondervan, 1993).

3. Some elements of or rough parallels to dispensationalism can be found in a handful of previous authors; nevertheless, the system as we know it is chiefly the product of John Nelson Darby's fertile imagination.

4. Dispensationalist authors disagree among themselves about the number and boundaries of these ages. The most widely recognized scenario is that suggested by C. I. Scofield (in the famous *Scofield Reference Bible* of 1909/17), which divides human history into seven dispensations: "innocency (Garden of Eden), conscience (Adam to Noah), human government (Noah to Abraham), promise (Abraham to Moses), Law (Moses to Christ), grace or the church age (from Christ's first to second coming), and the kingdom age or millennium" (Clouse et al., *New Millennium Manual*, p. 59).

ism is "premillennial" in part because it includes the belief that Christ will return on the clouds to gather believers to heaven several years prior to his millennial reign on earth (mentioned only in Rev. 20:1-10). It is this interpretation that is presupposed in the enormously popular *Left Behind* novels of Tim LaHaye and Jerry Jenkins.

The seedbed of dispensationalism was a series of conferences in the 1820s and 30s on the subject of "unfulfilled prophecy."[5] Special attention was given to the unrealized expectations of Israel's glory found in the prophets of the Hebrew Bible.[6] Over the centuries, Christian interpreters had dealt with this issue in a variety of ways, for example, by asserting that God's promises to Israel were fulfilled *spiritually* in the church.[7] Much of Darby's appeal, both then and now, arises from his insistence upon biblical literalism. Darby believed that the prophetic oracles concerning Israel must be fulfilled to the letter. Because this fulfillment has not taken place, the dispensation to Israel cannot be complete.[8] But how can this be since, by Darby's own reckoning, we are already living in the next dispensation, the age of the (Gentile) church?

---

5. The origins of dispensationalism are chronicled in Grayson Carter's excellent study *Anglican Evangelicals: Protestant Secessions from the* Via Media, *c. 1800-1850* (Oxford: Oxford University Press, 2001), pp. 152-248.

6. See Chapter Three for a discussion of this issue.

7. A key element of traditional dispensationalist thinking is the segregation of Israel and the church, which are thought to exist as discrete entities in separate dispensations. This view clashes with the NT idea that Gentile Christians have been incorporated into Israel; see, for example, Paul's metaphor of the olive tree in Rom. 11:13-24 and his references to Christians as children of Abraham (e.g., Rom. 4:16-18 and 9:7).

8. Hence the euphoria of many dispensationalists at the creation of the modern state of Israel in 1948. The notion that Israel must become a nation for Christ to return is nowhere stated in the New Testament. Mark 13:14 par. refers to the "desolating sacrilege" of Daniel (8:11; 9:27; 11:31; and 12:11), which has led many to think that the Jerusalem temple must be rebuilt and thus, by implication, Israel restored. (See Chapter Five.) The parable of the fig tree (Mark 13:28-31 par.) is widely cited in this connection, but it is only by a considerable leap of interpretation that it can be taken to refer to the reestablishment of Israel. Instead, the fig tree relates to "all these things" (v. 29), namely, to the "messianic woes" of vv. 5-25, and not to the rebirth of Israel. (These same interpreters seldom note that the gathering of the saints *follows* the period of tribulation in Mark 13.) The symbol of the fig tree is apt since "the peculiarly bare appearance of the fig tree in winter, followed by its early blossom, makes it stand out in Palestine as a harbinger of spring" (I. Howard Marshall, *Commentary on Luke* [Grand Rapids: Eerdmans, 1978], p. 778).

Darby's solution is ingenious: the present age is really only a "parenthesis" interrupting the age of Israel.[9] Once the church is whisked off the scene at the time of the rapture, the dispensation to Israel will recommence and all remaining prophecies will be fulfilled.[10] Hence we discover the need for a two-part return of Christ: the first completes the dispensation to the church and the second the dispensation to Israel.

To their credit, the dispensationalists had put their finger on an important problem, namely, the relationship between Israel and the church in the plan of God. Their dissatisfaction with Christian supercessionism[11] is highly commendable, although their convoluted solution created as many difficulties as it solved. The presupposition of biblical inerrancy[12] has been the primary stumbling block to their effective resolution of this problem; nevertheless, dispensationalists are to be commended for recognizing and caring about this issue long before it appeared on the radar screen of most other Christian interpreters.

The problem of unfilled prophecy is not the only biblical difficulty addressed by dispensationalism. Another obstacle to a literal interpretation of the Bible is the conflict between heavenly and earthly visions of God's future reign. This tension was already present in pre-Christian Judaism, which favored an earthly expectation but which also accommodated a belief in heaven as the final destiny of the righteous (e.g., 1 Enoch 104:1-5; Daniel 12:3). Both views are also represented in the early church, which is unsurprising given its Jewish origins. For some New Testament writers, the return of Christ was associated with the establishment of a physical kingdom (Rev. 21); others regarded it as the occasion at which Christ would gather believers to heavenly glory (Matt.

9. According to Darby, the church was necessitated by the Jews' rejection of Jesus. Had the Jews accepted Jesus as their messiah as they were meant to, the crucifixion and resurrection would not have occurred. Understandably, many Christians have looked unfavorably on the notion that the events of Holy Week represent God's "Plan B."

10. Traditional dispensationalists believe that Daniel's prophecy of the seventy weeks (Dan. 9:20-27) was suspended at week 69 due to the crucifixion of Jesus. After the rapture, the prophetic clock will be reactivated and the postponed events of Daniel's vision will occur. It should go without saying that this is anything but a literal reading of the text.

11. That is, the idea that the church has superseded, taken over the place of, historical Israel.

12. See Chapter Two for an extended discussion of inerrancy, the belief that the Bible is without error or contradiction.

3:12; John 14:3).[13] Dispensationalists deal with this problem by positing two returns, the first heavenly and second earthly. It is a resourceful move for which there is no biblical warrant. The simple truth is that no New Testament writer, including the author of Revelation, speaks of two returns of Christ (see below).

Viewed from one angle, dispensationalism is an elaborate harmonization strategy necessitated by its authors' insistence upon taking the Bible "literally." The assumption that all biblical authors agree is maintained only by means of enormous invention, and dispensationalists are some of the most inventive interpreters ever to open a Bible. In such a system, conflicting biblical texts serve as invitations to theological creativity. (As the software programmer said, "It's not a bug; it's a feature!") Since all books are presumed to share the same outlook, the perspective of Revelation can be filled out with ideas taken from 1 Thessalonians, and so on and so on. The result is an eschatology that borrows from a wide range of biblical authors but which is actually foreign to all of them. Consider the following passage, found in the recent book *Are We Living in the End Times?* by Tim LaHaye and Jerry B. Jenkins:

> When the more than three hundred Bible references to the Second Coming are carefully examined, it becomes clear that there are two phases to His return. There are far too many conflicting activities connected with His return to be merged into a single coming. . . . Since we know that there are no contradictions in the Word of God, our Lord must be telling us something here.[14]

To accept that the biblical authors had even somewhat differing views of the future would, of course, threaten the notion that "there are no contradictions in the Word of God." That is what is perceived to be at stake and what, in no small part, drives the phenomenon. Dispensationalism is necessitated by fundamentalism, and fundamentalism is defended and propagated by dispensationalism. Like bees and flowers, they are in perpetual symbiotic relationship.

13. See the discussion on pp. 176-77 above.

14. Tim LaHaye and Jerry B. Jenkins, *Are We Living in the End Times?* (Wheaton, Ill.: Tyndale, 1999), pp. 98, 100. (Page 99 contains a chart titled "Locating the Tribulation Period.")

Looking for the Rapture

Doubtless, the great majority of Christians who believe in a premillennial "rapture of the saints" are good people who want only to believe what the Bible teaches about the return of Christ. Unfortunately, what the Bible teaches is not the rapture. Let us briefly consider the most commonly cited biblical texts, the most prominent of which is 1 Thessalonians 4:16-17:

> For the Lord himself, with a cry of command, with the archangel's call and with the sound of God's trumpet, will descend from heaven, and the dead in Christ will rise first. Then we who are alive, who are left, will be caught up in the clouds together with them to meet the Lord in the air; and so we will be with the Lord forever.

What ultimately stands behind these verses is the vision of the coming of the Son of Man in Daniel 7:13-14. According to Daniel, the Son of Man will come to earth to rule over an everlasting kingdom. It is entirely possible that Paul had in mind that very expectation. It is interesting that the word he used for "meet(ing)," *apantēsis,* is a technical term "used of citizens, or a group of them, going out of the city to meet a visiting dignitary and then escorting him back into the city."[15] Paul may well have employed the word in precisely that sense. If so, he wrote this passage to address the Thessalonians' concern that deceased believers would not participate in Christ's kingdom. On the contrary, Paul would console, the dead will be the first to meet Christ, after which they will be joined by all other believers, who together will accompany Christ to earth. Hence verse 14: "[T]hrough Jesus, God will bring with him those who have died" (see also 3:13).

One passage that might shed light on these verses is Romans 11:26-27, which paraphrases Isaiah 59:20-21a: "Out of Zion will come the De-

---

15. Abraham J. Malherbe, *The Letters to the Thessalonians: A New Translation with Introduction and Commentary,* The Anchor Bible, vol. 32B (New York: Doubleday, 2000), p. 277. Malherbe cites the example of Josephus, *Jewish Antiquities* 11:26-28, where a priest awaits "the *parousia* [coming] of Alexander in order to go out and meet [*hypantēsis*] him." The same word is used in Acts 28:15 for the meeting of Paul and his Christian escort outside of Rome.

liverer; he will banish ungodliness from Jacob. And this is my covenant with them, when I take away their sins." The expectation of God's (or the Messiah's) appearance at and reign from Mount Zion is a typical feature of apocalyptic thought (cf. Rev. 14:1; see pp. 89-92 above). It is reasonable to suppose that Paul shared this view.

In a sense, however, it is irrelevant whether Paul thought that believers would accompany Christ to earth or to heaven. The more important datum is that Paul nowhere mentions two returns of Christ. An instructive passage, if it indeed was written by Paul,[16] is 2 Thessalonians 2:1-12, which envisages a single coming *following* the period of "messianic woes."

> As to the coming of our Lord Jesus Christ and our being gathered together to him, we beg you, brothers and sisters, not to be quickly shaken. . . . Let no one deceive you in any way, for that day will not come unless the rebellion comes first and the lawless one is revealed. . . . (vv. 1-3)

The same perspective is evident in some other NT writings, for example, in Mark 13:19-20, 24-27:

> For in those days there will be suffering, such as has not been from the beginning of the creation that God created until now, no, and never will be. And if the Lord had not cut short those days, no one would be saved; but for the sake of the elect, whom he chose, he has cut short those days. . . . But in those days, after that suffering . . . they will see "the Son of Man coming in clouds" with great power and glory. Then he will send out the angels, and gather his elect from the four winds, from the ends of the earth to the ends of heaven.

Clearly, it is the expectation of these passages that the gathering of the saints will occur only once — after the expected period of "tribulation."

Premillennialists often argue for a pre-tribulation rapture by invoking Revelation 3:10:

---

16. On the question of the authorship of 2 Thessalonians, see Raymond Brown, *An Introduction to the New Testament* (New York: Doubleday, 1997), pp. 590-98.

Because you have kept my word of patient endurance, I will keep you from the hour of trial that is coming on the whole world to test the inhabitants of the earth.

This verse is addressed to the church of Philadelphia, whose exemption (whatever the author might have imagined it to be)[17] was a reward for its "patient endurance." It is only with Herculean exertion that "pre-trib" advocates are able to bend this verse to their will. Writes Tim LaHaye,

> The message of Christ to the church at Philadelphia was not only for that little church but also to the "open door" church — that is, the evangelistic, missionary-minded church, which started about 1750 and will exist right up to the time Christ comes to rapture His church.[18]

It is astounding how far from the literal meaning of a text "biblical literalists" will stray for the sake of defending their interpretive system. Against their commitment to that system, no inconveniently incompatible passage stands a chance.

As is the case elsewhere in the New Testament, there is only one return of Christ in the book of Revelation.[19] Moreover, the "first resurrection" (20:5) is said to occur at the inauguration of the millennial kingdom and includes only those "beheaded for their testimony to Jesus" (20:4). If the author had maintained the hope of an imminent resurrection and rescue of the saints, it is passing strange that he failed to mention it, especially given his unmistakable pastoral concern for his

17. The word "trial," *peirasmos,* is the same word that is usually translated as "temptation" in the Lord's Prayer ("Lead us not into temptation . . ."). Rev. 3:10 could mean either that the believers at Philadelphia will be given power to withstand the coming trial/temptation or that they will be spared facing it.

18. LaHaye and Jenkins, *Are We Living in the End Times?* p. 108.

19. LaHaye argues that the rapture is assumed by Revelation since the church is not mentioned from chapters 5 to 18 (*Are We Living in the End Times?* p. 112). If so, then why is the earthly church admonished to endurance in both Rev. 13:9-10 and 14:12-13?

One source of confusion is the fact that the author of Revelation imagines that the souls of the martyrs have already ascended to heaven (e.g., Rev. 6:9), where they are told to "rest" (v. 11); nevertheless, the "first resurrection" does not occur until chapter 20 (see above).

readers. Instead, he repeatedly called for the endurance of believers in the face of present and future hostility.[20]

The other key texts cited in defense of the rapture are Matthew 24:40-41 and Luke 17:34-35, which speak of a sudden division of humanity ("Two women will be grinding meal together; one will be taken and one will be left," etc.). Only by tearing these verses from their context can one possibly think that they refer to an initial, secret return of Christ. In fact, both passages are attached to discussions concerning the very *public* coming of the Son of Man. In Luke we are told forthrightly that "as the lightning flashes and lights up the sky from one side to the other, so will the Son of Man be in his day" (17:24). Similarly, according to Matthew (paralleling Mark 13:26-27, quoted above),

> Then the sign of the Son of Man will appear in heaven, and then all the tribes of the earth will mourn, and they will see the Son of Man coming on the clouds of heaven with power and great glory. And he will send out his angels with a loud trumpet call, and they will gather his elect from the four winds, from one end of heaven to the other. (Matt. 24:30-31)

In both passages, the return of Christ is, like the flood at the time of Noah, also an occasion of judgment. It is crystal clear that neither author had in view a separate rapture of the church that precedes Christ's "third coming" as ruler and judge.

In sum, contemporary America's most popular Christian eschatology is unscriptural. Ironically, in their effort to interpret the Bible literally and consistently, proponents of the rapture have mangled the biblical witness almost beyond recognition. At the end of all their theorizing and systematizing, it is the Bible itself, this wonderfully diverse and complex witness to God and Christ, that has been left behind.

Conclusion

Ideas have consequences. At best, belief in premillennial dispensationalism heightens devotion to God and increases awareness of the ur-

---

20. E.g., Rev. 1:9; 2:2-3, 10, 19; 3:10-11; 13:9-10; and 14:12-13.

gency and importance of one's spiritual commitments. It also moti-
vates evangelism. One cannot deny the fact that its proponents have
been successful at bringing others into the fold, however much one
might question their methods.

At worst, such belief is a form of escapism. The hope of impending
departure can lead believers to abandon interest in the world and its
problems. The expectation of deteriorating conditions prior to the
soon-approaching rapture is morally corrosive, encouraging pessi-
mism, fatalism, and the forsaking of political responsibility.[21] Disen-
gagement from the problems of the world is ethically indefensible, but
it is all too common among today's prophecy elite. Their books tell us
that nuclear war is inevitable, that the pursuit of peace is pointless,
that the planet's environmental woes are unstoppable, and so on.[22]
One of the quirkiest passages in the whole of the Tim LaHaye canon is
the following, taken from a discussion of Ezekiel 38-39:[23]

> It does not seem as if time is on Russia's side. If she is going to be
> the major power that Ezekiel forecasts her to be, she had better
> make her move soon, or she won't be able to do so. If Russia is to
> attack Israel, she had better do it soon![24]

It is wrong to be morally complacent. Still worse is hoping for, even
abetting, the advance of evil. Statements such as the above, whatever
their intention, come dangerously close to doing just that. I trust that
the Kremlin is not listening; nevertheless, millions of Christians are.
We do not know how or when God's purposes for the world ultimately
will be fulfilled. We can however say with absolute certainty that we
have no right to be acquiescent in the face of injustice or to be gleeful
in the face of suffering.

More than a century and a half ago, John Nelson Darby wrote, "I
believe from Scripture that the ruin is without remedy." Believers
should expect only "a progress of evil."[25] All of us are the beneficiaries
of those Christian reformers who ignored Darby and got on with the

---

21. On the very ancient origins of this idea, see Chapter Four.
22. See the summary in Clouse et al., *New Millennium Manual*, ch. 6.
23. On Ezek. 38-39, see pp. 66-68 above.
24. LaHaye & Jenkins, *Are We Living in the End Times?* p. 92.
25. Cited in Carter, *Anglican Evangelicals*, pp. 220, 226.

business of fighting slavery, opposing child labor, and campaigning for the enfranchisement of women — the business, that is, of making this world a little more like the dominion of God. For the time being, there remains more than enough such work for all of us.

> *Blessed are those servants whom the master will find at work when he arrives.* (Matt. 24:46)

Bibliography of Works Cited

Achtemeier, Paul J. *Inspiration and Authority: Nature and Function of Christian Scripture.* Peabody, Mass.: Hendrickson, 1999.

Allen, Charlotte. *The Human Christ: The Search for the Historical Jesus.* New York: Free Press, 1998.

Allen, Leslie C. *Ezekiel 20–48.* Word Biblical Commentary, vol. 29. Dallas: Word, 1990.

Allison, Dale C. *Jesus of Nazareth: Millenarian Prophet.* Minneapolis: Fortress, 1998.

Anderson, Bernhard W. *Understanding the Old Testament.* 4th ed. Englewood Cliffs, N.J.: Prentice-Hall, 1986.

Barrett, C. K. *Jesus and the Gospel Tradition.* London, SPCK, 1967.

Barth, Karl. *The Epistle to the Romans.* Translated by E. C. Hoskyns. Oxford: Oxford University Press, 1933.

Blaising, Craig A., and Darrell L. Bock. *Progressive Dispensationalism.* Wheaton, Ill.: Bridgepoint, 1993.

Boring, M. Eugene. *Revelation.* Louisville: John Knox, 1989.

Brown, Raymond. *An Introduction to the New Testament.* New York: Doubleday, 1997.

Carter, Grayson. *Anglican Evangelicals: Protestant Secessions from the Via Media, c. 1800-1850.* Oxford: Oxford University Press, 2001.

Charles, R. H. *The Apocrypha and Pseudepigrapha of the Old Testament.* Oxford: Oxford University Press, 1913.

———. *The Book of Enoch.* London: SPCK, 1997.

Clouse, Robert G., Robert N. Hosack, and Richard V. Pierard. *The New Millennium Manual: A Once and Future Guide.* Grand Rapids: Baker, 1999.

Collins, John. *The Apocalyptic Imagination: An Introduction to Jewish Apocalyptic Literature.* 2nd ed. Grand Rapids: Eerdmans, 1998.

————. *Daniel.* Hermeneia. Minneapolis: Fortress, 1993.

Cook, Stephen L. *Prophecy & Apocalypticism: The Postexilic Social Setting.* Minneapolis: Fortress, 1995.

Cross, Frank Moore. *Canaanite Myth and Hebrew Epic.* Cambridge, Mass.: Harvard University Press, 1973.

Deissmann, G. Adolf. *Light from the Ancient East.* Translated by Lionel R. M. Strachan. Rev. ed. New York: George H. Doran, 1927.

de Jong, Marinus. *God's Final Envoy: Early Christology and Jesus' Own View of His Mission.* Grand Rapids: Eerdmans, 1998.

Dyrness, William. *Learning about Theology from the Third World.* Grand Rapids: Zondervan, 1990.

Efird, James M. *Daniel and Revelation.* Valley Forge, Pa.: Judson, 1978.

Ehrman, Bart. *Jesus: Apocalyptic Prophet of the New Millennium.* Oxford: Oxford University Press, 1999.

Funk, Robert W., et al. *The Five Gospels: What Did Jesus Really Say?* New York: HarperCollins, 1997.

Garrett, Susan. "Revelation." In *The Women's Bible Commentary.* Edited by Carol A. Newsom and Sharon H. Ringe. Louisville: Westminster/John Knox, 1992.

Hanson, Paul. *The Dawn of Apocalyptic.* Philadelphia: Fortress, 1975.

Harris, Stephen L. *The New Testament: A Student's Guide.* Mountain View, Calif.: Mayfield, 1988.

Hays, Richard B. "The Corrected Jesus." *First Things* 43 (May 1994): 43-48.

————. *Echoes of Scripture in the Letters of Paul.* New Haven: Yale University Press, 1989.

————. *The Moral Vision of the New Testament.* San Francisco: HarperCollins, 1996.

Hill, Craig C. *Hellenists and Hebrews: Reappraising Division within the Earliest Church.* Minneapolis: Fortress, 1992.

————. "Restoring the Kingdom to Israel." In *Shadow of Glory: Reading the New Testament after the Holocaust.* New York: Routledge, 2002.

————. "Romans." In *The Oxford Bible Commentary.* Oxford: Oxford University Press, 2001.

Hurtado, Larry W. *One God, One Lord: Early Christian Devotion and Ancient Jewish Monotheism.* 2nd ed. Edinburgh: T. & T. Clark, 1998.

Jewett, Robert. *A Chronology of Paul's Life.* Philadelphia: Fortress, 1979.

—————. "Coming to Terms with the Doom Boom." *Quarterly Review* 4, no. 3 (1984): 9-22.

Johnson, Luke T. "The Humanity of Jesus: What's at Stake in the Quest for the Historical Jesus?" In *The Jesus Controversy: Perspectives in Conflict*, pp. 48-74. Harrisburg, Pa.: Trinity Press International, 1999.

—————. *The Real Jesus: The Misguided Quest for the Historical Jesus and the Truth of the Traditional Gospels.* New York: HarperCollins, 1996.

Koester, Helmut. "Jesus the Victim." *Journal of Biblical Literature* III (1992): 3-15.

Kyle, Richard. *The Last Days Are Here Again: A History of the End Times.* Grand Rapids: Baker, 1998.

LaHaye, Tim, and Jerry B. Jenkins. *Are We Living in the End Times?* Wheaton, Ill.: Tyndale, 1999.

Linafelt, Tod. *Shadow of Glory: Reading the New Testament after the Holocaust.* New York: Routledge, 2002.

Lindsey, Hal. *The Late Great Planet Earth.* Grand Rapids: Zondervan, 1970.

Malherbe, Abraham. *The Letters to the Thessalonians: A New Translation with Introduction and Commentary.* The Anchor Bible, vol. 32B. New York: Doubleday, 2000.

—————. *Moral Exhortation: A Greco-Roman Sourcebook.* Philadelphia: Westminster, 1986.

Marshall, I. Howard. *Commentary on Luke.* Grand Rapids: Eerdmans, 1978.

Meeks, Wayne A. *The Writings of St. Paul.* New York: Norton, 1972.

Meier, John P. *A Marginal Jew: Rethinking the Historical Jesus.* Vol. 2. New York: Doubleday, 1994.

Meyer, Ben. *The Aims of Jesus.* London: SCM, 1979.

Richard, Pablo. *Apocalypse: A People's Commentary on the Book of Revelation.* Maryknoll, N.Y.: Orbis, 1995.

Ringgren, Helmer. "Prophecy in the Ancient Near East." *Israel's Prophetic Tradition: Essays in Honour of Peter R. Ackroyd.* Edited by Richard Coggins, Anthony Phillips, and Michael Knibb. Cambridge: Cambridge University Press, 1982.

Robinson, J. A. T. *In the End, God.* London: James Clarke & Co., 1950.

Sanders, E. P. *The Historical Figure of Jesus.* London: Allen Lane, 1993.

—————. *Jesus and Judaism.* London: SCM, 1985.

Saucy, Robert. *The Case for Progressive Dispensationalism.* Grand Rapids: Zondervan, 1993.

Stanton, Graham. *Gospel Truth? New Light on Jesus and the Gospels.* London: HarperCollins, 1995.

Throckmorton, Burton H. *Jesus Christ: The Message of the Gospels, The Hope of the Church.* Louisville: Westminster/John Knox, 1998.

Tiffany, Frederick, and Sharon Ringe. *Biblical Interpretation: A Roadmap.* Nashville: Abingdon, 1996.

Vermes, Geza. *The Complete Dead Sea Scrolls in English.* London: Penguin, 1998.

————. *Jesus the Jew.* London: Collins, 1973.

Wink, Walter. *Naming the Powers: The Language of Power in the New Testament.* Philadelphia: Fortress, 1984.

Witherington, Ben. *The Jesus Quest: The Third Search for the Jew of Nazareth.* Downers Grove, Ill.: InterVarsity Press, 1995.

Wright, N. T. *The New Testament and the People of God.* Minneapolis: Fortress, 1992.

Index of Modern Authors

Index of Subjects

Index of Scripture and Other Ancient Sources